>>

THE
COMPLETE
GUIDE
TO

DIGITAL
GRAPHIC
DESIGN

NEW EDITION

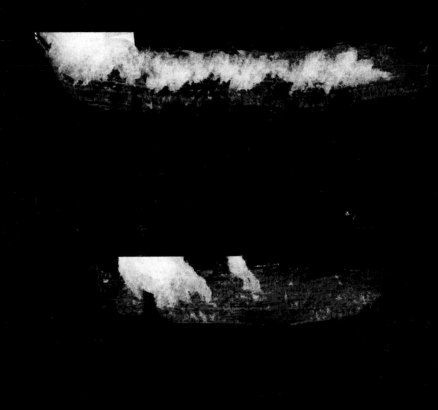

THE COMPLETE GUIDE TO >>

DIGITAL GRAPHIC DESIGN

NEW EDITION

Consultant Editors
Bob Gordon and Maggie Gordon

 Thames & Hudson

First published in the United Kingdom in 2002 by
THAMES & HUDSON LTD
181A High Holborn
London WC1V 7QX

www.thamesandhudson.com

© The Ilex Press Limited 2002 and 2005

Revised edition 2005

This book was conceived,
designed, and produced by
THE ILEX PRESS LIMITED
3 St Andrews Place
Lewes
East Sussex BN7 1UP

ILEX is an imprint of The Ilex Press Ltd

Art Director: Alastair Campbell
Designer: Jonathan Raimes
Design Manager: Tony Seddon
Project Editor: Lachlan McLaine
Revised Edition Editor: Adam Banks
Picture research: Heather Vickers
Contributors: Jonathan Raimes, Ian Chilvers,
Richard Gooch, Keith Martin, Sue Perks,
Jonathan Smith, Paul Springer, Phil Taylor

British Library Cataloguing-in-Publication Data
A catalogue record for this book is available from
the British Library

ISBN 0-500-28560-8

Printed and bound in China

For more information on this title visit:
www.web-linked.com/cggduk

00

CONTENTS

01 **02** **02** **03** **04**

INTRODUCTION

Design finds its way into every aspect of daily life. From the look of clothes, buildings, and consumer goods to reading matter, entertainment, interior and exterior environments – almost every form of modern communication and production – graphic design plays an important part. It is almost impossible to avoid being bombarded by visual messages.

'Digital', 'graphic', and 'design' have become three very potent words in our vocabulary. There can be few people living in the developed world whose life has not been touched or influenced by information and design technology. Personal computers and the ubiquitous silicon chip have found their way into the homes and workplaces of millions of people irrespective of background, age, or culture.

One of the most common words bandied about as an all-encompassing descriptor is 'digital'. This is almost inevitable, since computers depend on streams of electronically generated 'digits' to function. So we have digital telephone lines, digital printing, digital radio and digital television, among the many areas connected with information, communication, and design. Virtually all data, whether it is in the form of words, numbers, images, sound, or movement, can be digitized and transmitted using a range of technologies. Digitization has created a common method of recording and transmitting data, allowing a high level of interactivity across many forms of media.

This interactivity allows sound, image, text, and other creative elements to work together in a single context, and has radically changed designers' working methods by providing access to the vast storehouse of knowledge on the Internet and corporate intranets and enabling them to send and receive a range of media electronically via email from their own computers.

Digital data transmission speeds are constrained by the size of files, the medium through which data flows, and the speed at which computer processors can handle the information. But every day sees an improvement in all of these areas – files can be compressed more efficiently, broadband Internet connections and high-speed wireless networking are being used more and more, and processor speeds are getting faster and faster. Together with increases in transmission speeds, there is a growing convergence of media, which is bringing about a merging of personal computing, television, radio, telephone, publishing, games, web, email, and ecommerce. Computer and TV monitors are getting larger, with crystal clear flat-screen technologies replacing CRT, while mobile phones and other portable devices gain full-colour displays. This takes us into an era where the quality of visual content will play an increasingly important role in the way we communicate to a wider range of audiences. The quality of visually received information is the responsibility of the digital graphic designer.

Much of what is published in print or on screen has a tendency to be visually discordant or jumbled, partly because of the speed with which it can now be generated and delivered. In this information- and message-orientated world, it is increasingly important for the graphic designer to strive for order and clarity. Understanding how audiences react to visual material, their levels of concentration and comprehension, and how they can be influenced by cultural or fashion trends is key to the problem-solving process. Equally important is understanding how eye and brain work together in scanning and processing words, pictures, and the subtler visual cues of form, colour, and composition.

Since prehistory, humans have used signs and shapes to communicate information and ideas about the real world as well as to express what they saw in their imagination. While the earliest scribes could perhaps be described as the first 'graphic designers' – arranging text in a logical and efficient way – it was the invention of printing, with its potential for mass production, that formed the bedrock for graphic design as a recognizable trade.

The development of movable type in the mid-15th Century, widely attributed to Johann Gutenberg, radically changed the design of letter shapes. Whereas the handwriting of the scribe had evolved slowly and gently over centuries, with as much emphasis placed on composition and embellishment as on letter forms, type design now became a relatively fast-moving commercial process. Letter shapes were standardized, and it was necessary to devise different varieties to help convey meaning.

Graphic design continued to evolve as a hybrid activity, owing as much to mathematics, engineering, and psychology as to the fine arts. Changes in art, fashion, and taste, dramatic advances in reprographic technologies, and the changing demands of commerce and lifestyle exerted massive influence, along with the creative contributions of innumerable artists, typographers, designers, and stylists. Yet the overwhelming impression given by the more influential graphic designers of recent times is of a calculated reluctance to draw on history. Following World War I, members of the

There are, however, several aspects of graphic design that remain relatively unaffected by technology. These include generating and developing ideas and concepts, design and typographic principles, and creative problem-solving – all attributes that distinguish graphic design from other professions. Happily, digital technologies have provided many first-class tools for exploring, extending, and realizing ideas in faster, more flexible, and more cost-effective ways.

Printing has traditionally dominated the way in which graphic designers work: fields such as packaging, exhibition design, and advertising are largely defined by the different printing processes associated with them. But the printing methods that

Digital developments have given designers a range of first class tools for exploring, extending, and realizing ideas in faster, more flexible, and more cost-effective ways.

Bauhaus School saw history as dead convention, and preferred to redefine or reject the parameters within which their predecessors had worked. All avant-garde thinking – a major component of graphic design – is driven by the need to escape from the past in order to explore the possibilities of the future.

The emphasis of this book is on *digital* graphic design, a field created by the development not of the computer itself but of the 'graphical user interface' (GUI) – the means by which users can interact with graphic symbols on screen. The Apple Macintosh in particular, by adopting a GUI in place of text-based operation, allowed the innovation of a graphical screen display to be exploited for the creation of graphical content, and thus digital graphic design was born.

Since the launch of the Mac in 1984, the digital revolution has overtaken traditional graphic design working practices with extraordinary speed. Many specialist trades and crafts have become almost entirely redundant. Much of the responsibility for the technical aspects of production has shifted to the computerized desktop, and designers themselves are required to master an ever-expanding new skillset, ranging from the operation of different software packages to the digital representation of colour and the processes involved in reproducing digital content in print and on screen.

dominated the major part of the twentieth century have seen rapid revolutions. During the 1960s, offset lithography took over from the labour-intensive letterpress printing, and within a decade became the most common form of reproduction. This major change was followed closely by computerized typesetting, which was finally absorbed into personal computer systems.

Today, a PDF (portable document format) file containing all the information necessary to output a printed document – whether a single black-and-white page to a colour magazine – can be transmitted directly to the printer's factory floor, where computerized equipment either makes plates ready for offset litho printing, or outputs the job directly to paper using a digital press. Colour calibration can be performed automatically throughout the process, from obtaining images from cameras and scanners to outputting them on press. In practice, designers will – and should – still discuss a complex job with the printer, who will oversee some of the finer technical settings. The fact remains that it is now an everyday event for pages, posters, signs, and even three-dimensional objects to be produced with virtually no separation between the designer and the final result.

Digital technology is by now so well established that many young designers may question whether the word 'digital' need even be used. But graphic design finds itself in a state of permanent revolution. Web design, for instance, is a discipline less than a decade old, yet its basic methods have already changed beyond recognition as new generations of software have been developed and new standards, both technical and practical, adopted. Who knows what media we may be designing for, and with what tools, in another decade? As the saying goes: 'If we can see into the future, then we're not looking far enough ahead.'

THE ROLE OF THE DIGITAL GRAPHIC DESIGNER

bring presentations to life. Many of the chores associated with repetitive design or editing tasks have been reduced considerably by automated features built into most applications: search and replace, spellchecking, graphic and typographic 'style sheets', and 'content management' systems, to name just a few. If you can't find a feature that automates a repetitive task, you can probably create it yourself by recording a sequence of commands as a 'macro', 'script', or 'action'.

Paradoxically, in an era that has seen many industries and professions having to specialize in order to survive, the digital graphic designer has been required to diversify. The most significant growth is in the explosion of the Internet and multimedia industry. Many graphic designers are fully engaged in webpage design involving typography, imagery, animation, movies, and even sound. The computerization of graphic design work, with the development of numerous disparate, yet often overlapping, software programs has greatly enlarged the

As graphic designers can work across so many fields, they need to be familiar with a wide range of different production and manufacturing processes and related support professions and skills. This may include photographers, illustrators, musicians, writers, and film-makers, as well as technical specialists in web design, database programming and other fields. Digitization of sound, image, animation, movies, and production processes has enabled professionals to collaborate and work across an increasingly wide spectrum.

The emergence of the personal computer and desktop publishing programs, together with their wide availability to

Professional graphic design will continue to thrive because ideas and innovation, good composition, and a creative eye cannot be 'packaged'.

range of work in which 'graphic' designers can be involved. In addition to the rich creative elements of many programs, there are numerous built-in productivity and labour-saving features. Many previously specialist areas of graphic design now share similar software programs for image and text origination.

The digital power readily available to the designer is immense. Every aspect of a project can be created and finished to a high professional level on a single Apple Macintosh or PC workstation. Not only has the origination process been made easier, but the ways in which the finished result can be previewed by both designer and client has transformed the way creative people work. Affordable colour proofers show how printed materials will look; technologies such as PDF files allow instant transmission and distribution; walk-through software previews three-dimensional creations; packaging software folds and makes up packs from flat designs; and slide shows and movies

non designers, could have signalled the beginning of the end for the practising graphic designer. Photography, as a profession, could also have died out as high-quality automatic cameras became accessible and easy to use for anybody and everybody. However, like professional photography, professional graphic design will continue to thrive because ideas and innovation, experience, the instinct for composition, and a creative eye cannot be 'packaged' as an off-the-shelf product for clients lacking the relevant skills and talent.

Graphic design is an immensely exciting and vibrant activity in which to be involved and, as such, is a rewarding profession to follow. But it requires vision, stamina, and good humour combined with creativity, innovation, and analytical and methodical ways of working. Designers need a working knowledge of budgets, manufacturing, and reproduction processes. Successful graphic designers aim to devise inventive solutions to visual communication problems in response to clients' needs, and in order to do so often work closely with clients in formulating a brief and working strategy prior to starting any visual work. A good understanding of human nature and the cultural environment, as well as the ability to lead or be a team player as required, together with a keen eye for detail, distinguish the truly excellent designer from the average.

THE COMPLETE GUIDE TO DIGITAL GRAPHIC DESIGN

The aim of this book is to both inspire and inform the reader by exploring a wide range of visual communication and graphic design contexts while introducing essential, related design methodology and concepts on which to build. It explores the diversity of graphic design and showcases the work of inventive and talented designers using digital media for the development, realization, and production of projects.

The Complete Guide to Digital Graphic Design demonstrates different facets of digital graphic design and seeks to demystify some of the technical jargon that is often associated with computing and the design world.

The introductory pages show examples of work from a wide range of visual communication contexts, setting the scene for further in-depth exploration within individual sections.

Part One, Design Basics, explores some of the fundamental principles that underpin good and efficient graphic design. This section is, in essence, 'away from the screen' as it involves thinking and creative processes related to idea generation and informed design decision-making. It includes an appreciation of the 'building blocks' essential to good graphic design: shape and form, spatial awareness, what type is and how to work with it. The emotive use of colour and how colour can work for the digital designer is also looked at, as a powerful tool rather than just decoration.

Part Two consists of sub-sections that explore defined areas of surface graphic design. These include: Design for Print, Packaging, Signage, Advertising, and Exhibition and Display Design.

Part Three looks at web design for the Internet, intranets and multimedia. This part is particularly useful for those who may feel somewhat swamped by the terminology in this area. It shows clearly how designers have to respond and adapt to a fluidity of display by different web browsers and computer platforms, and explains the significance of new standards of good practice for accessibility to disabled users.

Leading practitioners from each field take an in-depth look at their specialist areas. Where equipment or software, additional to the core list introducing these sections, is considered important, this is highlighted. Specialist processes, which include four-colour, offset lithographic printing, are discussed, together with the related creative and support professionals as appropriate. At the end of each section, a case history is explored and the key creative and production stages involved in arriving at the final design are explained.

Part Four takes a focused look at the technical intricacies of Colour, Type, and Image Making.

The use of colour is discussed in the Design Basics section but it is essential for the practising graphic designer to understand how colour is created and why, for instance, different sets of primary colours are used for discussing monitor matters (RGB) from those used in printing (CMYK). As mixing, controlling, and adjusting colour plays such an important role in graphic design, the attributes and terminology of colour and how it works are looked at closely.

Digital type, too, has a language of its own. The Design Basics section covers working with type from an aesthetic and functional point of view, but on a technical level the graphic designer has to appreciate how type is handled by the computer. What are bitmap and outline fonts, for example? How can fonts be delivered along with documents, whether for printing or viewing? Typefaces and font files, managing fonts, font libraries, buying fonts, and font copyright are also explained.

Computer programs have made retouching, montaging, and technical and fine art image making readily accessible to the designer and artist. The essential way in which bitmap programs work compared to the very different vector-based programs is made clear. The creation of special effects, the use of painting programs or drawing programs and how they interact with each other is discussed and explained.

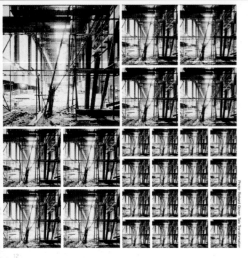

lucy bullivant:musing on the contemporary museum   >When museums outgrow their institutional facilities, they don't necessarily have to marry old and new by extending on one site. The satellite idea creates a complex field of activity less bound by place. Architecture grounds each one in a context – it's down to the staff to design the field. Everyone is an architect in this business nowadays.   >The term museum implies the facilities of collection, endowment, preservation and curatorial pedigree. It doesn't automatically signify retailing elements. Is the term 'hybrid' architecture a simplification of the need to create a dynamic relationship, in formal and programmatic terms, that endures in a climate of change?   >Contemporary museum design pitfalls: gratuitous and not so revelatory form-making [every museum architect should reveal as well as display], and seduction by the myths of flexibility. If neutrality is an illusion, flexibility is a holy grail.   >Curators have to be very flexible, even de-curate the architecture, but everyone works better with parameters.   >Museum design now bridges the physical and the virtual worlds. How do we describe such an architecture, and how does it change the way we see museums? Improvisational tactics in lieu of physical facilities: the virtual friends' room [how far can you go with 'the museum without walls'? One mouse for every friend, perhaps, which is also a camera into all the other spaces, or is that another typology altogether]?   >The contents and ambience of a museum [whether more masculine or more feminine] are frequently disturbingly various: the architecture cannot afford to be, but nor should it entirely lose the mystery of the gathering place, of chosen, untouched objects from the underworld. In this distillation, there is no other kind of secular solace.   >The Centre Pompidou – that quintessential expression of the democratizing of knowledge and culture, a child of its time [1977]. But, [referring to the new renovation], how do you update utopia when it's lost its original meaning, its ethos of cultural democracy? Now, with the new pay to enter policy, you can't see one of its best exhibits, the views of the city of Paris, for free any more.   >Don't forget take away museum experiences. Where tv is going [consumer choice], museums are following: at Frank Gehry's soon to be completed Pop Music Museum in Seattle visitors make their own customised disk from a sound bank to play later.   >We have a museological climate where retailing elements frequently impinge on cultural pleasure, as harmlessly diverting as a form of museum downtime as they usually are. 'The ace caff with the museum attached' allows us to carry out more of our personal lives in these spaces. The museum community is interested in civic values in a place they want to feel is theirs too. After all, the fortunes of outdoor public space have waned, and perhaps the museum is a better, more rainproof place anyway in which to renew the idea of the civic agora.   >Museums in the city: the relatively rare building of a new street smart metropolitan museum or its extension redefines the local urban fabric, causing its value as real estate to soar.   >We need 'trickle down' on occasion to work more slowly [yes, developers], not to upset context into a total face lift that excludes the locals. On the other hand, if museums don't get above themselves, something else is bound to fill the space.   >Cultural multiplex at one end of the spectrum, single theme museums at the other: you can't generalise. Isn't it reassuring that museum architecture as a subject and as a response is too rich and too layered to be conveyed in a rhetorical, 'talking to your one circulation choice walk', acoustiguide recording?   >Lucy Bullivant is an architectural writer and curator, Archis and Domus correspondent, and director of >enter, her international exhibition/events consultancy.

herbert girardet/urban futures:rethinking the city   >At the start of the new millennium cities and their resource use dominate life on earth. In the last 100 years, human numbers have grown fourfold, whilst both the world economy and urban populations have grown about 15 fold. Today, half of us live in cities while most of the rest depends on urban markets for their economic survival. One species now uses about half of nature's entire annual production, and we are increasingly undermining the integrity of the global environment. We have to rethink how we run our urban economies, energy, transport and waste systems, and the way we construct our buildings. If sustainability was the main frame of reference for the way we plan urban spaces, structures and processes – how would things change?   >Given the vast scale of urbanisation today, cities would be well advised to model their functioning on natural ecosystems. These are generally systems of permanence, whereas currently man-made systems are defined by high levels of entropy. Cities have a linear metabolism, consisting of the flow of resources and products through the urban system. Nature's own ecosystems have an essentially circular metabolism in which every output by an organism is also an input which renews the whole living environment of which it is a part. The web of life hangs together in a 'chain of mutual benefit'. To be sustainable, cities have to develop a circular metabolism, minimising waste discharges, and using and re-using resources as efficiently as possible.   >Thinking differently is an important starting point in the process of remodelling our cities. The real challenge however is to act differently. People all over the world are working on how to make their cities more sustainable, in both environmental and social terms. This exhibition is intended to enhance that process in the city that started it all: London. It is, at present, a city of vast global dependencies. Its ecological footprint extends to an area the size of the UK, about 125 times its own surface area. If all the world's cities demanded such vast surface areas to supply themselves three planets would be needed rather than the one we have.   >It makes sense for people to live in cities. They have the potential for great resource efficiency through closed-loop economies, diversity and mutuality. In the past, economic growth has meant automatic growth in the consumption of resources and services of all kinds. Sustainable development, in contrast, requires new solutions to ensure that economic well-being is founded on efficient use of resources, minimising pollution and waste. New energy systems can support technologies we inherited from the past. It is clear that many new local jobs can be created on the way. In the exhibition the main focus is on these areas where the potential for change is greatest. These sections form an agenda for constructing the future sustainable city.   >The quest for sustainability requires a strengthening of local democratic processes. Methods such as neighbourhood forums, action planning and consensus-building should be widely used, because they usually lead to better decision making. Community groups, local and central governments are increasingly aware that efforts to improve the living environment must focus on cities and urban lifestyles. Eco-friendly urban development could well become the greatest challenge of the twenty-first century, not only for human self-interest, but also for the sake of a sustainable relationship between cities and the biosphere on which humanity ultimately depends.

act differently:living city

Cities, occupying 2% of the world's land surface, consume 75% of the world's resources and discharge 75% of the world's waste

London's total ecological footprint extends to around 125 times its surface area

Living City events

Mayoral Candidates Interviews
14 April to 04 May
decide who to vote for by viewing videos of the candidates policies on sustainability.
RIBA Architecture Gallery

Living City Forum
Tuesday 09 May
6.30pm
with Herbert Girardet, Patrick Bellew of Atelier Ten, Robin Murray of Ecologika and Dickon Robinson of Peabody Trust. Chaired by Paul Finch, Publishing Editor, emap. the event will outline practical steps to take forward possible outcomes of the Living City initiative.

Education Sustainability Forum
Tuesday 16 May
2.30pm to 5.30pm
Event for technology and design teachers in architecture.
Contact: Pamela Edwards, RIBA Education

Green Kids Workshop
Saturday 10 June
11am
Bring the children to the Architecture Week family day at RIBA. This workshop, run by the Centre for Sustainability, is free.

Left: **A double-page spread for the Royal Institute of British Architects' Annual Report. Such multipage book work relies on a strong underpinning grid structure and clear typographic signposting to guide the reader and maintain interest.**
Design by Studio Myerscough, UK

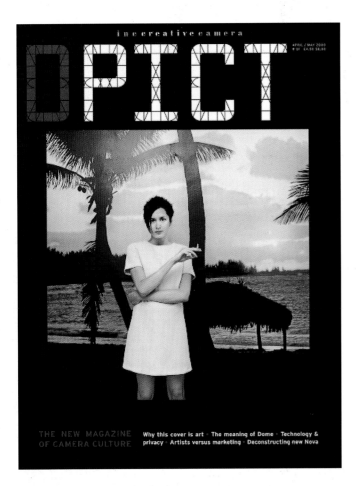

Above: *DPICT*, a creative photography magazine, was able to take advantage of IBM's Infoprint Colour 100 printer and print 560 different, personalized covers for its launch edition. The computerized selection, delivery, and output of discrete text and imagery is beginning to alter our perception of volume publishing as new printing technology is exploited.
Design by *DPICT*, UK

Right: The Providian 2000 Annual Report focused on the financial services company's employees and the cities where they lived and worked. In doing so the report humanized what might otherwise seem a faceless corporation. The sensitive and creative imagery and interesting assembly of disparate typographic elements is facilitated by the flexible tools of the page-layout application.
Design by Cahan and Associates, USA

DESIGN FOR ADVERTISING

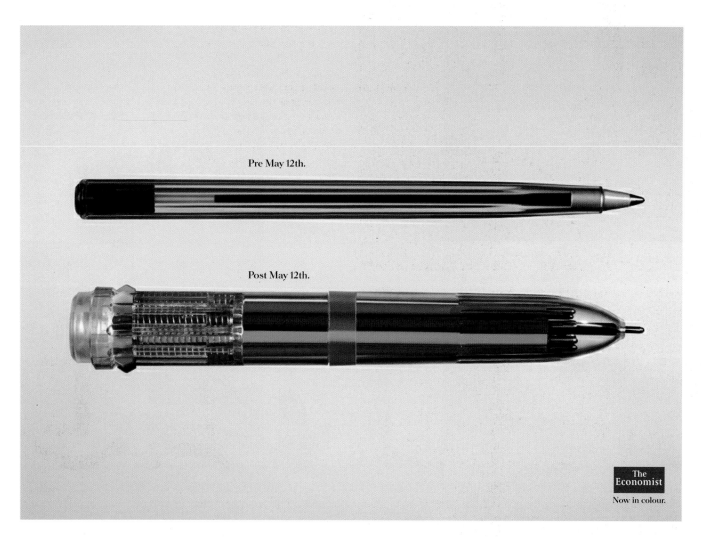

Pre May 12th.

Post May 12th.

The Economist
Now in colour.

Left and above: A series of British Airways posters by M & C Saatchi displayed in London Underground stations. Digital printing allows for customized, large-format posters, made in small quantities, providing advertisers with opportunities for focusing on specific target audiences.
Design by M & C Saachi , UK

Top: Double-page spread advertisement for *The Economist* magazine, 'Now in Colour'. A simple photographic image to make a powerful point.
Design by Abbott Meade Vickers, UK

Left: This advertisement works by association: the slick engineering used to produce London's Millennium Wheel to that of the Audi. In advertising this is called 'borrowed interest'. In visualizing the composition, the image would have been mocked up either as a Photoshop collage or as a 'moodboard' (usually rendered in marker and pencil). Note the treatment of the sky (the negative space), flattened in tone and colour to make the body text legible.
Design by Bartle Bogle Hegarty, UK

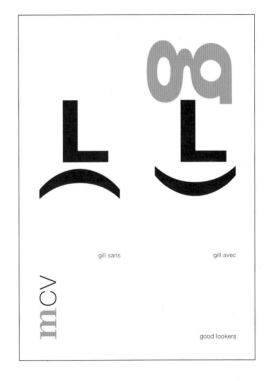

Left: Claimed to be the world's largest building graphic at over 150 metres high, this promotion, for the Dutch national football team, was produced by large-format digital printers VgL who printed 4500 panels covering 10,000 square metres. Printed on 3M Perforated Window Marking Film (PWMF), the graphics do not prevent people from seeing out through the building's windows.
Design by Wieden and Kennedy, Netherlands

Above: This full-page magazine advertisement for the recruitment consultants MCV, aimed at creatives proves the power of simplicity and wit.
Design by Peter Stimpson, UK

DESIGN FOR PACKAGING

Left: The catalogue for an exhibition of fashion design by Jill Ritblat was wittily designed to be carried as a handbag.
Designed by Area, UK

Right: When packing becomes an invitation. For the opening ceremony of Zeum, an interactive arts centre in San Francisco, invitees received a velvet drawstring bag containing a brick of modelling clay elegantly wrapped in the invitation itself.
Design by Cahan and Associates, USA

Above: Wrapping paper is highly flexible and, ultimately, the simplest form of packaging. This example, designed by Summa for a Spanish supermarket, uses colour coding to identify delicatessen items, meats, vegetables, fish, and bread products.
Design by Summa, Spain

Right: **Making a virtue out of simplicity, this entirely typographic solution by Simon and Lars for a small bakery reflects the fresh, uncomplicated, yet upmarket product.**
Design by Simon and Lars, UK

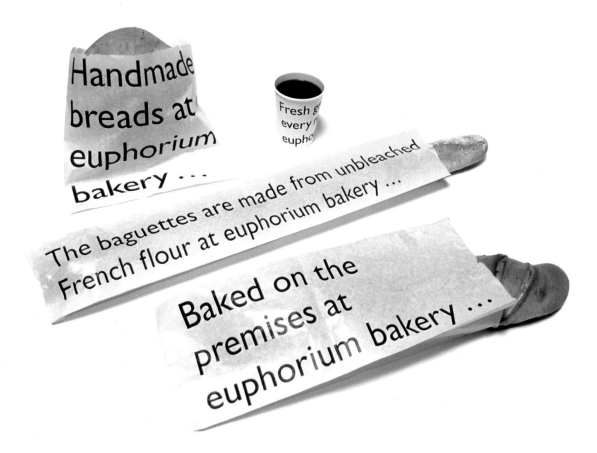

Right: **The Veuve Clicquot champagne laminated cardboard 'Magic Box' unfolds to create a strong, insulated and perfectly watertight ice bucket.**
Design by Veuve Clicquot, France

DESIGN FOR SIGNAGE

Left: Taking digital design quite literally, the interior and exterior graphics for Apple Computer's research and development campus borrow pixellated imagery from the company's distinctive graphical user interface.
Design by Sussman/Prejza & Co, USA

Below: Signage has sometimes to be subtle and understated in order to fit into interior environments. Choice of materials and scale of presentation is all-important, as can be seen here in the elegant freestanding lobby sign.
Design by Sussman/Prejza & Co., USA

Right: These signage icons for various sporting activities installed in the Nishi Kasai district, Tokyo, are integrated into street furniture, which seeks to minimize their intrusion without compromising their effectiveness.
Design by Edogawa Ward, Japan

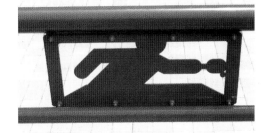

Left: This signage system reflects the strong colours used for the Georges Pompidou Centre in Paris and creates a special energy for a building devoted to the promotion of the visual arts.
Design by Integral Ruedi Bauer & Associés, France

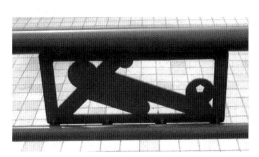

Below: Signs are not always explicitly designed as such. This decorative element on a Swiss school has become a familiar landmark and works much as a purpose-built sign would.
Design by Niklaus Troxler, Switzerland

DESIGN FOR EXHIBITION

Above: **The Newseum, located in Washington D.C., deals with all aspects of news-gathering and reporting. The exhibition design incorporates the illuminated front pages of newspapers and a video newswall as well as computer stations for interactive learning. The visually dynamic space reflects the constant flow of information, news, and data in the modern world.**
Design by Ralph Applebaum Associates, USA

Above: **The design of the Xerox trade stand is dominated a 10-metre-high example of the memorable, partly pixellated, capital X that represents Xerox everywhere.**
Design by IDEO, USA

Left: This curving wall, created for a University of Rochester exhibition, demonstrates how design for exhibition can be a liberating pursuit – unconstrained as it is by paper size formats or the ubiquitous rectangle of the computer monitor.
Design by Poulin & Morris, USA

Above: The 'Power of Maps' exhibition at the Cooper Hewitt National Design Museum in New York incorporates exhibition panels that reflect the folding nature of maps and how they are used.
Design by Pentagram, USA

DESIGN FOR THE INTERNET

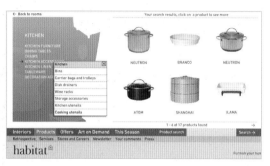

Above: www.habitat.co.uk
This Macromedia Flash-based website for the famous interiors store reflects its aesthetic values while efficiently presenting a large and regularly updated range of products. On the home page, animated sequences introduce each new season.
Design by Digit, UK

Left: www.allyourprey.com
British designers Richard Bacon and Martin Thompson created a website in their own distinctive style to showcase their photography and illustration work.
Design by AYP, UK

Above and top: www.identikal.com
Designers Adam and Nick Hayes are best known for their fresh, modern typefaces and illustrations. Their self-designed website not only shows their work, but also incorporates an ecommerce section offering fonts and other merchandise for sale.
Design by Identikal, UK

FRONT | ISSUES | NEWS | ★ SPECIALS | 🛒 STORE

K10k backissues

Kaliber Frontpage - A yummy grabbag o' design goodies

Backissue selecta

Issue 0151

Freedom of Expression
...
by Adriana de Barros

ISSUE DESCRIPTION

Have you ever thought about the concept: Many artists today want to have freedom of expression, but once they create their own art piece, they don't want others to copy it?

ISSUE REQUIREMENTS

IE 5.0 | NN 6.0 | FLASH | NONE

ISSUE RATINGS

HUMOR		COMPLEXITY
SMOOTHNESS		INNOVATION
AVERAGE		no. of ratings: 491

Specials

★ KALIBER SPECIALS

PHOTOPACKS | ONDISPLAY | PXLPATTERNS

37 top images

FLASH IN THE CAN 2004
FABULOUS FLASH FUN IN TORONTO, CANADA

★ KALIBER MATCHMAKER

RANDOM | LIST PROJECTS | WHAT IS THIS ?!!

Japan4 Redesign

Desc: We're a consortium of disc jockies located ...

Needed: Graphic Designer

★ GLOBAL EVENT LOCATOR

LISTING | CALENDAR | SUBMIT

Upcoming Events

Nov 29 - Dec 05
Last Lemon & Harold' ...
Animations, sculptures line-drawings, ...

Dec 01 - Dec 03
FlashForMexico

n this important festival, Flash of Me ...

★ GENERIC MEDUTAINMENT

TRAILERPARK | MOODSTATSSTATS

01	De-Lovely
02	The Burial Society
03	The Terminal

News

🗞 KALIBER CONTROL TOWER & GOOD VIBE NEWSFEED

NEWSFEED | CUSTOM | LINKS | AUTHORS | SUBMIT LINK

CHRIS PAPASADERO [FWIS]

Finally! An earth-friendly computer for $100

18 hours old - Nov. 27, 2004 at 13:09

CURT CLONINGER [LAB404]

from Avenida Paulista in São Paulo -- Deep/Young Ethereal Radio Broadcast #14: Brazil

02 days old - Nov. 26, 2004 at 5:15

CALVIN HO [ATOMICATTACK]

You don't like your car? Change it.

03 days old - Nov. 26, 2004 at 0:34

DANIEL KOH [AMATEUR PROVOKATEUR]

B.I.O. (by invitation only) series 1 are now

REFRESH ⇄ | SEARCH THE MUTHA ▼

Store

NEW K10k TEES   ID #005

NIELSEN ESPECIAL

MOODSTATS APP   ID #002

Now also for OS X
MONITOR YOUR MOODS

KALIBERUCKUS™   ID #003
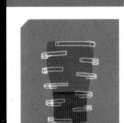
TYPOGRAPHIC BABY

---

k.net
an online magazine,
d meeting-place for
s. The site's layout –
'blog', with stories
on the fly – carries
ation than the image-
es that once seemed
sign-conscious
nique visual identity.
Council, USA

nessstorehouse.com
brewer's visitor
lin uses Flash
, and interactivity to
multimedia tour.
ation, UK

GUINNESS STOREHOUSE

A COPPER HAS A 600 BARREL CAPACITY, 1...
SO EACH COPPER HOLDS...
88 PINTS,

04
WHAT'S THE MYSTERIOUS PROCESS?

04
WHAT'S THE MYSTERIOUS PROCESS?

DRINKING. THE FINAL STAGE IN THE GUINNESS PROCESS. BUT WHAT COMES BEFORE?
JUST START THE BREWING MACHINE AND YOU'LL DISCOVER HOW TO BREW THE PERFECT PINT.

▸ TERMS & CONDITIONS
▸ PRIVACY POLICY

HOME

GUINNESS

» Terms & Conditions · » Privacy Policy · » Responsible Drinking · » Site Map   © 2004 GUINNESS4 STOREHOUSE

» Home » Info » Tickets » Explore » Meetings » Shop » Stories   » Deutsch » Italiano » Español » Français

DESIGN FOR MULTIMEDIA AND GAMES

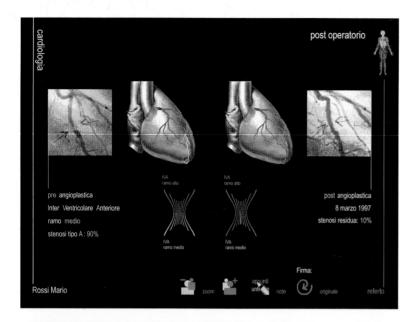

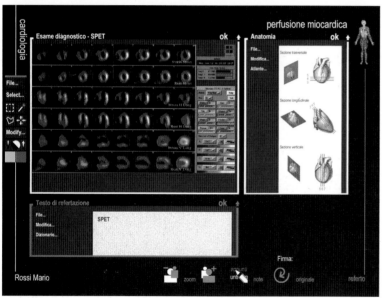

Above: **Multimedia can be used to produce effective educational tools for many specialist professions. These screens are a sample from an interactive multimedia project aimed at explaining the use of technical imaging equipment for medical diagnosis.**
Design by Maddalene Beltrami and the Ospedale Maggiore di Milano, Italy

Below: InterStitch created this title sequence for the feature documentary film, *Aging in America*. The film was a seven-year project to chronicle the varied perspectives of elderly populations. The broader project comprised a book, a travelling photography exhibit, and the film. For the title sequence, details from photographs were animated in three-dimensional space with lighting, shadows, and typography.
Design by InterStitch, USA

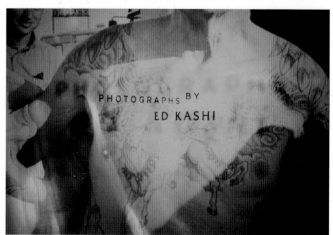

Below: This animation formed part of a winning bid for a project development competition. Created in Adobe Premiere, it was presented on a laptop and via an LCD projector.
Design by RTKL

Top: *Need For Speed Underground 2*
Computer game design is an arena where digital graphics are often pushed to their technical limits. Development is a team exercise, and the graphic designer may have only a limited role in the process, but visual design can have a huge impact on the success of the finished game.
Design by Electronic Arts, USA

Above: *Championship Manager 4*
All games require some element of user interface design, and for some, such as management-based titles, it is central to gameplay. Here the skills of the multimedia designer come to the fore. The challenge is to present information and choices with perfect clarity within the overall look and mood of the game.
Design by Eidos, UK

DESIGN BASICS

Basic design principles are the building blocks of graphic communication. To appreciate their value and relevance it is best to begin by looking at their particular characteristics away from an applied context.

Graphic designers find themselves working at both large and small scales across increasingly varied areas at local, national, and international levels. The flexible, innovative perspective they need must be underpinned by basic principles if they are to make informed design decisions and aesthetic judgments. These principles are common to other design disciplines and provide a valuable constant in the midst of the continually developing opportunities with which the graphic designer is presented.

PART 01. DESIGN BASICS

CHAPTER ONE

THE VALUE OF DESIGN BASICS

Left: **Promotional brochure for the** *Museo de Arte Contemporaneo (MARCO)* in Monterey in Mexico. The square, derived from the shape of the building, forms the basis of the museum's logo and overall visual identity.
Design by Lance Wyman, USA

Above: **Circular architectural forms soften the large ticketing area in Chicago airport and offer an organic-looking background to the starkly contrasting rectangular information panels, ensuring that the latter stand out.**
Design by Carol Naughton & Associates, USA

PRIMARY SHAPES The familiar shapes – square, circle, and triangle – together with their three-dimensional derivatives – cube, sphere, and pyramid – underpin all the structures seen around us. There is very little that will not break down into, or visually relate to, some form of primary shape.

The square, like the cube, is a wholly static form with no directional pull. It can be used to frame, exclude, include, attract, or define area, or for modular division, and it will sit comfortably in almost any arrangement of multiples. Even when rotated and in a more dynamic, diamond form, it retains its inherent, fixed quality. Minor modification to a linear square will, however, begin to direct the eye and also create associations. For example, if the corners are opened, or if a side is removed or tilted, the eye will move into the shape and associations of exit or entrance will be made. An extended square, or rectangle, directs the eye along, up or down its length and beyond, making the eye look for common alignments.

The circle has two main attributes – it provides a powerful focus for the eye and at the same time invites it to take a circular journey round either itself or a circular layout of any kind of element. By contrast, a series of circles suggests self-contained units and so makes the eye 'jump' from one unit to the other, quickly tiring it. Although circles do not easily fit together, the eye can be made to spin across the surface by physically linking a series of circles. The pace of the spin is controlled by the size of circle.

The triangle is a balanced and completely stable form in both two- and three-dimensional form, but also suggests a dynamic energy, even when equilateral. Unlike the circle or square, the proportions of a triangle can be radically altered to give it directional force without affecting its basic shape. The eye finds this directional force difficult to ignore.

It is important to understand the significant influence that these key forms have on the viewer's perception. Such an understanding will enable the designer to organize confidently the form and content of a design in order to communicate a visual message.

Kieler Woche   1997

21.- 29. Juni

Above: **The primary shapes and bright colours that underlie the concept of this 3D, giant-sized children's hospital sign are familiar things with which a child can comfortably identify. Variations on the playful and cheerful signage theme are used through the system.** Design by Emery Vincent Design, Australia

Left: **This poster for a sailing regatta uses a simple, primary shape inspired by both sails and flags used in the regattas. Cropped and overlapping, the shapes evoke a sense of celebration.** Design by Niklaus Troxler, Switzerland

POINT, LINE, AND AREA are the basic elements used in all graphic design and, as with primary shapes, the way in which they are used will affect the overall perception of any communication. Most basic visual design decisions involve some representative combination of these shapes and elements. These may be used explicitly or implicitly, and with varying levels of complexity.

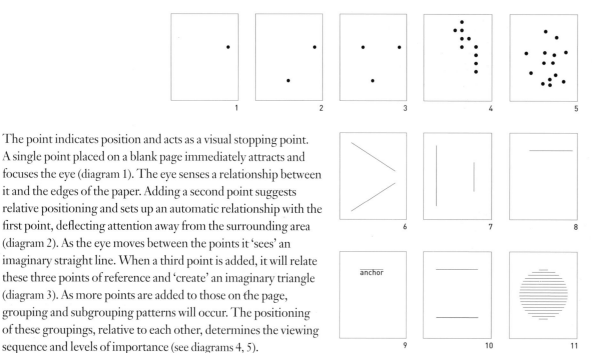

Diagrams:
1. A point of focus.
2. Points suggesting a line.
3. Points suggesting a shape.
4. Organized grouping of points leading the eye from start to finish in an ordered way.
5. Random grouping of points. This causes the eye to scan the area constantly looking for starting and finishing points.
6 & 7. Lines creating an illusion of depth.
8. Placing a line closer to one edge of an area will direct the eye along it.
9. Centring a line on a page closer to either the top or bottom will visually anchor it.
10. Lines may be used to direct the eye to a given area.
11. Rules of different lengths build an image. Lines of type can produce the same effect.

The point indicates position and acts as a visual stopping point. A single point placed on a blank page immediately attracts and focuses the eye (diagram 1). The eye senses a relationship between it and the edges of the paper. Adding a second point suggests relative positioning and sets up an automatic relationship with the first point, deflecting attention away from the surrounding area (diagram 2). As the eye moves between the points it 'sees' an imaginary straight line. When a third point is added, it will relate these three points of reference and 'create' an imaginary triangle (diagram 3). As more points are added to those on the page, grouping and subgrouping patterns will occur. The positioning of these groupings, relative to each other, determines the viewing sequence and levels of importance (see diagrams 4, 5).

Line essentially indicates direction and so leads the eye. It will also encourage the eye to continue beyond its length. It may be either implied through the juxtaposition of two elements, as with points, or actual, as in a drawn line, a line of text, a typographic rule or set of images or other elements. The strategic placement of several lines can create an illusion of depth (linear perspective) (diagrams 6, 7). Lines may also be used to suggest form, delineate, enclose or divide, emphasize, and act as a visual marker (diagrams 8, 9, 10, 11).

Area is a defined surface or plane, and it acts as a visual container, drawing attention to its content or edges. Graphic designers are concerned with area as a means of defining format and proportion and as a way of pacing

Left: With the competition of both web and CD-ROM, designers of brochures, catalogues, and promotional print are having to reconsider the possibilities of size, format, content, and surface quality. This inventive exhibition 'catalogue' mixes techniques and materials to produce a pack that works as a visual and tactile experience to inform and entertain. Design by Jo Stockham, UK

Right: Creating an axis through proportional division of space can be an effective way of visually coordinating radically different-sized elements within a single design concept, such as an exhibition or display.

Left: Historic and contemporary sites in downtown Manhattan are linked in a series of walking tours, each colour-coded and physically identified by coloured dots set into the pavement. The series of dots is distinct yet subtle enough not to intrude on the environment.
Design by Chermayeff & Geismar, USA

Right: Created for a group producing film commercials, the design of this letterhead was quirkily inspired by the white of the three shirts blending into the white of a conference table in a dimly lit studio. The small proportion of image to white space gives the design a dynamic that forms the basis of the group's visual identity.
Design by Alan Fletcher, UK

the viewing within a design at any scale. It is easy to be distracted by disparate elements on the surface without realizing that area is also a powerful element in its own right – 'empty' areas can create energy within a design – and can be used to direct the eye from one place to another. This energy is known as dynamic white space.

Choice of format (rectangular or otherwise) may be dictated by either job content or production practicalities or both. There are some time-tested formats that have proved to be particularly suited to a wide range of uses. Print, for example, makes frequent use of the international standard series of A and B paper sizes, which are based on a rectangle having sides in the ratio of 1:1.414, the latter remarkable number being the square root of 2. Repeated folding parallel to the short side allows paper in this

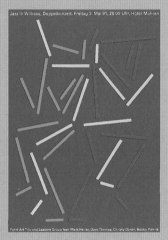

Above: Simple lines, strategically placed, symbolize saxophonist, dancer, and trumpet-player. Their dynamic positioning is designed to capture individual movements that combine to create a harmonious performance as a trio.
Design by Niklaus Troxler, Switzerland

proportion to be halved into further rectangles – all in the same 1:1.414 proportion – giving the designer a flexible range of proportionally related sizes with which to work.

Although screen-design formats generally follow the maximum allowable vertical and horizontal dimensions, there is no reason why this must be rigidly adhered to.

Equal division of an area conveys a static feel, whereas contrasting division communicates greater dynamism. The golden section has been used for centuries as a formula for creating harmony. In this formula, the relationship of the smaller area to the larger area is equal to the relationship of the larger area to the whole – approximately 8:13.

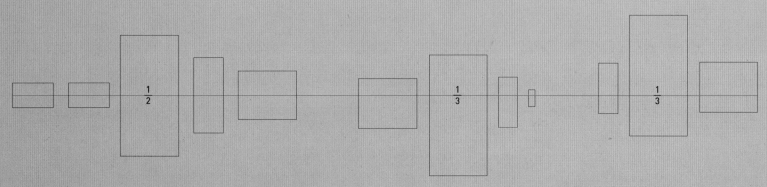

DYNAMICS, EMPHASIS, AND CONTRAST Visual emphasis is a means of specifically directing the viewer, ordering complex information by creating a visual hierarchy and highlighting elements. Four basic ways of creating visual emphasis are through the use of size, weight, colour, and disposition (placement).

Headline

Dos espacios que se aman, que se besan, pour una puerta que no se sabe si separa o une. Aquí todo tiene la suficente claridad y la deliciosa oscuridad de la armoniá. No nos sabemos dentro hasta que unos pasos más allá de la primera puerta, nos encontramos fuera del edificio; nunca sabemos qué es demasiado. Todo recuerdo de este viaje será el instante en que abandonamos esa sensación de recogimiento, memoria irrecuperable de un espacio inmenso, inmensamente fugaz.

Small print following definition of a man was written by R Buckminster-Fuller in 1938 "A self-balancing, 28 jointed adapter-based biped; an electrochemical reduction plant, integral with segregated stowages of special energy extract in storage batteries for subsequent actuation of thousands of hydraulic and pneumatic pumps with motors attached; 62,000 miles of capillaries...

Left: Typesize is generally used to rank text into levels of importance – in this case headline, body text, and small print. Drop caps (the large 'D') are used to indicate the start of a new section of text.

The skilled use of emphasis is essential to communicating with clarity and pace, and works to focus and progressively direct the viewer through or around a design. Emphasis, like all other design basics, should always be considered in relation to the design as a whole. Many examples of size, weight, colour, and disposition used as emphasis can be seen in newspapers and magazines where the visual pace is broken down into small parcels of information. These are identified (or emphasized) in many different ways, for example, by a heading (size), bold introductory text (weight), a coloured rule or tonal change in text setting (colour), placement or discrete arrangement of elements (disposition).

Size creates emphasis through contrast in proportions of format, type, image, relationship of elements, dimension (length and height), and volume (area and depth). Reducing an element to a small size on a large format can be just as powerful as enlarging it to fill the area, if not more so.

Weight suggests visual substance and mass, which can range from heavy or bold to light. It is often used in conjunction with size but works successfully when used across uniformly sized elements. Contrast in weight alone between individual words or lines can be effective in large amounts of text. Changes of weight between elements or blocks of continuous or display

Above: The contrasting type size and positioning of the headlines in this book spread, together with the diagonal, inward direction of the image, bring the reader directly into the experience. Using lower case letters at a large scale, tightly kerning them and reducing the scale of the surfer to match the letters, accentuates the emotion and drama. Design by Barney Pickard, UK

Right:
Diagram 1: The exact central placement of an element within an area will produce a fixed appearance.
Diagram 2: Placing an element close to the top edge of an area will encourage the eye to travel upwards beyond it.
Diagram 3: Placement to the left and a third of the way down will draw the eye downwards.

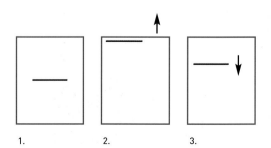

1.　　　　2.　　　　3.

Below: The Trocadero complex in London makes use of the latest technology to create an ambience of energy, excitement, and power within the seven-storey space. Natural light is excluded in favour of vibrant colour lighting. With more than a hundred different, independently controlled light sources, rotating billboards, a video wall, TV screens, sound, animatronics, lasers, and smoke machines, the Trocadero is a prime example of a digital entertainment destination.
Design: RTKL and Jonathan Spiers & Associates

La puerta con dos casas es lo permanente, inacesible. Esta casa de alforja se encuentra en el territorio de los acontecimientos simultáneos. Dos espacios que se aman, que se besan, pour una puerta que no se sabe si separa o une. Aquí todo tiene la suficente claridad y la deliciosa oscuridad de la armoniá. No nos sabemos dentro hasta que unos pasos más allá de la primera puerta, nos encontramos fuera del edificio; nunca sabemos qué es demasiado. Todo recuerdo de este viaje será el instante en que abandonamos esa sensación de recogimiento, memoria irrecuperable de un espacio inmenso, inmensamente fugaz.

La puerta con dos casas es lo permanente, inacesible. Esta casa de alforja se encuentra en el territorio de los acontecimientos simultáneos. Dos espacios que se aman, que se besan, pour una puerta que no se sabe si separa o une. Aquí todo tiene la suficente claridad y la deliciosa oscuridad de la armoniá. No nos sabemos dentro hasta que unos pasos más allá de la primera puerta, nos encontramos fuera del edificio; nunca sabemos qué es demasiado. Todo recuerdo de este viaje será el instante en que abandonamos esa sensación de recogimiento, memoria irrecuperable de un espacio inmenso, inmensamente fugaz.

Above: Text set in three different weights of the same typeface – light, regular, and bold. These variants can be effectively used to create a visual hierarchy with continuous text as well as to lend tone and texture (typographic colour) to text.

La puerta con dos casas es lo permanente, inacesible. Esta casa de alforja se encuentra en el territorio de los acontecimientos simultáneos. Dos espacios que se aman, que se besan, pour una puerta que no se sabe si separa o une. Aquí todo tiene la suficente claridad y la deliciosa oscuridad de la armoniá. No nos sabemos dentro hasta que unos pasos más allá de la primera puerta, nos encontramos fuera del edificio; nunca sabemos qué es demasiado. Todo recuerdo de este viaje será el instante en que abandonamos esa sensación de recogimiento, memoria irrecuperable de un espacio inmenso, inmensamente fugaz.

Left: The signage system developed for this hospital site uses distinctive colours and shapes directly influenced by the idiosyncratic design of the hospital building. The building has a strong identity of its own and the signs have to be very distinctive in themselves, yet visually link with it. This sign picks up the strong colour and quirky shape of a nearby red wall and is illuminated internally at night.
Design by by Tom Graboski Associates, USA

text will set up different spatial planes and can influence the viewing and reading order. Degrees of density and openness in text and the tonal value of images can be used to increase or decrease levels of emphasis.

The use of colour not only highlights, but also adds depth to every aspect of emphasis through association, mood, temperature, and emotion. Appropriate colour choice can be based on any one or a combination of these areas. Random choice or personal preference in the use of colour can wrongly emphasize or detract from the content or message. Interaction and / or contrast between individual colours together with the level of saturation (intensity) and brightness (tone) will significantly modify the degree and volume of emphasis (see Designing with Colour). Typographic 'colour' created by weight change from one body of text to another can also be used as a means of subtle emphasis or contrast.

Disposition, like colour, interfaces with every aspect of emphasis. It is so integral to visual communication that its potential is often undervalued. Disposition is inextricably linked to area and is concerned with the strategic placement of elements. It can subtly or dynamically draw attention to elements within the overall design area. For example, the small folio sitting on its own at the bottom or top of a page does not shout but is instantly found by the reader through its unique positioning. Similarly an indent (the placement or disposition

ONE
STEP
CONTACT
LENS SOLUTION

PEROXIDE SYSTEM

DISINFECTS & NEUTRALISES

FOR ALL TYPES OF CONTACT LENSES

superdrug

The Art and
Architecture of Light
Richard MacCormac
RIBA President-elect

Right: One of a series of posters in which the capital letter 'A' was used as the key design feature. In this example the size, angle, and distortion of the letter plays with the idea of a shaft of light contrasting with the predominantly black space.
Design by Pentagram, UK

Left: This contact lens solution packaging makes a clever play on the opticians' eye chart and uses the varying type sizes as a way of ordering and highlighting elements of the product.
Design by Williams Murray Hamm, UK

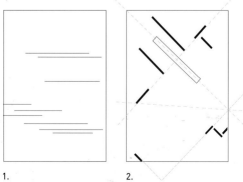

1.   2.

Left: 1. Asymmetrical placement works best if the elements are informally grouped with the space in-between and around used to lead the eye though them. 2. Diagonal arrangements need careful consideration in structuring in order to avoid causing the eye to dart from element to element. Setting up basic directional lines can help avoid this.

of the first word in sequences of paragraphs) quietly creates pace for the reader. It is surprising how successfully judicious use of disposition can work without recourse to other methods of emphasis. However, poorly considered placement of elements on a page can set up confusing dynamics that may hinder the reader.

Contrast is used to create and sustain visual interest, in the same way that tone and intonation add interest to speech. Without contrast, graphic communication would become dull and flat, with little to attract attention or sustain interest. Contrast draws on visual opposites or dissimilarity to emphasize, differentiate, set up competition, attract and change the reading pace. It can be both quantitative and qualitative, obvious or subtle. Its use should always be considered in direct relation to the concept and the design as a whole. As there is little limit to the areas in which contrast may be used, it can be helpful to look initially for potential within the main emphasis groups – size, colour, weight, and disposition.

Everyday visual opposites (loud and quiet, warm and cool, balance and motion) can also be a source of inspiration for graphic contrast. To be effective, contrast needs to be appropriate to the concept and be closely linked to emphasis. Overuse may result in a lack of focus in the design, with elements fighting for the viewer's attention and the eye being pulled in different directions.

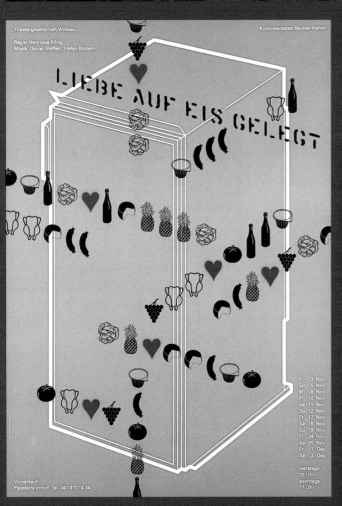

Left: This poster uses dramatic yet subtle contrasts in size, weight, colour, disposition, and proportion to communicate a sense of architectural modernity.
Design by: Tenazas Design, USA

Below left: This poster for an unusual theatre piece with a theme of food and love, based around a refrigerator, combines disposition and colour to highlight the key elements of the play. The subtle use of line to depict the refrigerator prevents its comparative size from overpowering them.
Design by Niklaus Troxler, Switzerland

Below: The colour palette created for this book was designed to underline the zen quality of tea. The palette was given to the photographer to help in selecting props so that some element of the colour chosen for the chapter openings would appear in the photograph.
Design by Chronicle Books, USA

Above: The idea of 'bigness' was the key concept for the design of this cookery book. Over-sized numerals are used to emphasize the large number of recipes in the book.

These shift vertically and horizontally, bleeding off the page, using disposition and cropping to reinforce the message.
Design by Chronicle Books, USA

THE MECHANICS OF TYPE The designer needs to understand how type is constructed and assembled as well as having an aesthetic appreciation of it. Letters of the alphabet are made up of complex combinations of straight lines and curves that give them their individual character.

Far right and below: **Comparison of the variation in cap and x-height between four typefaces of the same point size.**

All letters have common, notional points of reference in their physical make-up, regardless of the typeface design, style, or size. These notional points are the baseline (the line on which all letters sit), the x-height (the height of the lowercase letters), the ascender line (the extent of the vertical upstrokes of lowercase letters), and the descender line (the extent of the downstrokes of lowercase letters).

The terms used to identify the different parts and structures of letterforms within this notional framework help to ensure accurate recognition and reference (see diagram above). Some characters have detailing unique both to themselves and to the typeface, for example the ear of lowercase g or the tail of uppercase Q. However, although letterforms are recognized by these specific characteristics, the overall shape of the characters and the counter-shapes (enclosed areas) also contribute to the character of a typeface. Although there is considerable individuality within the different characters of a typeface, typefaces are designed to form a cohesive whole and give a global colour and texture when typeset. Appreciating the physical make-up of type helps the designer to identify points to look for and so facilitates typeface choice for different purposes.

Although the size of type is described by a common system (usually in points), you need to be aware that different typefaces at, say, 10 pt, may look quite different in size (see examples above). This happens because of the relative proportions of the characters. Helvetica, for instance, has a large x-height and comparatively short ascenders and descenders, whereas some Garamonds have

Times

La puerta con dos casas es lo permanente, inacesible. Esta casa de alforja se encuentra en el territorio de los acontecimientos simultáneos. Dos espacios que se aman, que se besan, pour una puerta que no se sabe si separa o une. Aquí todo tiene la suficente claridad y la deliciosa oscuridad de la armoniá. No nos sabemos dentro hasta que unos pasos más allá de la primera puerta, nos encontramos fuera del edificio; nunca sabemos qué es demasiado. Todo recuerdo de este viaje será el instante en que abandonamos esa sensación de recogimiento, memoria irrecuperable de un espacio inmenso, inmensamente fugaz.

Palatino

La puerta con dos casas es lo permanente, inacesible. Esta casa de alforja se encuentra en el territorio de los acontecimientos simultáneos. Dos espacios que se aman, que se besan, pour una puerta que no se sabe si separa o une. Aquí todo tiene la suficente claridad y la deliciosa oscuridad de la armoniá. No nos sabemos dentro hasta que unos pasos más allá de la primera puerta, nos encontramos fuera del edificio; nunca sabemos qué es demasiado. Todo recuerdo de este viaje será el instante en que abandonamos esa sensación de recogimiento, memoria irrecuperable de un espacio inmenso, inmensamente fugaz.

Bodoni

La puerta con dos casas es lo permanente, inacesible. Esta casa de alforja se encuentra en el territorio de los acontecimientos simultáneos. Dos espacios que se aman, que se besan, pour una puerta que no se sabe si separa o une. Aquí todo tiene la suficente claridad y la deliciosa oscuridad de la armoniá. No nos sabemos dentro hasta que unos pasos más allá de la primera puerta, nos encontramos fuera del edificio; nunca sabemos qué es demasiado. Todo recuerdo de este viaje será el instante en que abandonamos esa sensación de recogimiento, memoria irrecuperable de un espacio inmenso, inmensamente fugaz.

Garamond

La puerta con dos casas es lo permanente, inacesible. Esta casa de alforja se encuentra en el territorio de los acontecimientos simultáneos. Dos espacios que se aman, que se besan, pour una puerta que no se sabe si separa o une. Aquí todo tiene la suficente claridad y la deliciosa oscuridad de la armoniá. No nos sabemos dentro hasta que unos pasos más allá de la primera puerta, nos encontramos fuera del edificio; nunca sabemos qué es demasiado. Todo recuerdo de este viaje será el instante en que abandonamos esa sensación de recogimiento, memoria irrecuperable de un espacio inmenso, inmensamente fugaz.

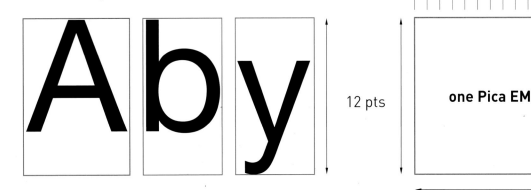

POINTS AND PICAS.
Right: The small unit, the **point**, is .35136 mm, about 1/72 of an inch. The larger unit, the **pica**, is made up of 12 points. All type sizes (measured over the overall body of the type) are specified in points. Larger distances, especially column widths, are traditionally measured in picas, although many digital designers now prefer to work in millimetres or inches.

12 pts

one Pica EM

12 pts

a relatively small x-height and longer ascenders and descenders. These differences in proportion result in different typographic colour when text is set – the bigger the x-height, the more open the texture and colour, making it essential to look at different sample settings. For the same reason, the number of characters that will fit on a given line length varies between typefaces at the same size. Even if this makes little difference to small amounts of copy, it can make a considerable difference to many pages of text.

THE POINT SYSTEM

Digital processing allows designers to work on screen in a range of interchangeable measurement systems, to their own choice. However, when dealing with type, most people find it more practical to work with a common system that allows everyone to grasp and quickly appreciate the values being talked about. The point system used for measuring type – unique to the printing industry – has, surprisingly, remained the same since the days of metal type. In the days of phototypesetting, an attempt was made to use millimetres as a basic unit for type measurement, but it was never taken up.

Type size, as shown in the diagram, is determined by the size of the type body (which, in the past, was a piece of movable metal) rather than by the actual letter. Nowadays, the body can be considered as the distance between the top of the highest part of the letterform (usually an ascender) to the bottom of the lowest (a descender), plus a notional amount of clearance, which varies from typeface to typeface.

The typographer's point is approximately 0.3 mm or 1/72 inch. Such a very small unit is necessary when describing very small sizes of type. However, attempting to express large measurement in points is cumbersome, so a larger unit of 12 pt, the pica em, is used. In many programs, it is possible to select pica ems or picas as a unit of measurement, for example, horizontal measurement for setting column widths. In practice, digital graphic designers will probably find themselves working in several measurement systems – points

for type, millimetres for area or page size, and inches for scanning resolutions (dpi).

The em (without the pica) is a measurement notionally based on the width of a capital M. Therefore, the value of the em is the same as the point size being used. Units of digital letter spacing and character construction are based on dividing the em of the given type size (be it 8 pt or 24 pt) into hundredths or thousandths – infinitely more subtle than in earlier times.

Below: Digital graphic designers often find themselves working with several measurement systems – points for type, millimetres for page sizes, centimetres as a familiar unit for sizing graphic elements, and inches for image resolutions (dpi). Fortunately, the software can convert effortlessly between all of these. Adding a suffix such as 'mm' or 'pt' (points) after entering a figure is enough to notify most programs that they should take a dimension as being specified in those units.

Preferences	
General	Units & Increments
Text	
Composition	Ruler Units
Units & Increments	Origin:
Grids	Points
Guides & Pasteboard	Picas
Dictionary	Horizontal: ✓ Inches points
Spelling	Inches Decimal
Story Editor Display	Vertical: Millimetres points
Display Performance	Centimetres
File Handling	Keyboard Incremen Ciceros
Updates	Cursor Key: Custom
	Size/Leading: 2 pt
	Baseline Shift: 2 pt
	Kerning: 20 /1000 em

Cancel   OK

DESIGNING WITH TYPE When working with type, the graphic designer automatically draws upon the influence of centuries of development. Typeface design evolved slowly as printing technology developed, but, given the flexibility of digital technology, recent typeface design has had few constraints. Radically different and new letterforms, often challenging typographic convention, have emerged alongside the redrawing and digitization of many classic typeface families originally designed for older typesetting methods.

Rather than being limited to a few fonts in a fixed number of sizes, the digital designer will typically have access to hundreds of typefaces that can be instantly scaled to any size required. Each font, moreover, is increasingly likely to contain extra characters beyond the basic alphanumeric set, including symbols, ligatures (letter combinations), fractions, accents, and even foreign alphabets.

Many typefaces fall into one the following broad groups: serif, sans serif, glyphic, decorative and display, script, blackletter, and contemporary. More recent, innovative digital typeface designs, however, follow their own rules and do not fit easily into these groups. The terms used are derived from basic characteristics such as whether or not the letters have serifs, the shape of any serif, the contrast between thick and thin strokes, and the angle of stress or axis of the letters. These characteristics combine to give a typeface its unique character, typographic colour, and rhythm. They should be carefully considered when you choose a typeface. Trying out different text settings is always useful in assessing the typographic colour and rhythm in a particular context (see page 36).

Although letterforms are necessarily restricted in shape and almost always monochromatic, it would be blinkered to

Zapf Chancery
ABCDEFGHIJKLMNOPQRSTUVWXYZ
abcdefghijklmnopqrstuvwxyz

Vag Rounded
ABCDEFGHIJKLMNOPQRSTUVWXYZ
abcdefghijklmnopqrstuvwxyz

Gridnik
ABCDEFGHIJKLMNOPQRSTUVWXYZ
abcdefghijklmnopqrstuvwxyz

Serpentine
ABCDEFGHIJKLMNOPQRSTUVWXYZ
abcdefghijklmnopqrstuvwxyz

Reactor
ABCDEFGHIJKLMNAOPQRSTUVWXYZ
ABCDEFGHIJKLMNOPQRSTUVWXYZ

Left: Adobe's Multiple Master font format made it possible to generate limitless variations in weight, proportion, and style on the same basic typeface. Although the technology never quite caught on, it has enabled the development of some remarkable – and uniquely digital – families of typefaces.
Design by Adobe, USA

Above: Recent innovative typeface designs (commonly produced digitally) follow their own rules and do not fit easily into the standard typographical family groups.

1. Old Face: marked axis inclined to the left, subtle change from thick to thin in the letterstrokes, bracketed serifs that are angled on the ascenders and an 'e' with a horizontal bar. Capital letters are sometimes shorter than ascenders.

2. Transitional: axis that is slightly inclined to the left (can also be vertical), bracketed serifs that are angled on the ascenders.

3. Modern Face: vertical axis, abrupt contrast between thick and thin letterstrokes, unbracketed (or minimally bracketed) hairline serifs.

4. Geometric Sans Serif: normally monoline letterstrokes, based on simple geometric shapes. Often with a single-storey lowercase 'a'.

5. Humanist Sans Serif: some contrast in the letterstrokes, based on inscriptional letterforms, with two-storey lowercase 'a' and 'g'.

6. Slab Serif: monoline or with minimal contrast in the letter strokes. Unbracketed, heavy serifs.

consider type as a limited graphic medium, because it can equally well be used in its own right as 'image'. In a context where pictorial images are inappropriate or do not exist, a heading, single word, or letterform can be inventively used as a graphic focal point to create interest, evoke mood, or set the scene for the rest of the design scheme. Visual onomatopoeia, in which type is made to suggest the meaning of the word visually and 'talk' to the viewer, is also an engaging way of getting the message across.

DECIDING ON A TYPEFACE

Typefaces are the voices of words and determine the visual tone of the text. The success of typographic communication depends as much on the choice of typeface as on the use of space and layout. Deciding on one typeface over another is a matter of visual judgement, fitness for purpose, and style. A close look at the basic characteristics of different typefaces within the broad groups will help to make the choice more manageable. A typeface can be specifically chosen to reflect, or contrast with, the content and mood of the text in relation to feel of the overall design, but care should be taken to

Above: **The giant type on these signs at the Melbourne Exhibition Centre works as a powerful graphic element. Although cropped and placed at odd angles, the type still retains its legibility. This dynamic typographic signage is integral to the building, adding to its unique and unmistakable character.**
Design by Emery Vincent Design, Australia

ensure that this does not conflict with the message or overpower the look of the text. Identifying the purpose and context of the text – advertising, signage, packaging, print, Web, or multimedia, the audience and the location in which it will be read – will inform the choice of size, weight, and style of type.

Type is used for informing, entertaining, providing reference, instructing, directing, or otherwise involving the reader in some way. Each of these contexts will require a different level of concentration and reading pace, and both of these factors are relevant to the choice of typeface. For example, road signage has to be instantly recognizable: using a decorative face for a directional road sign might dangerously distract the driver's attention from the road while he or she deciphers the information. Reading may be sustained (as for a book), intermittent (as for a magazine, on a website, package, or exhibition panel) or focused (as for a set of instructions or reference source). Text may need to be read under compulsion (as for a warning), or as an option (as for a disclaimer). The choice of size, weight, and style of the typeface, as well as the typeface itself, should be linked to the reading pace. For example, it would be inappropriate to set instructional text in small, closely spaced, bold type: the difficulty in reading and understanding would be reflected in the reader's attitude to the task.

It is generally felt that serif, rather than sans serif, typefaces are easier on the eye and less tiring to read over lengthy continuous text. Magazines commonly break the rule, but complete novels are not often set in sans serif. Discussion of the relative merits of serif and

Interstate Light Compressed
Interstate Compressed
Interstate Bold Compressed
Interstate Black Compressed
Interstate Light Condensed
Interstate Light Condensed Italic
Interstate Condensed
Interstate Condensed Italic
Interstate Bold Condensed
Interstate Bold Condensed Italic
Interstate Black Condensed
Interstate Light
Interstate Light Italic
Interstate Regular
Interstate Italic
Interstate Bold
Interstate Bold Italic
Interstate Black
Interstate Black Italic

Below: Lively, characterful letterforms, symbolizing the past, present, and future of the New York Public Library, combine to celebrate the start of the Library's second century. The widely varying

Left: A selection of typefaces from the extensive Interstate family. Using related typefaces within a document will help to ensure a professional-looking result.

Right: Variants in weight and proportion are shown in this example of a MultipleMaster font which maintains the intrinsic character of the letter style. MultipleMaster fonts are very useful where a broad typographic hierarchy is required without loss of character.
Design by Adobe Systems, USA

Below right: This office space and facade for Gensler Design, San Fransico, reflects the company's own design approach. Innovative graphics are used throughout the interior, where individual workstations are mixed with shared work areas. Giant dingbats above the entrance make for unusual typographic imagery. The only sign identifying the company is very small and can be seen on the lower right hand side.
Design by Gensler, USA

Below: The stark contrast in size gives this CD cover a range of levels of interest in type as image and information. Individual letterforms were enlarged and the resulting abstracted shapes layered using PhotoShop. The typeface (developed specially for the project) creates a visual tension between the heavy rounded letterforms and the crisp arrow-shaped countershapes.
Design by Swifty Typografix, UK

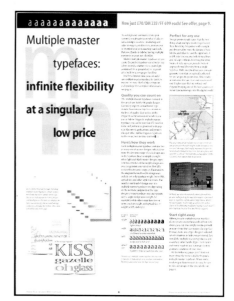

styles and sizes of letterforms are strong and interesting enough to work both individually or together in monochrome or colour at very different scales, making them highly flexible and suitable for merchandising and packaging.
Design by Chermayeff & Geismar, USA

Right: Exaggerated kerning and a degree of baseline shift transform a simple word into a powerful typographic impasse in this spread from the book *Just One More*. The size and scale of the letters in relation to the page, together with the sharply contrasting text sizes, reinforce the message.
Design by Barney Pickard, UK

Modernism, as we have know it, has served as the aesthetic, spiritual and moral conscience of our time. It embodies the essentially democratic idea of the creative artist as the inventor of a personal style, a unique vision of the world.

Modernism, as we have know it, has served as the aesthetic, spiritual and moral conscience of our time. It embodies the essentially democratic idea of the creative artist as the inventor of a personal style, a unique vision of the world. Modernism fosters a dynamic

sans serif text faces will inevitably continue. Display faces are suitable for setting a few words at a large size, rather than continuous text. Quirky or gimmicky typefaces are usually best reserved for display work. Text faces can be scaled to display sizes, but care should be taken to consider whether the letterforms still look well proportioned, and the overall character spacing (tracking or range kerning) may need to be reduced.

Most typefaces are designed with a basic roman (upright) and true italic style (or oblique, for sans serif faces) and perhaps one or two other weights (light, bold, etc). Those intended for professional text setting, however, may have extensive families of weights ranging from extra-light to ultra-black and of styles ranging from condensed to expanded. This can be useful when complex information needs different levels of emphasis; it will ensure that changes of type will work well together stylistically. The aim should be to choose a small set of ideal weights for a given purpose, however, not to mix dozens of variants.

TYPE FOR SCREEN DISPLAY

Text for monitor display must be set at sizes larger than for print, since small letterforms cannot be formed legibly by the restricted number of pixels on screen. Similarly, typefaces with fine serifs are unsuited to screen display at text sizes: fine detail is lost in the rendering. Many type manufacturers now offer faces optimized for screen display, such as AgfaMonotype's ESQ (Enhanced Screen Quality) series. The colour of background and type needs extra consideration; coloured or dark backgrounds can ease monitor glare.

THE PERFECT DAY
40 YEARS OF *SURFER* MAGAZINE

Above: **Negative leading** between the three words of this book title creates a simple typographic image that echoes the image of a perfect ride, on the perfect wave, on the perfect day. The full bleed used with the image is designed to give readers a sense of being on the board themselves, inside the gigantic curl.
Design by Regina Frank / SDA Creative, USA

SPACING TYPE

Type is spaced both horizontally and vertically. Vertical spacing, or 'leading' (to rhyme with 'bedding'), is measured in points from the baseline of one line of type to the baseline of the next. The amount should balance continuity and legibility.

Horizontally, each character is spaced proportionally to its width, using units as small as one-thousandth of an em. Digital typeface designers program special adjustments to the spacing or 'kerning' of difficult pairs of characters – such as AV and Te – into their fonts, and software will apply these automatically as type is set. Even with a well-kerned font, however, it will occasionally be necessary to make one-off adjustments to kerning, particularly in headlines.

Increasing or decreasing the spacing across several words or lines is known as tracking or range kerning, and can be used to alter the visual 'colour' of the typeface or on rare occasions as a cheat to help fit the text to the space available.

When text is justified across a column (see page 47), rules must be set up and carefully tweaked to tell the software how spacing is to be adjusted to achieve the required line length. Word spacing can be controlled independently to help balance excessive character spacing against unsightly gaps.

The space between lines of type is known as leading

Word
Kerned

Word
Unkerned

Logo

Colours

Air Freshener

Agency / Wink
Client / Sky Wash Detial and Lube
Date / Summer 2000
Art Direction, Design / Erik Torstensson
Photography / Sesse Lind
Icons / 500 GLS

Typeface

Neue Helvetica 35

Neue Helvetica 55

Business Card and Compliment Slip

Letterhead

Service Menu

Icons

Complimentary Wash Card

Complimentary Wash

The world's most luxurious car-care facility

Posters

Thank You Card

Thank You!

Save 15% next time

Above: A company logo is very often only the first step in creating a corporate identity. This range of elements from a corporate identity design for Skywash – a car-wash company based in Atlanta – illustrates how a whole range of graphics can be developed by cleverly picking up on key elements of the logo.

Design by Wink Design, USA

42

THE DESIGN PROCESS Design is normally carried out in response to a need, and inevitably involves a certain amount of planning. The parameters may not always be clear in the first instance, as clients can have difficulty in pinpointing their exact requirements. Graphic designers are normally employed to bring their individual creative ability and practical understanding to solving a particular problem.

Acquiring an insight into the clients' businesses is an important part of informing the creative process. This can often be done simply by listening to and learning from clients, who usually know their own businesses intimately. Sometimes a client may be convinced that a particular medium or context is the best way to promote a product or service but, after careful analysis of the brief by the designer, an entirely different medium or approach may emerge as more suited to the actual, rather than the perceived, needs of the client.

The designer needs to make a reasonably accurate assessment of the size and complexity of the job and level of budget allocation. It is, for instance, unwise to embark on a corporate identity design without first agreeing which specific elements are going to need design consideration – is it a logo or letterhead, or will there also be a requirement to look at packaging, vehicle livery, and uniforms, a signage system, website, and design standards manual? Even a small-scale design can involve unexpected work, such as having to include,

Above: **This poster formed part of an in-store campaign for a department store that aimed to move away from clichés and express the real spirit of Mother's Day – a lie-in or a half-hour to herself will mean more than just tokens of appreciation.** Design by Williams Murray Hamm, UK

Above left: **The idea for this classic poster grew out of the designer setting his own parameters in response to a wide-open brief for Designer's Saturday in London. The event combined business and fun as the inventive and witty transformation of the primary shapes suggests.** Design by Alan Fletcher, UK/USA

or rework a highly complicated diagram. Preliminary inquiries have to be made as to the feasibility and timescale of any reprographic and production processes from the completion of digital artwork before a realistic timetable can be worked out and agreed with the client. These initial planning stages are all essential to the design process. The only real drawback to digital design is that it allows designers to explore endless variations of ideas and colourways in a process where time is usually at a premium and decisions have to be made quickly.

When it comes to the creative element of the design process, there is little doubt that paper, pencil, and digital software can work well in partnership. Paper and pencil are valuable basic tools for the digital graphic designer – much creative inspiration can come from doodling and note-making both on- and off-screen. Whichever starting point you use, your creative approach should always be informed by the brief. Basic guidelines for possible approaches can be set up by identifying from within the brief the answers to four simple questions. This exercise will also help you to clarify your intentions for the design.

The questions are:

What	– is the message to be communicated?
	– is the reason for the brief?
	– is the problem to be solved?
Why	– does the client want to communicate the message?
Where	– is the message going to communicate, and under what conditions?
Who	– is the intended audience or market?

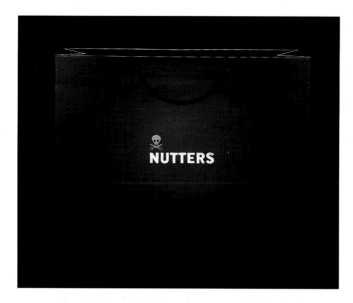

Working out and evaluating the answers to these questions should give you a springboard for idea generation that will help you maintain a reasoned link between the brief and even the most lateral approaches. One or more key words, images, or points should emerge from the analysis. These can be used as the basis of short but intensive visual brainstorming sessions on paper or screen to help start ideas and associations flowing.

Drawing need not be restricted to paper for these sessions, as many designers find working with a digital tablet creates a natural progression from hand to screen. But, whichever method you use, the value of drawing as a tool for visual thinking and exploration is important to recognize. Thinking through drawing focuses the mind and, as it rarely throws up 'finished' or resolved ideas, its flexible immediacy can suggest alternative routes for exploration, allowing for 'happy discoveries' along the way. For this reason, put down every response that comes to mind, whether or not the relevance is immediately clear – often, it is not! Wit and humour can also play an important part in graphic communication, and they often make for entertaining, informative, and memorable designs.

When working in a three-dimensional field, any initial two-dimensional creative thinking can be developed through the making process with small-scale maquettes and mock-ups or by using a three-dimensional modelling program.

Drawn or doodled ideas, whether on paper or screen, should be stored, and those with potential should be researched and developed further without imposing too many constraints. Although ideas are generated by the creative intellect, they normally need some form of reference to underpin them, as the imagination cannot always be relied on for accuracy. Access to the Internet is extremely useful for this purpose – the World Wide Web offers a vast storehouse of knowledge and visual references that can both inform and

Above left: **This masculine identity was designed for the re-launch of 'Nutters', the London clothiers founded by maverick tailor Tommy Nutter in 1969, whose trademark look was created through dramatic and humorous twists on classic English style.**
Design by Bryn Jones, UK

Above: **This double-layered book jacket features an outer layer printed on heavyweight tracing paper, designed to play with the books' theme visually and to physically involve the reader as the book is opened.**
Design by Chronicle Books, USA

stimulate the design-making process. Digital-image libraries offer downloading facilities, and it is possible to download royalty-free images. Ideas should always be thoroughly explored until they are fully resolved, and all research should be kept as it can sometimes throw up different ideas worth following.

When an idea seems right, the designer should assess how it can be realistically applied to all the components of the job. Decisions as to choice and use of type, images, and colour then need to be made. If you do not have the typeface you feel is suitable, font manufacturers have many browsable websites where it may be possible to find a face that fits your particular requirements. To assess colours and make choices, alternative colourways can be set up and viewed in most graphic art software packages. Images and graphics may either be supplied by the client or may need to be commissioned by the designer. They in turn may also help to generate ideas and influence the final design (see Image Selection and Image Creation).

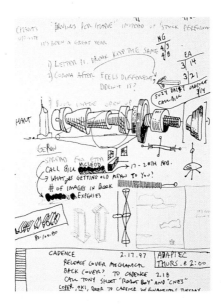

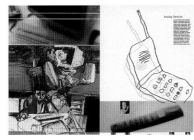

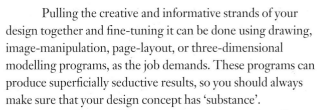

Above: **A page of ideas, notes, visual thinking, and thought exploration – an essential part of the design process, helping to generate and develop ideas as well as clarify intentions. Finding a 'story' that will lend itself to visual interpretation is often a challenge to the designer. For this report for Cadence Design Systems, the aim** was to show conceptually the unique role of the company and the irony that difficult situations in a complex industry create growth opportunities. In the completed report, the headline and velour cover inventively encapsulate the aim, with the images reflecting the global and everyday use of Cadence technology.
Design by Cahan & Associates, USA

FEELS DIFFERENT,
DOESN'T IT?

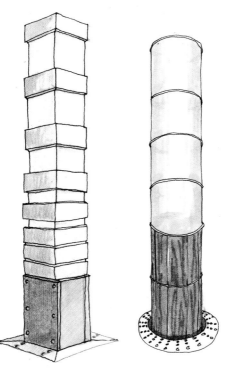

Left and right: **Initial ideas sheet for sculptural light towers designed to define and frame entrances to the new scheme for Principe Pio, one of Madrid's main rail station and metro interchanges. The design combines ideas of movement, destination, and connection with angled signage elements that further enhance the idea of dynamic movement. Bold colour reflects the modernity and elegance of the space. Design development and refinement for presentation visuals were done in Illustrator 9.0. Rendering effects were applied in PhotoShop 6.**
Design by RTKL

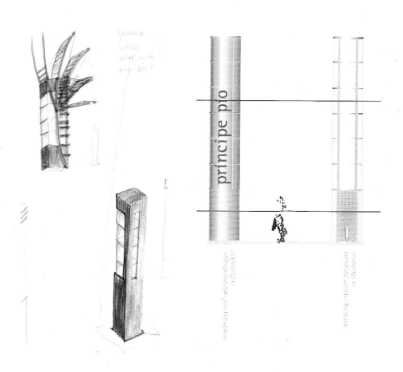

Pulling the creative and informative strands of your design together and fine-tuning it can be done using drawing, image-manipulation, page-layout, or three-dimensional modelling programs, as the job demands. These programs can produce superficially seductive results, so you should always make sure that your design concept has 'substance'.

Most clients will have computing set-ups that allow you to communicate by email and to send visuals in a digitally viewable form. The graphic designer should be in a position to make PDF files, which can be viewed on any computer, and should also have a commonly used compression program. Once initial ideas have been approved or modifications agreed, the detailed design for each and every component of the job can be finalized before work can be prepared for production.

Every production process demands varying amounts of execution from the designer, but it will inevitably involve a digital file being prepared in a graphic arts program. The designer's file may be used directly to drive a printing device or a process with little or no intervention from the printer or anyone else. This raises two very important points. First, the content of your digital files must be correct in every aspect, with type and image information appropriately supplied. Second, it is extremely valuable to develop a good working relationship with your supplier, and ensure that there is a clear indication and understanding of responsibilities. Never assume that everything created digitally is going to be perfect – it is absolutely essential to have proofs for all print work, regardless of how small or big the job may be. Never rely on output from your studio printer being identical to that of the printer's or bureau's device.

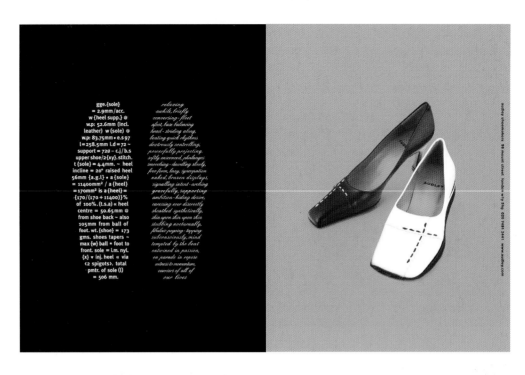

Left: **Advertisement for Audley shoemakers.** The concept for this intriguing ad cleverly plays on the idea of the two sides of the brain – emotional and rational – to parallel the company philosophy. Design by Lippa Pearce, UK

Below: Although display type set vertically is economical in one way, it puts added reading strain on the eye as it is forced to jump unnaturally downwards, from letter to letter.

V
E
R
T
I
C
A
L

HORIZONTAL

LEGIBILITY VERSUS READABILITY

Continuous text needs special attention, as it contains large amounts of detailed information that needs to be easily understood. Readability is concerned with the speed and ease with which the reader can assimilate and retain information printed on the page or screen. Although individual components (letters) may be legible, this does not automatically mean that reading is easy. Readers perceive words not simply as sequences of letters, but as groups of letters and words. These letter and word groupings facilitate speedy recognition as the eye scans the text. Anything that contributes to the breaking up or the slowing down of this scanning process makes for harder and more tiring reading. For example, exaggerated tracking (character and word spacing) will disrupt the normal shape of words (recognizable letter groupings) causing strain to the eye and brain.

Character and word recognition are more easily achieved with upper- and lowercase letters, since they create a greater range of word-icon shapes and individuality than uppercase alone. Capital letters all appear to occupy equal spaces when set in a line of text, so the words they form are more difficult to discern at a normal reading speed. The relative weight of type can also affect legibility. Medium weights are easiest to read because of the visual balance between the counter-shapes and letterstrokes. Extreme weights of both light and bold type are more difficult and tiring to read as the contrast between the letterstrokes and counter-shapes is distracting.

Modernism, as we have known it, has served as the aesthetic, spiritual and moral conscience of our time. It embodies the essentially democratic idea of the creative artist as the

Modernism, as we have known it, has served as the aesthetic, spiritual and moral conscience of our time. It embodies the essentially democratic idea of the creative artist as the inventor of a personal style, a unique vision of the world.

Modernism, as we have known it, has served as the aesthetic, spiritual and moral conscience of our time. It embodies the essentially democratic idea of the creative artist as the inventor of a personal style, a unique vision of the world.

Modernism, as we have known it, has served as the aesthetic, spiritual and moral conscience of our time. It embodies the essentially democratic idea of the creative artist as the inventor of a personal style, a unique vision of the world.

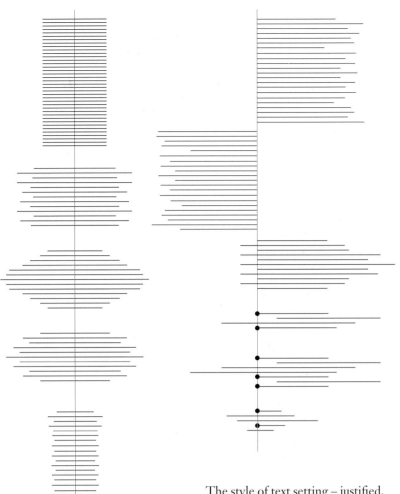

Above left: Setting justified type to an overly narrow measure throws up exaggerated letter spacing to fill the measure and makes for difficult and tiring reading.

Left: A comparison of over-long and readable line lengths.

Bottom left: Tight tracking makes an interesting but illegible typographic pattern. Loose tracking weakens the horizontal character of lines of type and so slows and hinders reading.

Left: Digital technology allows almost limitless possibilities with text-setting styles. However when working with continuous text, even in small amounts, it can be helpful to establish an axis to give the design structure. These diagrams show a range of variations than can be useful.

Below: Lowercase letters have individual key characteristics which tend to be in the top half of the letterform. These characteristics are more important to letter and word recognition than those in the bottom half. This is particularly noticeable in serif typefaces where the tops of letters are more easily identifiable. In sans serif designs, there can be greater similarity between the top half of letters
Design by Brian Coe, UK

The style of text setting – justified, flush left or right, centred or asymmetric – together with line length, also has an effect on the readability of text. In reading any length of text, the eye is generally more comfortable in returning to a straight left-hand edge. However, small groupings of text can normally be read in most of the setting styles. Justified setting (text that is aligned at both sides) is not suitable for very small blocks of text, where ugly word spacing will occur. Justification can also sometimes create difficulties with hyphenation and word spacing in longer, continuous text unless this is carefully controlled. Hyphenation at line ends can sometimes create an unnecessarily 'spotty' look and should be avoided where possible.

Line length also affects how text is read. If lines of text are too long, the eye has difficulty in returning to the start of the next line. Conversely, if lines of text are too narrowly set, the eye is made to progress too quickly from line to line and may skip lines, interrupting the flow of comprehension. Although these disturbances will have little effect over a few lines, they will tire the eye over large amounts of text. As a rough guide to line length, an average line of text in the English language reads comfortably with approximately sixty-three to sixty-five characters (counting word spaces as characters).

Digital technology enables both display and text type to be very flexibly set into shapes. Running text round images is also easily done. However, in working with either, care has to be taken to maintain coherent, readable text by controlling each individual line-break.

Display type is normally restricted to a few words and presents fewer problems due to its size, weight, and dominant position in the design area. The designer should, however, look carefully at the spaces between characters and words in larger type sizes. Pairs of letters may need kerning to aid readability. Where several words are involved, one or more word spaces may need to be optically balanced – to counteract the effects produced by the shapes of the last and first letters of the words at either side, which may be exaggerated at display sizes.

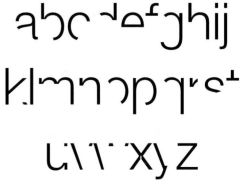

Æ æ Q Q

ſi ſſ ſt w aa ee

ö ç å é á ê

1 2 3 4 5 6 7 8 9 10
1 2 3 4 5 6 7 8 9 10

EXTENDED OR EXPERT SETS

Many digital typefaces have extensive ranges of characters well in excess of the basic set of letters, numerals, punctuation marks, and symbols included as standard in most fonts. Where these are included within a single font file, the font is said to have an extended character set. The Unicode character encoding system, now the industry standard, encompasses a huge range of characters in many languages, although this is no guarantee that a particular font will include them. OpenType fonts can also store multiple glyphs (letterforms) for each character. For example, there may be 'optical' variants designed for use at a different range of sizes (such as text and display); or a ligature glyph may represent multiple characters, such as 'ffi'.

Many of the fonts on the market predate these technologies, and any additional characters are supplied as a separate font, known as an expert set. In either case, the serious typographer is provided with a range of extra letterforms that share the inherent form and structure of the basic typeface.

Another example of an alternative glyph is a swash character: a decorative version of a letter with an exaggerated sweeping entrance or exit stroke that may overlap the preceding or following character. Swash characters can add a flourish to the start or the end of a word. Capitals ('swash caps') are common, but some designs include swash initial, terminal, and even medial lowercase letters (see above).

Non-lining or old-style numerals, which ascend and descend like lower-case letters rather than lining, are another useful option. Specially designed small capitals are essential for setting text in small caps, as ordinary caps reduced in size will not match the weight and proportion of other characters.

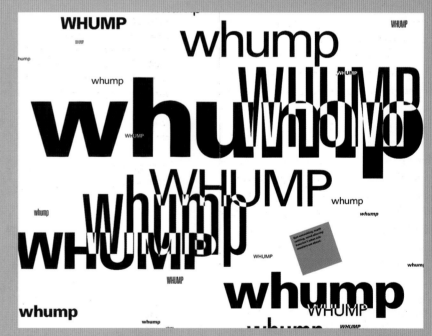

Above left: **Some of the alternative glyphs available in expert font sets. Most expert sets include 'old style' non-aligning numerals, which rise above and below the x-height and baseline. This style of numeral works well within text, as it is less disruptive to visual continuity. It can also be softer to read in tabular form, although lining numerals are often preferred for technical and financial material.**

Above: **This page, from a brochure for Entec, creates a precise yet complex typographic 'sound image' which reflects the nature of the product: high-fidelity speakers. The three-dimensional, broad-ranging nature of sound is suggested through strong contrast in size, weight, colour, and type style and semi-abstraction of parts of the letterforms.**
Design by Mauk Design, USA

LAYOUT The design area or page format and margins are the basic components of layout, which – like everything else in the design process – should always be informed by the content of the job and the creative approach. How and where the end-product is to be used or viewed must be taken into consideration in deciding a suitable size and format.

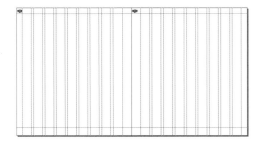

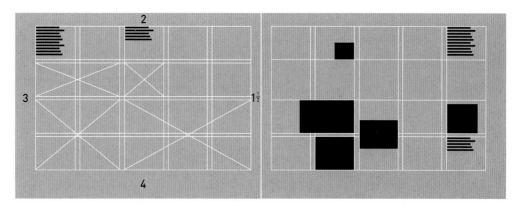

Size and format can range from pocket to wall-size, in both two and three dimensions. When designing for the Web or multimedia, where the overall maximum area is predetermined, consideration of the page proportions should still be given.

In almost every design context, the graphic designer will need to set up an appropriate page or design area structure (see above). This is normally done in a page-layout program, and it initially involves making a series of interrelated design decisions: width of the top, foot, and side margins (essentially there for handling purposes and for leading the eye), the number of columns for text and image organization and, where appropriate, the number of pages or surfaces that may be involved. Once these

Above: **Structuring the design area across a series of pages or surfaces so as to give maximum flexibility without losing continuity is important to holding the viewer's attention. Margin proportions will vary depending on the design context as in the diagram above, but as a guideline, the foot margin is normally double the head margin and the fore-edge margin half the width of the back margin.**

decisions have been made, the page structure can be set up as single or facing pages in templates (or master pages in desktop publishing programs) to allow automatic repetition of the original structure across numerous pages.

Multipage surface design benefits from adding a further underpinning structure or grid to the basic page. This is done by subdividing the basic page structure into sets and subsets of equal vertical column widths. The greater the number of divisions or columns, the greater the flexibility. The modularity that is created can be used invisibly to structure the relationship of quite disparate elements, with some running across several or all of the columns. If the complexity of the job requires additional underpinning, a horizontal grid can be constructed in a similar way. A grid system can be particularly useful in helping to keep a sense of continuity across a range of different pages, sizes, scales, or formats. Corporate identities, exhibitions, advertising campaigns, and multimedia can all benefit from the controlling influence of a grid system.

Diagonal layouts can be very powerful but need to be kept simple as they may hinder the reader if too many elements are involved.

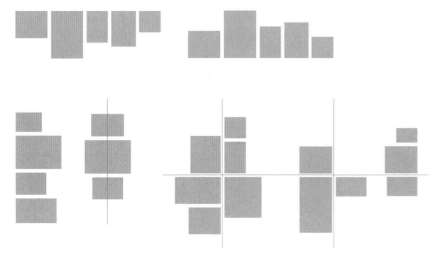

Left: **Most graphic design work involves a number of different sized and proportioned elements which have to be coordinated within a given area. This diagram shows 'hanging', 'sitting', vertical and centred alignments together with combined horizontal and vertical axes around which different clusters of elements can be grouped cohesively.**

DOCUMENT SIGNPOSTING Most graphic design includes working with some element of text or copy. Most copy needs ordered presentation, so before any design work starts the designer should work through it to establish some basic organization or hierarchy.

Breaking the copy down into digestible passages, if only by white space, will automatically pace the reader. Controlling the space between elements will determine the reading sequence. Hierarchical conventions will direct and signpost the reader through, for example, a book, via the title page, the contents page, the page numbers (folios), chapter headings, subheadings, paragraphs, and footnotes.

Designing a website will often involve developing an ordered, functional, and user-friendly navigation process to take the viewer through the various pages. In advertising, the hierarchy of information may be as simple as a main heading and strapline, whereas an instruction manual may contain many layers of information. Developing a visual hierarchy will order information and make it easily accessible. The exercise will normally include typeface and style together with varying levels of emphasis for other elements through the use of size, weight, colour, and disposition. Even the structuring of the basic paragraph needs many decisions about detailing (see diagram).

Bullet points (circular, square, or triangular) and selected dingbats (for example, Wingdings) can be used to highlight and draw attention to listings, instructions, or blocks of text, but the level of emphasis should be compatible with the rest of the text and overall context. The size, weight, or colour of bullets and dingbats should complement, rather

Type face	Column width
	La puerta con dos casas es lo permanente, inacesible. Esta casa de alforja se encuentra en el territorio de los acontecimientos simultáneos. Dos espacios que se aman, que se besan, pour una puerta que no se sabe si separa o une.
Indents	Aquí todo tiene la suficente claridad y la deliciosa oscuridad de la armoniá. No nos sabemos dentro hasta que unos pasos más allá de la primera puerta, nos encontramos fuera del edificio; nunca sabemos qué es demasiado.
	Alignments
Type size	Todo recuerdo de este viaje será el instante en que abandonamos esa sensación de recogimiento, memoria irrecuperable de un espacio inmenso, inmensamente.
Type style	*La puerta con dos casas es lo permanente, inacesible. Esta casa de alforja se encuentra en el territorio de los acontecimientos simultáneos. Dos espacios que se aman,*
Leading	
	Inter paragraph spacing
Case	AQUÍ TODO TIENE la suficente claridad y la deliciosa oscuridad de la armoniá. No nos sabemos dentro hasta que
Tracking	unos pasos más allá de la primera puerta, fuera del edificio; nunca sabemos qué

than compete with, the other elements in the design, and should direct the reader to and through the points in a relevant sequence.

Frames and rules are devices that can help to isolate, contain, formalize, contrast, and draw attention to text, image, or area. The weight, style, and colour of the line used to make a frame will control the level and intensity of focus, but the design and proportion of the frame should be integrated with the main context. Framed text or other elements often appear within a main body of text, but they should still be capable of being read independently. To achieve this, the framed text needs to be set to a narrower width than the main text to allow for the thickness of the frame and a reasonable space

Below: **Where it is essential that the viewer reads the design in a particular sequence, subtle grouping - through the use of white space one-and-a-half to two times the spacing between the individual elements in a group – will naturally guide the eye through the grouping sequentially. When elements are butted up to each other, the eye will read the surface as an entity in itself.**

Below: Size, type style, icon, disposition, and typographic devices are combined to visually pinpoint key locations in the wayfinding system for the American Museum of Natural History in New York. Clarity in the design is essential in preventing visitors from getting lost in the huge building.
Design by Lance Wyman, USA

Right: Examples of conventions that are used to make sense of copy and so guide the reader through documents.

HEADINGS	CAPTIONING	NUMBERING	INDEXING
Chapters	Illustrations	Pages	Index
Sections	Photographs	Paragraphs	Table of contents
Major topic	Charts	Foot notes	Glossaries
Headings	Diagrams	Cross-referencing	Appendices
Subheads	Tables		Bibliographies
Sub subheads			

QUOTATIONS			PUNCTUATION
Speech			Pace
Extracts			Sense

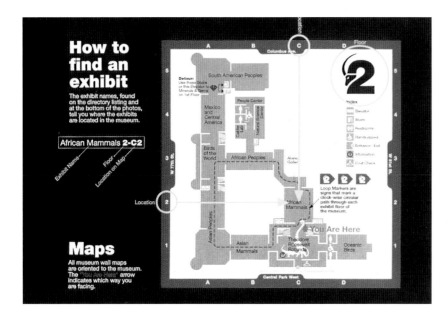

between it and the text. Surrounding white space can suggest a frame (as with margins on a page) through the placing of single element within a large area. Decorative frames should be used sparingly as they can easily distract attention from the content.

Desktop publishing programs make a distinction between rules that can be placed before or after paragraphs and underlining, which is a feature of the type style (character underlining or word underlining).

Typographic rules have considerable potential in their own right as design elements and need not be restricted to being used in conjunction with paragraphs. They can direct and arrest the eye, physically divide areas or separate elements, pace the viewer, and be a facilitating device in leading the eye along the horizontal, vertical, or diagonal direction. When placed above, below, or to the side of an element, a rule has an anchoring effect on it. The level of focus and emphasis created in this way can be accentuated or diminished by modifying the relative size, colour, texture, or weight of either the rule or the element. If different weights of rule are used in the same design area, they should be distinctly contrasting – if they are too similar in weight, they may look like a mistake or be indistinguishable from each other. Whichever type of frame or weight of rule is used, it is generally better to keep the scheme simple.

Above right: The impenetrable nature of the Berlin Wall is graphically conveyed in this exhibition display through the use of heavy typographic rules carrying tightly contained, reversed-out type.
Design by Ruedi Bauer and Pippo Lionni, Germany/France

Above right: A contrasting rule will anchor text to it. This device can be continued within the same design with different column widths to give an overall visual structure. A further rule placed after space below text or images will help to contain them.
Right: Within a design that uses marginal headings or two different column widths, a combination of vertical fine and bold rules can help to determine the reading hierarchy.
Bottom right: Rules can be a useful device for both separating and coordinating different elements within a design.

IMAGE SELECTION The client may provide the designer with a set of images that are integral to a particular job, which leaves the designer with no say in the content or design of the image and little say in the selection. However, the designer does have control over how the images are used and, when selecting from a range of existing images, he or she should ensure that the selection 'tells the story' appropriately.

Right: The paintings used in this Corporate Membership Program for the National Gallery in London were all selected from the Gallery's vast collection of new and old works. The repeated use of strip images plays on the title and human nature – the reader's desire to see more.
Design by Agenda, UK

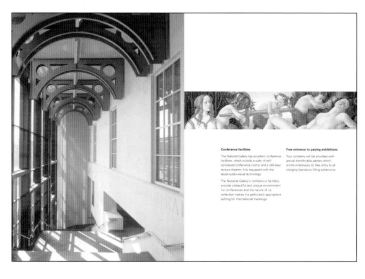

Above: Strong images and a bold message were used in this Maxygen annual report to illustrate how the company's new technology, molecular breeding – which imitates the natural process of classical breeding to achieve desired genetic characteristics – is not worlds away from farming.
Design by Cahan & Associates, USA

Initial impact may be of prime importance, but drawing the viewer in through secondary and tertiary levels of interest should also be considered. There are, however, some occasions when it is better to invest in a completely new set of images. The designer can then advise on them or be involved in selecting them or commissioning them from a photographer or illustrator. As coordinator of all the elements in a design and manager of the process, the designer has a responsibility to prepare a focused brief outlining the aims, purpose, format and context of the image-making. This should be agreed with the client and photographer or illustrator, and supplemented with detailed instructions concerning appropriate file formats and resolution values (see Image Creation).

Every aspect of an image should contribute in some degree to the overall message and mood of the design. Images may clarify, contrast, enhance, and partner text or other elements, but they should never be used as gratuitous 'add-ons'. Scaling and cropping images and deciding on a presentation method (colour, black and white, duotone, cutout, squared-up) need considerable care and attention, and should also bear a direct relevance to the overall design. Judicious cropping can substantially affect the visual impact and balance of the image itself, as well as influencing the message and other design elements.

Below: **The nature of the high-tech company, Geron, which develops treatments for age-related diseases, is humanized in this annual report companion design with its dramatically contrasting images, captioned with the subjects' small handwritten text. It is an approach with which readers can easily identify.**
Design by Cahan & Associates, USA

Bottom: **In this book spread the image is used to inform the typography in which the horizontal lines and colour are picked out and continued through onto the facing page.**
Design by Chronicle Books, USA

Chapter 8 : THE END of the RAINBOW

J. A. Bauer Pottery Co., Los Angeles
Plainware mixing bowls (left).
c. 1930.

Meyers Pottery, Vernon
California Rainbow mixing bowls (center). c. 1935.
Japan. Cactus salt and pepper shakers, unmarked. c. 1930s.

Meyers Pottery, Vernon
California Rainbow low bowls (right), unmarked. c. 1935.
California Rainbow casserole (lower center).

J. A. Bauer Pottery Co., Los Angeles
Cyclinder vase (foreground).
c. 1950.

If ever a Golden Age was misnamed, it was California Pottery's. Except for some gilt trim from Sascha Brastoff, the treasures of that period are of little intrinsic value. They're just some molded earth sealed with a few nonprecious minerals. Although pottery is currently enjoying a collector/decorator revival, the worth of these once insignificant objects is best measured in terms of the pleasure they give to those who use, collect, or simply admire them. The fact that after all this time they are being used, collected and remade confirms their relevance to the way we live now.

For years collectors had been baffled: despite their best efforts they had been unable to learn anything about the creator of the pottery signed "Barbara Willis" that some of them prized. Then, in 1995, a woman in her seventies wearing a straw hat over bright red hair pointed to a vase at a Los Angeles flea market and said: "That's mine. I'm Barbara Willis. I made that." It turned out that Ms. Willis had closed her North Hollywood pottery in 1958 and was living happily in Malibu. After her "discovery" she began producing again, hand-thrown pieces this time, but in the same signature combination of intense glazes and exposed

DESIGNING WITH COLOUR Colour is the element that brings an added, almost magical dimension to visual communication. It reflects the everyday world and human experience, giving the designer a strong common language with which to express mood, emotion, and significance.

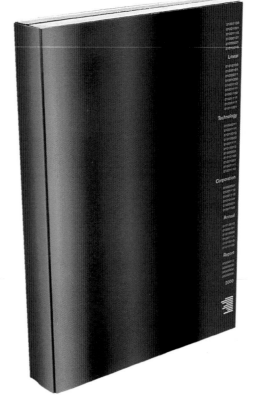

Far left: **Colour has been used to great effect in this commercial for Proctor & Gamble *Vibrant*. Brightly coloured fabrics dance and swirl in perfect sync with an operatic soundtrack against a black background to illustrate that 'colour sings'.**
Design by Grey Worldwide, UK

Left: **This inventive annual report for the Linear Technology Corporation is made up of two contrasting books – *Digital* and *Linear* – packaged in this bright sleeve. The *Digital* book is monochrome and only contains indecipherable streaming ascii code. The *Linear* book dramatically makes the point that 'Digital means nothing without Linear' through pages of brilliant digital colour and succinct, accessible black text on pure white.**
Design by Cahan & Associates, USA

The digital graphic designer has an almost limitless colour palette with which to work and evoke specific responses in the viewer. Colour can be used as appeal, inspiration, entertainment, a focus, or an identifying marker.

Colour is always relative and never works in isolation. The viewer responds to colour within a context and in association with other colours and graphic elements. Environmental and lighting conditions affect the way colour is perceived, which is a particular consideration when choosing colours for packaging, signage, and exhibitions.

Colour can be used as a means of identification and coding, as in pie and bar charts, where a range of different elements of equal importance need to be identified. In such contexts, care should be taken to mix colours (hues) of similar tones (brightness) and intensity (saturation) to avoid giving undue emphasis to any one element. In a situation where it is necessary to create levels of relative importance, a change in colour intensity or brightness or both can be used as a hierarchical device.

Combining complementary colours (true opposites on the colour wheel) will set up a natural vibrancy if a sense of excitement and energy is needed. To use colour emotively, it is essential to have an understanding of the design subject matter and the audience to which it is directed, so that colour choice can be appropriately related. Colours can be considered as warm or cool, soft or hard, light or dark, passive or active – all of which characteristics can be used individually or in association with each other. Mood is greatly affected by colour temperature.

Colour association forms an important part of colour language in all areas of graphic design. This can be seen in the way that greens are used for freshness, blues and whites for hygiene, red for danger, and purple for richness. There are many examples of colour combinations that are associated with politics, nationality, sport, religion, or cultural and social conventions. The designer has to be aware of all of them, in order to avoid creating confused messages. For example, red and green are recognized across the world as symbolizing 'stop' and 'go'.

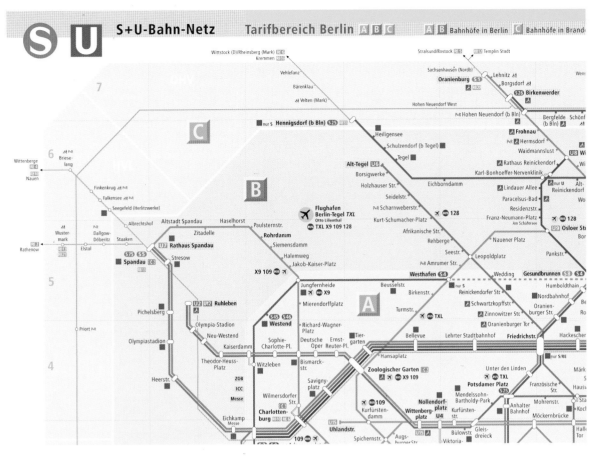

Left: Colour coding in diagrammatic maps ensures a clarity of communication and quick recognition that can be flexibly applied to related graphics and signage.
Design by MetaDesign, Germany

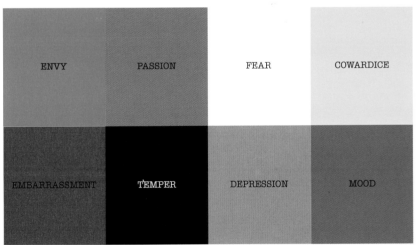

| ENVY | PASSION | FEAR | COWARDICE |
| EMBARRASSMENT | TEMPER | DEPRESSION | MOOD |

Above: Colour and meaning varies widely according to different cultures. For example in much of Asia white is associated with death whereas in the West it is associated with purity. These associations and differences can be useful in making unusual connections or changing perceptions depending on the design context.
Design by Alan Fletcher, UK/USA

Below: The distinctive colour choice and minimalist packaging design for Apollo Lager deliberately breaks away from traditional beer packaging to coolly reflect the product name and the associated space travel theme in a memorable, understated way.
Design by Cahan & Associates, USA

L	0	2	9	16	23	30
M	0	3	10	17	24	G
M	0	4	11	18	25	1
G	0	5	12	19	26	U
V	0	6	13	20	27	G
S	0	7	14	21	28	N
D	1	8	15	22	29	0

It is impossible to provide a set of rules for particular harmonious colour combinations since these change according to different environments, fashions, and culture. The designer may consider setting up disharmonies as a way of creating shock or provocation, which may be a perfectly legitimate way of communicating a message.

Graphic art software provides tools for selecting and mixing colours in a variety of models. These give the designer unprecedented control over colour creation and usage (see Colour). The hue, saturation, and brightness (HSB) model is particularly useful as it enables the creation either of different hues of the same brightness and intensity or of varying intensities or brightnesses of the same hue.

Designers should be aware that their colour perception can be affected if they set strong background colours for their monitors. Large areas of colour and poor lighting in the working environment will have a similar effect on perception. It is advisable, therefore, to set the monitor to a neutral grey when working intensively with colour, and to paint design studios in neutral colours.

Left: The combination of green background and fluorescent ink used to print the tiny numbers on the June page of this Olivetti calendar, was so dazzling that the Italian printer wore sunglasses while working with the job! The powerful colour combination that suggests red flowers in a green field is primary and the information secondary. This emphasis is used to bring the feel of summer into the office environment.
Design by Alan Fletcher, UK/USA

TYPE AND COLOUR

All the uses of colour to express mood, emotion, or significance can be equally well applied to type. Colour may be used to modify the way in which type works: bold type can be softened, hierarchies can be developed without recourse to change of size or weight, text can be enlivened, and typographic emphasis can be subtly enhanced.

When designing with coloured type on a coloured background, the designer must consider the choice of colour combination carefully in order to ensure legibility. In general, type and background need to be significantly contrasting. Dark type on a

Right: These unusual curved vertical signs for a drycleaning and laundromat business mimic laundry drying on a line. The freely drawn imagery combines with crisp type and fresh colours for this 'new concept in clean clothes' – the idea being that doing the laundry should be fun, not a chore. The colours are carried through the clean lines of the interior and branded merchandise.
Design by Ashdown Wood Design, Australia

Left: Colour and type reflect the 'straight-talking' policy of TKB Solicitors, enlivening and humanizing the traditional, rather formal, perception of the legal profession.
Design by the The Partners, UK

Left: Black was an unusual but distinctive choice for a coordinating element in the new, Suma supermarket identity in Barcelona. Together with special lighting, it is used as a means of focusing the eye on the many different colours of their merchandise. The graphics on these staff aprons show colour used as coding for fish, meat, and vegetables.
Design by Suma, Spain

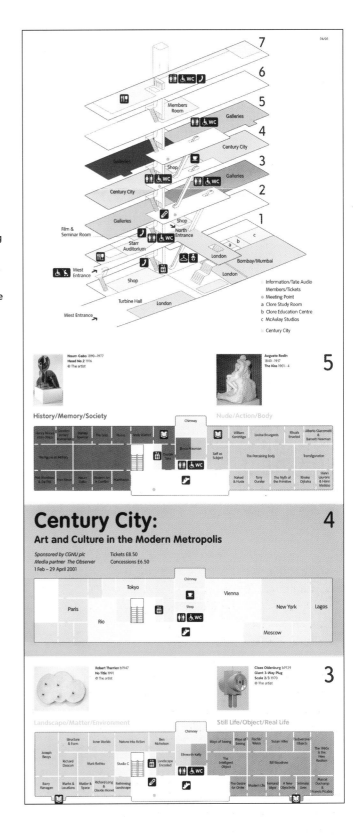

Right: Subject areas are grouped together into discrete gallery displays in the Tate Modern, London. Each is identified in the plan (or on the website) by a unique colour used in both the titles and floor plan, facilitating visit planning and wayfinding through the vast building.
Design by Halmes Wood, UK

pale background, rather than on a white background, will result in less glare (particularly with screen-based designs, for example on webpages). Type and backgrounds of equal brightness (tone) will reduce legibility considerably. Colour can be used with type to create a sense of progression and recession, to enhance spatial quality and suggest depth and perspective. The reading pace and sequence of text and display type can be further controlled through the use of colour.

Setting type in dark colours may be unsuccessful if the letters have a small surface area with which to carry colour; the result may appear to be a poor version of black. Type, particularly text type, has little surface area compared to the background surface on which it appears, so dark-coloured type generally appears darker and light-coloured type generally appears lighter. A heavier weight of type can be used to compensate for this phenomenon.

Interestingly, the millions of easily accessible digital colours have also brought a revived energy to the use of black and white that should not be underestimated.

SURFACE
DESIGN

The roots of graphic design lie in our desire to communicate information – more especially by the arrangement of type and pictures on a printed page. Although the development of digital technology has made the possibilities virtually limitless, graphic design and print remain inextricably linked.

Graphic design for the medium of print embraces an extensive and varied range of products. These include promotional applications such as brochures, leaflets, flyers, direct mail, catalogues, and posters. Business communication tools include stationery, newsletters, training manuals, reports, or menus. The publishing industry, producing magazines, books, and newspapers, is still one of the largest sectors employing graphic designers.

With ever-increasing market and client pressure to create eye-catching, innovative ways of presenting printed information, there are jobs that call for more specialized print processes. The use of materials other than paper – plastic, metal, or even fabric – is also becoming more prevalent.

The processes that take the concept to the printed product affect many design decisions made at concept stage. The choice of paper or other media, or the size of the print run, will dictate not only the type of print technology used but also the way the production files are created – including the appropriate choice of type and the size of the halftone dot.

The computer has shaped not only conceptual design, by encouraging freedom of layout and the breaking of typographic conventions, but also the linear process of transferring the design from screen to printed page. The traditional boundaries of the design-for-print process have been blurred. The designer equipped with a PC, or more commonly an Apple Macintosh, linked to a desktop scanner, a colour output device, and a high-speed Internet connection can take conceptual ideas through to press, and today even the printing press itself may be a digital device.

With the adoption of Adobe's PDF (portable document format) as a medium for delivering press-ready documents, there need be virtually no human intervention between the designer and the printed product.

PART 02. SURFACE DESIGN.

CHAPTER ONE

DESIGN FOR PRINT

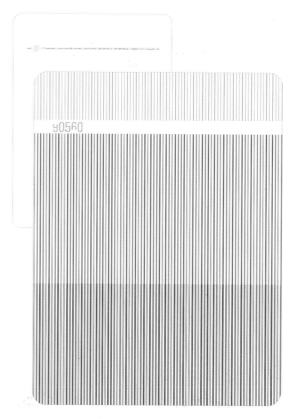

Left: **Visual identity for Yosho.com. The design utilizes a series of stripes printed as 'spot' colours. The colours were chosen to translate accurately into four-colour process tints when incorporated into other printed elements, such as a brochure that contains photographic imagery.** Design by Segura, USA

Far left: **Effective use of colour, type, and imagery for the cover of *Show* Magazine. The choice of colour for large, flat areas is very important as some hues are less intense when printed as process separations rather than specific PANTONE inks.** Design by John Brown Citrus Publishing, UK

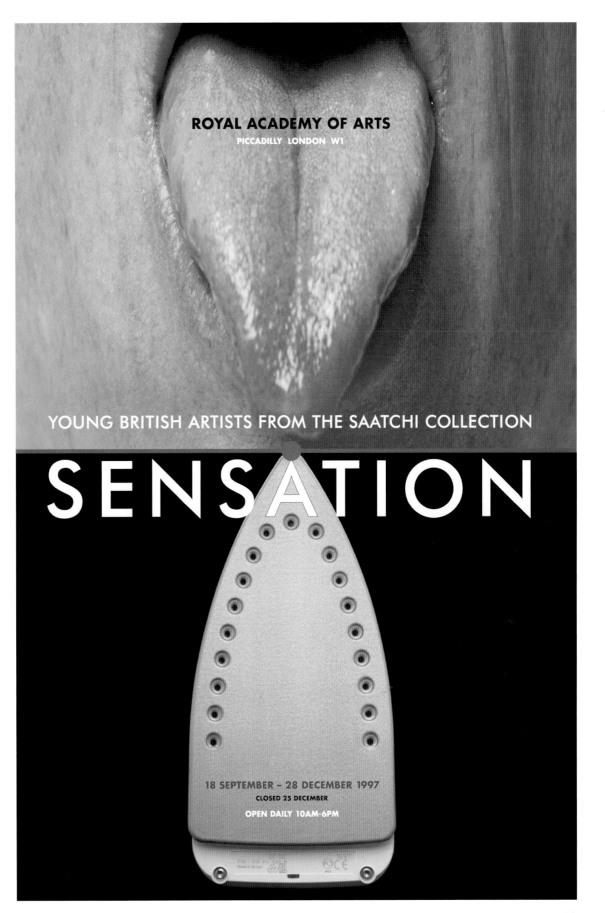

Right: Cleverly chosen imagery created a powerful visual pun in this poster, which contributed to the notoriety of a groundbreaking exhibition of new British art.
Design by Why Not Associates, UK

THE SOFTWARE Over the past few years, there have been significant developments in software dedicated to both design and production, providing more streamlined digitally driven systems that take design directly to print. As a result, the definition of 'publishing' has been greatly extended.

DESKTOP PUBLISHING

Desktop publishing (DTP) applications have evolved from the fundamentals of word processing into fully fledged design tools, streamlining the creation of layouts in which all text and pictures can be precisely manipulated, and simplifying the construction and management of long documents. Text can be imported and then styled to the designer's exact requirements. Virtually limitless type attributes can be applied, and H&Js (hyphenation and justification), horizontal and vertical scaling, leading, kerning, and tracking can all be finely tuned.

The leading DTP applications are available in both Apple Macintosh and Microsoft Windows formats. Serious graphic designers will almost invariably use a Mac; the main exceptions are PC-based administrative workers who need to produce well-presented documents, and designers in fields such as CAD (computer aided drawing) who need certain specialist programs that are unavailable for Mac.

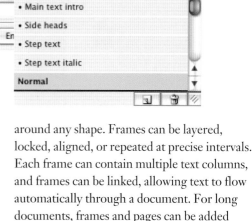

Adobe PageMaker was the first DTP package of note, but during the 1990s was overtaken by QuarkXPress as the choice of professional designers and major publishers. PageMaker has now been superseded by InDesign, which is rapidly growing in popularity. Both QuarkXPress and InDesign are vector-based, dealing primarily with 'line work': those elements of page layout – including type, rules, and tint boxes – that can be represented by scalable geometric descriptions. InDesign, however, integrated the ability to manipulate images and add effects such as transparency and soft shadows. Quark has caught up with a number of similar capabilities, albeit not quite so comprehensive or seamless.

Common to these applications (along with a few low-cost DTP programs available only for Windows) is the use of frames. Picture and text frames can have their exact position defined and can be pre-formatted with type, tint, border, and run-around specifications, allowing the designer to lay out documents with fixed structures independently of content.

Frame tools include rectangle, circle, and polygon shapes, all drawn simply by clicking and dragging. Using frames defined with Bézier curves, text can be made to run within or

around any shape. Frames can be layered, locked, aligned, or repeated at precise intervals. Each frame can contain multiple text columns, and frames can be linked, allowing text to flow automatically through a document. For long documents, frames and pages can be added automatically to suit the length of the text.

Flexibility is further enhanced by the use of layers, a feature previously seen in drawing and image-editing programs. Layers can be on or off, locked or unlocked, in view or out of view. They can be exported and printed independently. Multiple layers serve a number of purposes: for example, you can create several editions using different languages, or add notes and comments without affecting the layout.

Colour technologies that, only a few years ago, were the preserve of the high-end prepress market have been incorporated into DTP software. Industry-standard ICC colour management is built in, helping to preserve

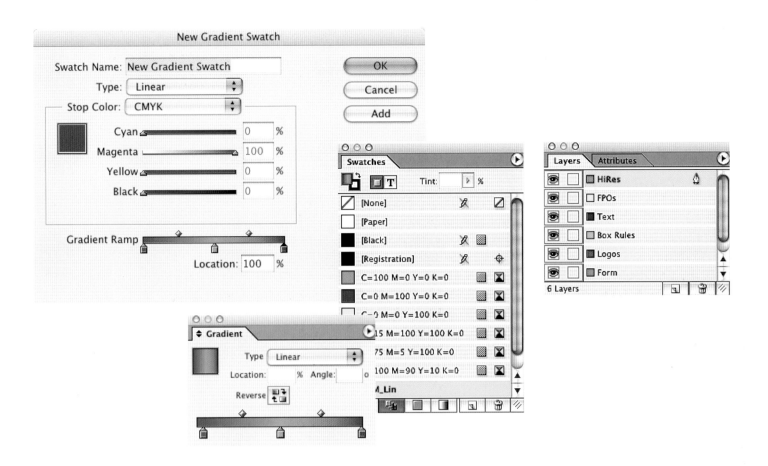

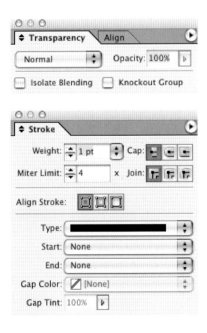

Opposite and this page: **Despite their very different birth dates and histories, QuarkXPress and InDesign share many features in common. Fairly similar toolboxes and onscreen dialog boxes are used to modify elements on the page, show and adjust positions and dimensions, and store attributes such as colour specifications and style sheets. Nonetheless, switching between the two programs is quite a disorienting experience for most designers.**

fidelity when pictures are imported from other software or directly from devices such as cameras and scanners. Special colours can be set up as spot colours, to be output on separate plates, or colour specifications such as PANTONE can be converted to the nearest four-colour process values.

Despite their growing feature set, DTP programs are rarely used alone. Photoshop is needed to adjust images and convert them to the required colour format and resolution, while detailed graphics are produced using programs such as Illustrator or Macromedia FreeHand. Built-in features can be supplemented, however, by a wide range of third-party 'plug-ins' or 'extensions' that add tools or automate specialist tasks.

MAKING READY FOR PRESS

The document file generated by a DTP program usually includes only the line work, with a low-resolution preview of imported images. To send the job for printing, the designer must gather together the picture files and fonts required for final output. This chore is automated by a feature called Collect for Output in QuarkXPress or Package in InDesign.

A more sophisticated approach is 'preflighting', which not only collects the required files but also ensures that images are of a sufficient resolution, colour specifications are

Left: A magazine layout in InDesign. Notice the selected text box, which can be resized using the 'handles' on its corners. Its position can be checked and adjusted in the *Control* palette below (similar to QuarkXPress' *Measurements*).

Left: InDesign uses a system of 'palettes' which can be docked to one side of the screen, and tucked out of sight when not required, or 'floated' as independent boxes that can be placed anywhere on the screen for convenience.

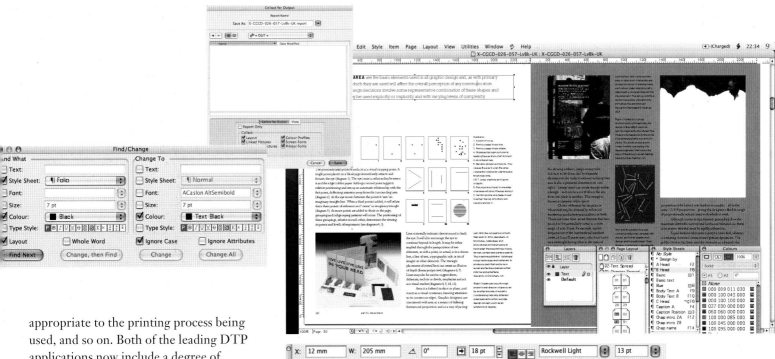

appropriate to the printing process being used, and so on. Both of the leading DTP applications now include a degree of preflighting, but separate programs such as Markzware Preflight Professional offer more advanced checking, typically in fields such as magazine publishing where it is vital that each page is reproduced perfectly every time.

Collecting for output and preflighting are still relevant when documents are supplied to the printer as PDFs (see page 70), because the PDF file will not be created successfully unless all files and settings are present and correct. Adobe Acrobat, the standard program for generating PDFs, provides increasingly sophisticated preflighting, while, again, various third-party alternatives are available.

In some cases high-resolution images may not be available to the designer – for example, because photos are not yet scanned – so layouts are created using low-res versions or sketches, referred to as 'positionals' or 'FPO' (for position only). These are replaced later by the prepress bureau. With OPI (open prepress interface), the bureau can pre-scan photos, keeping a high-res copy of each, and send low-res images back to the designer for layout. When the finished DTP file is output, the high-res images are automatically substituted. This avoids designers having to handle large files, but with today's faster computers and higher-bandwidth communications, OPI is less often required.

Above: Some of QuarkXPress's productivity features: the style sheet setup dialog boxes can be used to record individual text styles once the designer is satisfied with the layout. These can be appended to any other document. The *Find/Change* feature can change individual words, punctuation, font or size throughout the document with a single click. *Collect for Output* places all required files into one allocated folder in order to send them to the printer or output house. The *Measurements* bar shows all the attributes of the selected box.

PRODUCTIVITY FUNCTIONS

Productivity and consistency are greatly improved by features such as style sheets and master pages. Paragraph and character style sheets expedite the styling of text. Headlines, cross-heads, standfirsts, body text and captions, for example, can each be assigned a paragraph style sheet comprising all aspects of type formatting. Changes can then be made globally by amending the relevant style sheet. Each style sheet can also be 'based on' another, making it even easier to change, for example, the typeface used throughout a publication. Character styles can be applied to individual letters or words. As part of a style sheet's options, text can be locked to a fixed 'baseline grid', ensuring lines of type in different frames are aligned.

Production can be further streamlined by using master pages, which may contain text, picture boxes, and guides. Each new page inherits items from a chosen master page, including (optionally) a page number that changes automatically. The designer can create any number of master pages, allowing several alternative layouts to be used within a document, and InDesign users can also base one master page on another, with any changes to the 'parent' propagating to the 'child'. Pages can be set up singly or facing each other in spreads, and special layouts such as gatefolds can be accommodated. Master pages, style sheets, colours, and H&J settings can be appended from one document to another; QuarkXPress users can work within a 'project' that may comprise several different layouts sharing master pages, style sheets, colours, and so on.

PREPRESS

Until recently, most commercial printing involved producing film separations from which printing plates were created, and this meant the designer would require the services of a prepress bureau or a printer's own reprographic department. Today, an increasing number of documents are sent to press digitally: platemaking equipment for offset litho printing works directly from the designer's files, or the job is output on a digital press – usually based on inkjet technology – with no plates required. This is not to say that bureaux are a thing of the past. Although desktop scanners have greatly improved, only high-end bureau equipment will guarantee professional image reproduction from materials such as 35mm transparencies. A bureau can also be invaluable in managing the conversion of files to Acrobat PDF format (see page 70), although printers are increasingly likely to offer help with this.

It is important to have a good working relationship with your bureau and/or printer. You will need to know exactly what they expect from your files, whether PDFs or DTP documents collected for output. The bureau will be able to advise on what settings you should make to speed up production, keep costs to a minimum, and make sure that the end result will print without mishap. Issues range from the fairly obvious to the highly arcane, so initiating a discussion is always better than making an assumption. If colour tints or images 'bleed' off the page, for example, the amount of bleed (usually 3–5 mm) needs to be agreed with the printer and set up accordingly in your documents. While too little bleed can mean unsightly gaps, too much can cause output problems.

Fonts are a perennial bugbear of prepress work. Never use the 'faux' italic and bold type style functions in your software, as the RIP (see page 69) will probably ignore or misinterpret them; you must use true italic and bold fonts. Check whether TrueType or OpenType fonts can be used; in many cases only PostScript fonts will work reliably. When the job is sent, make sure all the fonts are collected for output: it is an infringement of copyright to supply the fonts to the bureau

Above: **Ultra-high-resolution drum scanners are a big investment, and remain in the domain of the bureau, but desktop scanners costing less than £10,000 are starting to rival their capabilities.**

Below: **Among the arcana of prepress, the screen angles of colour plates must be set correctly to avoid unsightly moiré patterns.**

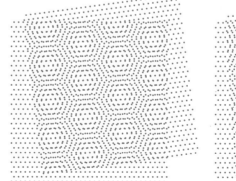
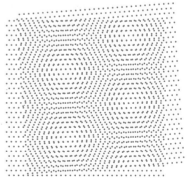

or printer unless it already owns them (see Font Copyright, page 186), but it is vital to ensure they have precisely the same versions you have used. Sending jobs as PDF gets around this issue, since you can 'embed' the fonts used in a document. If the bureau is likely to be asked to make last-minute text corrections, however, problems can arise. Only a 'subset' of each font is normally included, leaving out unused characters to reduce file size, but this means the omitted characters will not be available. Some new fonts also have their digital 'permissions' set to prevent them being used, when embedded, for any purpose other than viewing or printing, meaning the bureau will be unable to make changes unless a purchased copy of the font is installed.

The bureau or printer can manage other issues that the designer may not wish or need to be involved with. Trapping is the function of overlapping edges of colour areas

Right: Imposition for a typical sixteen-page section. Eight pages are printed on one side; the paper is then turned and printed again on the other side. In practice, if your document is short enough, a single plate can be made showing both sides of all the pages. This is printed on one side of the paper, which is then turned and printed with the same image on the other side. Cutting the sheets in half results in two identical stacks of finished pages, which are folded and trimmed as normal to make up the publication.

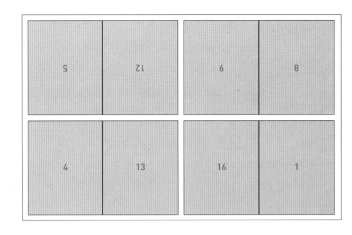

to compensate for poor registration on press. Each colour can have its own custom trapping, and blocks of colour can either 'knock out' any underlying graphics or overprint them (black normally overprints). Even if you set your own trapping preferences in your DTP software – perhaps for a one-off purpose such as ensuring a black graphic knocks out – you may find the imagesetting RIP overrides them. Although Adobe Acrobat now allows you to preview separations and overprints in PDFs on screen, not all RIPs meet the latest PDF standards. Here the designer, bureau (if any) and printer must all work together to get the right result.

IMPOSITION

A document of more than two pages will normally be viewed on screen as a series of double-page spreads. When a multi-page

Above: One side of a section ready to be trimmed, folded, and assembled. The result will be sixteen consecutive pages. Designers generally work on spreads within their layout software, seeing what will appear on the finished pages, with the technicalities of imposition left to the bureau or printer.

document is printed, however, the pages will be arranged on a larger sheet to be cut and folded into sections. A page has two sides; a single fold creates four sides; fold again and you have eight sides; and so on. Printers' sections are, therefore, made up of multiples of four. The commonest section size is sixteen pages, with eight pages printed on each side, although some web offset litho presses can print larger sections. The planning of this process is called imposition.

Imposition is usually carried out by the bureau, before running the film, or by the printer prior to platemaking. You should be aware of the most economical use of paper, and plan the page count accordingly – another conversation to have with the printer. Then draw a 'flatplan', a simple diagram indicating the content and position of each numbered page in each section. Using DTP software, you can print a flatplan showing a thumbnail image of each page for easy reference.

Because each side of each section is printed separately, some variation in colour and alignment is inevitable between pages in different sections; there may also be slight variation across each side. If the design of a spread incorporates an image that crosses over the gutter, the two halves will be separated when printed, and when the publication is bound a slight misalignment or colour variation may be apparent.

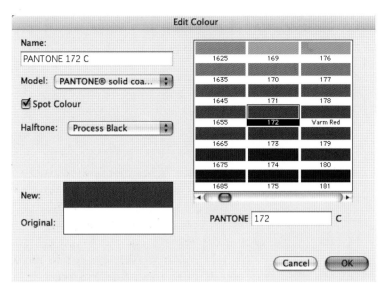

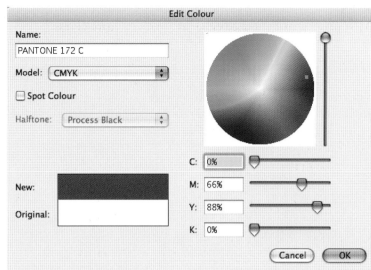

SPECIFYING COLOUR

Most colour documents are printed using the four-colour process, or CMYK. Graphics are broken up into percentages of cyan, magenta, yellow, and black inks, each printed in turn using a separate plate. These 'separations' can be generated by your DTP software, but your bureau or printer may use other means. PDF files can contain separations, but are more commonly created as composites, with the critical stage of separation left to the printer.

Spot colours – specific inks applied to blocks of type or graphics – have their own plates. Any spot colours defined within a document but not used should be deleted to ensure plates are not generated unnecessarily. In the past, the names given to spot colours within software were not significant, since the designer would brief the printer on the inks to be used. Increasing automation makes it advisable to stick to the naming conventions of an ink library such as PANTONE. If images or artwork containing spot colours are

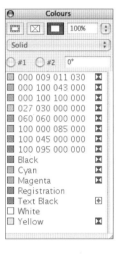

Above and left: **QuarkXPress offers comprehensive colour management. Conversion can be made from one of the proprietary spot colour system palettes to CMYK, ready for four-colour print output. A floating on-screen dialog box shows the selected colour at a glance.**

imported into DTP software from other programs, the colour names must be an exact match to those set up in your layout, or elements in the 'same' colour will appear on different plates.

Colour systems such as PANTONE can be used to help choose colours even if your document is to be process printed. Select a PANTONE swatch from the list displayed in your software, then pick the option to convert it to the nearest CMYK values. Bear in mind that not all colours can be reproduced accurately; you can buy PANTONE swatch books that show how the process versions compare.

For solid black areas, a denser colour can be achieved by underprinting a 'shiner' colour, such as 100% cyan, on the same area. Since 100% black overprints by default, you can do this simply by duplicating the graphic, colouring it 100% cyan, and sending it behind. Spot colours can be strengthened using a 'double hit', printing the same plate twice in the same colour.

Below: **For four-colour process printing, the colour bar is used by printers to assess the performance of the press, giving information such as dot gain. Printed away from the image, it is later trimmed off.**

RIPS

Most page layouts, supplied either as a 'native' QuarkXPress or InDesign file or as a PDF, are output to an imagesetter through a raster image processor or RIP (pronounced 'rip'). This device – usually a PC or Mac running specialized software – changes the outlines of the type and drawings from PostScript, the vector-based programming language used by computers to describe page layouts, into a bitmap (an array of dots) that can be printed by a filmsetter or digital press. Part of the RIP's job is to manage the creation of the 'halftone' patterns into which images and tints are broken up for printing. Although the DTP files may contain instructions to the RIP, the printer's RIP may not understand all of them or may be set, for very good reasons, to ignore them. 'Late binding' is a term used to describe last-minute changes made within PostScript files while they are in the RIP, such as adding trapping and imposition information.

Files that are 'RIP friendly' will be processed faster, and in some cases – particularly where you have an ongoing relationship with a bureau or printer – this may help keep reprographic charges low. For instance, if you use Photoshop to prepare bitmaps of the required size and orientation, rather than scaling and rotating in your DTP software, the pages will RIP faster. This must be balanced against the extra work for you and the flexibility you may be giving up.

More important is the need to supply files that will go through the RIP without errors. Not all image formats that can be imported into QuarkXPress or InDesign can be reliably ripped. The best format will depend on your bureau or printer's equipment, but will usually be EPS (encapsulated PostScript) or TIFF, pre-converted to CMYK rather than RGB colour. The ubiquitous JPEG format is not well suited to press work, although JPEG compression can now be applied within EPS and TIFF files, and will be correctly handled by many RIPs. TIFF files with LZW compression retain full image quality (unlike JPEGs) while saving considerable file space, but as with JPEGs the compression will take extra time to rip.

Below: **A bureau is no longer an essential part of the prepress chain, but may still be required to produce high-quality scans. Page layouts, stored either in the native format of a standard DTP package or as PDF files, can be sent directly from designer to printer and output, via RIP, directly to film or digital press without any further human intervention.**

When using a digital press, however, you may be asked to leave images in RGB format, and high-quality JPEG files may work fine.

Attention should also be paid to the widths of lines and rules. Strokes set to 'hairline' or less than 0.25 pt may print much finer than you expect, or may disappear on press, as may tints of less than 5%.

DELIVERING THE GOODS

If you and your printer both have broadband Internet, many documents can be emailed, transferred via FTP (file transfer protocol), or exchanged using Apple's iDisk facility. Larger files can be couriered or posted on recordable CD or DVD, or proprietary disk formats such as Zip or REV. High-volume users may consider a subscription-based digital delivery service such as WAM!NET.

For electronic transmission, files should be compressed using a program such as Allume StuffIt on the Mac or WinZip on the PC. These utilities allow a folder containing all the relevant files to be quickly compressed, typically to around half its actual size, thus potentially reducing transmission time. Zip format (unrelated to Zip disks) is usual for PC users, StuffIt (.sit) for Macs.

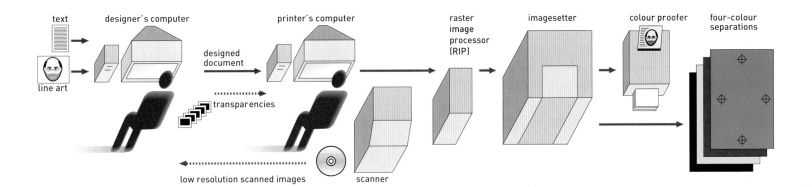

text | designer's computer | printer's computer | raster image processor (RIP) | imagesetter | colour proofer | four-colour separations
line art
designed document
transparencies
low resolution scanned images
scanner

SCREEN TO PROOF 2 Adobe introduced the PDF (Portable Document Format) as a universal file type for transmitting and printing business documents. It is now the standard format for distributing cross-platform manuals, technical drawings, marketing information, and proofs. PDF has been heralded as the key to the future of prepress, eliminating film, plates, and repro bureaux.

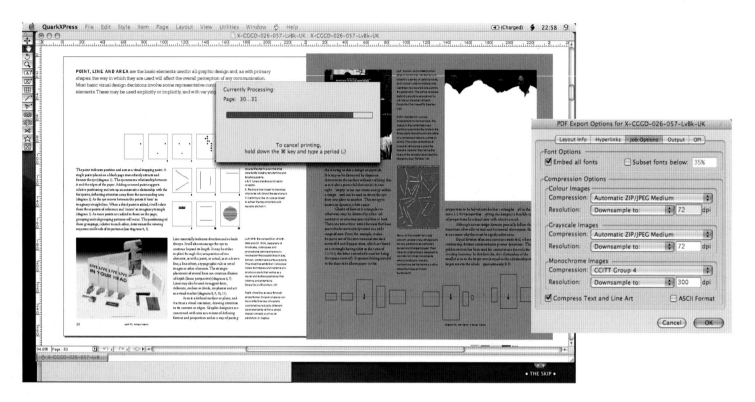

THE FUTURE OF DIGITAL WORKFLOW

PDF is a secondary file format, created from other files. Instead of sending separate page layout, font, and image files to the filmsetter, designers are able to use all these files to create a single PDF document file. The total file size is much smaller, making it quicker to transfer electronically, and can be output to any proofing device and eventually run on any press.

However, there are hazards that inhibit this perfect scenario. It is all too easy, for example, to let unconverted RGB images slip through to the final file, resulting in a monochrome image when the printer rips the file. There are options for automatically converting images to CMYK, but these can also produce unpredictable results. Designers may neglect to embed all the necessary fonts, or may set the wrong image compression options, resulting in poor-quality output. After being left out of early PDF specifications, trapping and overprints can now be correctly handled, but not all RIPs are up to date.

To realize the dream of 'blind exchange' – designers sending PDFs to press without any need to thrash out problems with the printer – a number of standards have been agreed and incorporated into PDF creation software. These

Above: **All Adobe's graphics applications support direct conversion to PDF. Other software usually requires the file to go through Acrobat Distiller, although you may still be able to initiate this process with one click. PDFs can be output directly from QuarkXPress, and Mac users can output PDFs from any application thanks to a feature built into Mac OS X, although the level of control is not really sufficient for prepress work. The distilling process is almost instant for simple files, but can take minutes for large documents.**

include PDF/X-1a, which demands that certain items must be included in the file – such as fonts, images, and essential specifications like trim and bleed – and prohibits others that could cause errors. In short, it pre-empts many of the problems identified in the previous pages. On the other hand, PDF/X-1a also prohibits ICC colour management (see page 194), which is itself a valuable tool for ensuring printed pages appear as you intended!

As time goes by, more and better PDF standards will be established, but an equally useful approach is for your printer to supply its own preferred PDF specification for you to work to. This is the method adopted by some Internet-based print services, which offer low prices on print jobs on the basis that you, the client, will prepare and submit PDF files ready to run. Despite the potential pitfalls, the results usually turn out fine.

PROOFING Only the designer knows how he or she expects the final printed product to look. The proof is the last opportunity to check for text errors, misalignment, and colour problems, and it is ultimately the designer's responsibility to clear it.

For most of the history of desktop publishing, proofing was typically done from film, using plastic laminate systems such as Matchprint and Cromalin, often called 'dry proofs'. Coloured powders or pre-coated sheets matching the process colours are exposed using filters and laminated together onto white paper.

Although dry proofs can only approximate press output, they are accurate enough to be used as 'contract proofs' to which press output should be matched. These types of proof are expensive, but cheaper than a 'wet proof' produced on a flatbed proofing press. Wet proofing has the advantage that the actual paper stock selected for the job can be used for the proof.

Over the past few years, digital colour management and inkjet technology have made it possible to generate accurate proofs quickly and at low cost. Options range from desktop proofers with built-in RIPs, from under £1000, through solutions based on similar hardware with advanced RIPs, to high-end packages such as Creo's Veris. Bureau-produced inkjet proofs are sometimes referred to as 'Iris' proofs, after an early brand-name solution, but there are now dozens of options. The quality of the RIP is at least as important as that of the hardware connected to it; basic inkjet printers, though they may offer high resolutions and impressive photo printing, rarely even support PostScript, meaning that page layouts are output quite differently from the prepress chain, if they can be output at all.

If you invest in a proofer, learn how the system works and make sure your workflow is properly colour managed (see page 194). You can then feel confident in taking the proof as a reliable guide, and making changes if colours don't look the way you want them.

Above: Wet proofing typically includes a full set of 'progressives', colour proofs printed in the same order as the process colours on the final press. Each colour printing is shown separately and also overprinted with the other colours.

Proofing systems compared (**** = excellent *** = good ** = average * = poor)

System	Speed	Quality	Cost
Matchprint	*	****	££££
Cromalin	*	****	££££
High-end inkjet	**	***	£££
Inkjet with RIP	***	**	££
Basic inkjet	***	*	£
Digital press†	**	****	££

†With a digital press, it is often cost-effective to run a single copy on press as a proof

COLOUR AND THE HALFTONE

Whether you use spot or process colour in your design depends on the job. Spot colour will give better specific colour matching and more vibrant flat colours, but only CMYK can reproduce colour photos. Sometimes you will need to add a spot colour to a CMYK job, either for a special effect such as metallic or fluorescent, or because a client demands an exact PANTONE colour for its identity. This means additional printing impressions, which will drive up costs. Packaging designs often use several spot colours, but they have a profit-driven imperative to grab attention and are printed efficiently in huge volumes.

There are two sets of primary colours, and neither is the red, yellow, and blue we all learned about in school. Computer and television displays emit light, and form colours by combining different amounts of the true primaries red, green, and blue (RGB); this is 'additive' colour mixing. The RGB system is also used by scanners and digital cameras, which have sensors dedicated to each primary.

Printed materials can only reflect light, so they use primaries which each absorb one of the RGB colours while reflecting other wavelengths; this is subtractive mixing. Cyan absorbs red, magenta absorbs green, and yellow absorbs blue. Black (which absorbs all light) is added to the set to reproduce black text cleanly and to help make deep colours without resorting to a muddy mix. Brighter, more stable colours can be achieved by using a technique called GCR (grey component replacement). Wherever the process colour

mix to create a particular colour requires equal amounts of all the primaries, a percentage of pure black is added instead. This results in better contrast and colour saturation in shadows.

The black plate is referred to as 'K', which can stand for 'key' and, more importantly, cannot be confused with blue.

Subtractive mixing does a poor job in certain areas of the spectrum, but this can be improved by adding more ink colours. The Hexachrome system uses slightly adjusted cyan, magenta, and yellow plus a vivid orange and green to give an excellent quality of colour reproduction, with subtle variations and greater range. Many everyday inkjet printers use alternative systems of six or more inks to improve colour quality. Using more than four colours on press, however, demands some fundamental changes to reprographic methods.

Printing plates can only hold discrete dots of ink, so to fill an area with 50% grey, for example, the plate must be stippled with dots filling half the area. Traditionally, 'continuous tone' images such as photos are broken up by optical screening into halftone dots that lie on a fixed grid, the size of each dot changing in proportion to the required tint. The fineness or 'frequency' of the screen is measured in lpi (lines per inch); newspapers may use 55 or 65lpi, to suit coarse paper, whereas a glossy magazine might use 133lpi.

To avoid moiré (see below), all the screens must be set at non-conflicting angles. With more than four plates, there aren't enough angles to go around. So, rather than halftoning, 'stochastic' screening must be used. Tiny dots, all the same size, are scattered pseudo-randomly across an area.

Below: Process colour halftone screens must be applied at different angles to prevent unwanted moiré patterns. Black is normally rotated to 45°, as this is the easiest on the eye; 90° is the most difficult to guarantee, so this is reserved for the less visible yellow; cyan and magenta are rotated at approximately 105° and 75°. Unfortunately, no similarly compatible set of angles exists for six or more plates. This is one reason for using 'stochastic' screening, also known as 'dithering', where dots of a small fixed size are scattered in random positions rather than using dots of variable size in a grid. In practice, to avoid unsightly clumps and gaps, the arrangement of dots must be carefully controlled rather than completely random. Inkjet printers use dithering, although some can also reproduce halftones as a simulation of press output.

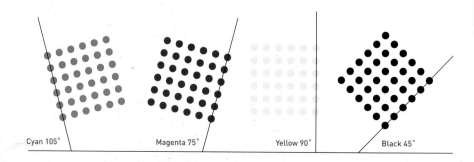

Cyan 105°   Magenta 75°   Yellow 90°   Black 45°

Above: **An image separated for four-colour process printing and enlarged (by approximately x 300,000) creates a 'rosette' pattern clearly showing the angles of the individual colour screens.**

Right: **An enlargement of a conventional mono halftone image reveals the dot pattern. A regular array of different-sized dots arranged according to the screen and screen angle being used. Smaller dots represent the lighter tones.**

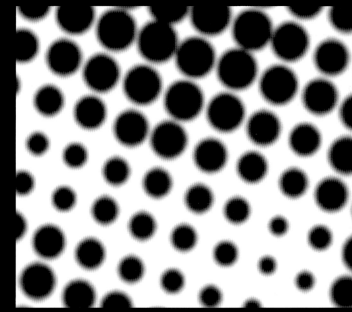

THE PRINTING PROCESS 2

The design-to-print workflow can now be executed totally digitally. However, the final step – the printing press – is still predominantly analogue. This is also the stage over which the graphic designer has least influence. Knowing how the finished product will look and feel is an essential part of the design process, so the designer must have a basic knowledge of the various printing techniques available to achieve the desired result.

LITHOGRAPHY

Lithography is by far the most common form of printing today. Originally devised more than 200 years ago, its success is based on a simple principle: oil and water do not mix.

In offset lithography the image is printed from a rubber coated roller (blanket) to which the ink is transferred from the plate. The image is firstly created on a printing plate, either photographically or by using a CTP (computer-to-plate) digital system. CTP systems are not yet the standard, but this method is set to dominate within the next few years. When the photopolymer resin coating of the plate is exposed to ultraviolet light under a process camera, exposed areas are hardened. The unexposed areas are subsequently washed off during processing. Gum Arabic is then applied to the surface to make the non-image areas water-receptive and grease-repellent (ink-repellent). Plates can either be negative or positive working. Negative-working plates are much less expensive and are generally used for single-colour work. The same chemistry applies to negative-working plates but in reverse: it is the exposed areas that become unstable leaving the unexposed areas to print.

The thin metal, plastic, or paper plate is then wrapped around the plate cylinder of the press. As the cylinder rotates, it makes contact with rollers wet with water or a similar dampening solution and rollers conveying ink. The dampening solution prevents ink adhering to the non-printing areas of the plate. The inked image areas are then transferred to a rubber covered blanket cylinder, finally offsetting the image onto the paper as it passes between the blanket and impression cylinders.

The latest litho presses can be connected directly to the digital output source, eliminating both film and the platemaking stage, making the press another link in the digital chain. The 'rewritable' drums are unsuited to large numbers of impressions, however, and there are also some uniquely digital problems that may occur, such as ghosting and mottling.

Lithography is well suited to the four-colour printing process, since larger presses can print the four colours consecutively in a single pass. Indeed, modern commercial litho presses can print up to eight colours. Smaller presses are sheet-fed, but longer print runs such as books and magazines are offset onto paper fed from large rolls on a so-called web press.

The size of the halftone screen and the surface of the paper stock will determine the density of ink required in the litho process. Uncoated paper is more absorbent and will soak up more ink; to compensate for this, the dot size can be reduced in film production. Positive-working plates produce less dot gain and are generally preferred for web-offset magazine printing.

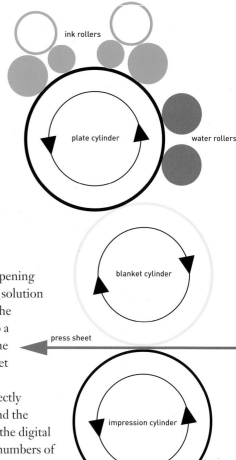

Above: Thick, viscous printing ink is forced through a system of rollers, making it semi-liquid. A thin layer is distributed over the plate. A fountain solution moistens the plate's non-image areas so that ink adheres only to the image areas. The plate cylinder revolves into contact with the blanket cylinder depositing an inked, reversed image. Paper passes between the blanket and impression cylinders, offsetting a right-reading image.

DREAMT IN HEAVEN. FORGED IN HELL. MADE IN LAS VEGAS.

TEXT BY STEPHEN BARRETT PHOTOGRAPHY BY GLENDA STUART

Left and below: In a typical web offset system, the paper is printed on both sides in one pass. A web press consists of up to eight consecutive units like this, one for each colour.

Above: A spread from the Canadian magazine Coupe, printed in four-colour process on a web-offset press. Magazines are commonly printed in sixteen page sections. Colour can be adjusted on the press electronically by increasing or decreasing the deposit of any of the four process inks to sections of the printing plates. However, once on press, localized colour changes to individual images are not possible.
Design by The Bang, Canada

ink rollers

ink rollers

plate cylinder

plate cylinder

reel

water rollers

water rollers

blanket cylinder

blanket cylinder

web

THE PRINTING PROCESS 3

The print industry is not limited to lithography; other processes offer the possibility of print on a wider variety of materials or creating more interesting, tactile effects. For straightforward, short-run jobs, meanwhile, new digital presses offer unrivalled efficiency.

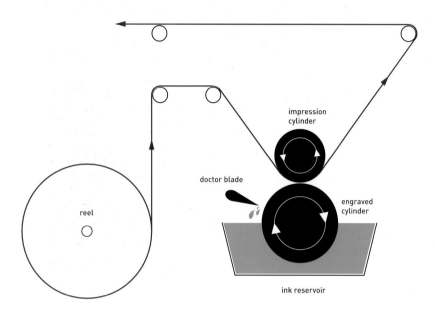

impression cylinder

doctor blade

reel

engraved cylinder

ink reservoir

GRAVURE

Possibly offset litho's biggest rival, this process is used to print everything from postage stamps to wallpaper. Gravure is an adaptation of the ancient etching method of reproducing tone. 'Cells' of different depths are cut into the surface of a cylinder, deeper cells holding and subsequently depositing more ink, rendering a darker image. As the ink from neighbouring cells tends to merge, the result is almost screenless in appearance.

Like offset litho, gravure can be printed onto a web. The process is digitally prepared: diamond styli in the engraving heads that cut the printing cells are driven from digital files. An engraved cylinder revolves in a reservoir of thin, solvent-based ink, flooding the surface. A flexible steel 'doctor blade' wipes the cylinder clean as it revolves, leaving ink only in the image areas. Finally, a rubber-covered impression cylinder presses the paper onto the engraved surface. One drawback of gravure is that type appears less sharply than with lithography.

LETTERPRESS

Once the most popular printing process, letterpress is now only used for specialized jobs or limited edition (short-run) books. The use of hot metal typesetting really survives only to

Above: A typical gravure press is web-fed. The engraved gravure cylinder rotates through an ink reservoir, and the surplus ink is wiped from the surface by a 'doctor' blade. The printed image is made by pressure between the plate cylinder and the impression cylinder.

Below: On a letterpress press the paper is placed face down on an inked block, or 'forme'. Pressure is applied by screw or lever.

produce a proof that can then be scanned and printed by offset litho to reproduce the traditional effect.

Letterpress machines have largely been converted to or replaced by flexography, in which the metal type trays of letterpress are replaced by a flexible rubber or polymer plate. Widely used in the packaging industry, flexographic (or 'flexo') presses are similar to gravure, using a series of rotating cylinders to collect ink from a reservoir and transfer it onto a web-fed printing material via plate and impression cylinders. Flexo presses can print on materials unsuitable for offset litho, such as cardboard, plastic bags, or waxed paper.

SCREEN PRINTING

Often associated with poster and art prints, the silk screen or screen printing process gets its name from what was originally a stretched silk cloth used to hold a stencil. This versatile printing process produces thick, opaque

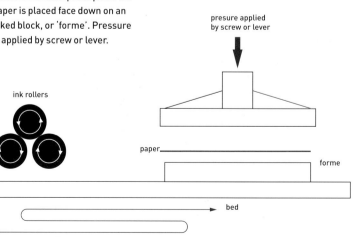

pressure applied by screw or lever

ink rollers

paper

forme

bed

Right: *O* by Frederico d'Orazio, PlaatsMaken. This plastic 'book' can be unfolded and blown-up into a human sized inflatable mattress. Text and graphics are screen printed onto the plastic.
Design by Frederico d'Orazio, Italy/Netherlands

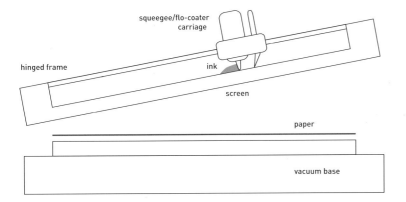

deposits of ink in brilliant colours, and can be used to print on virtually any material, including shop windows and the sides of vans, or even curved or uneven surfaces such as bottles, T-shirts, and printed circuit boards.

Modern screens are made from a fine polyester mesh, stretched on a metal or wooden frame. A simple line stencil is cut using a digitally controlled pen plotter that manipulates a knife. More complex stencils and halftones can be made using a film positive as in lithography. The screen is

Above: A common hand-operated screen printing press. The rubber-bladed squeegee is pulled over the surface of the screen, forcing the ink through the mesh onto the paper or material held in position on a vacuum bed.

coated on both sides with a light-sensitive polymer emulsion and exposed through the film with ultraviolet light, after which the image areas are washed away with water. The screen is mounted on the press and a rubber-edged squeegee forces the ink through the mesh, passing only through the 'open' image areas. Though fine screens are available, screen printing is not recommended for close registration or work involving very small type sizes.

DIGITAL PRINTING

Finally, we come to the latest output option and the one that seems closest to the goal of an all-digital workflow. Digital presses, based on various inkjet and 'dry ink' technologies, are rapidly increasing in popularity for economical short-run, full-colour work. Running at speeds up to around 10,000 copies an hour, they offer similar quality to offset litho and compete well on cost up to a few thousand units: litho costs far less per copy, but digital does away with job setup costs. Many of these presses can optionally create a different image on every sheet (see page 13), allowing huge scope for such tasks as printing personalized documents from mailing databases. On the down side, the range of paper stock that can be printed is more limited than with litho, and print can have an annoying tendency to rub off, particularly when subjected to heat.

FINISHING Once the job has been printed, there is one final stage before delivering the finished product. This is entirely mechanical, which may involve trimming, folding, collating, or binding. It must be considered early in the design process because it will affect the way the document is constructed and therefore the production budget.

Finishing can also include print-related operations such as die-stamping, embossing, varnishing, and laminating. Die-stamping and embossing use a metal die (engraved by a digitally controlled machine tool) to 'stamp' or press a relief image into paper or board. The image can be impressed with or without ink, to create subtle effects. Frequently seen on paperback book jackets, a metal foil can be combined with the raised impression, using a heated die. Die-cutting physically cuts out sections of the paper. Digitally controlled laser die-cutting is used to cut fine detail such as company logos in business stationery.

There are a number of ways to protect the printed page and make it scuff-resistant. Varnishes can be printed on the litho press to give varying degrees of gloss or matt finish. To add extra strength, a film lamination, again in matt or gloss,

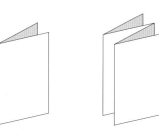

Above: **Some of the varied ways of folding. Left to right: Single fold four-page sheet. Accordion eight-page fold, Gatefold eight-page fold, Rollover eight-page fold.**

can be glued to the stock under pressure through a heated roller. Interesting design effects can be created by mixing spot areas of gloss and matt varnishes or by adding a varnish after the lamination is applied.

FOLDING AND BINDING

Once the print finishes have been applied, the stock is ready to be folded. Folding is accomplished using a buckle, knife, or combination folding machine. There is no limit to the number of folds employed, and interesting visual effects can be created by using a single sheet designed to fold into several smaller sections. After folding, multi-page jobs have to be gathered, bundled, and collated (put in order), prior to binding and guillotining. Other operations that may need to be considered are perforating or tipping-in (adding a single page to a multi-page publication).

Left: **Folding, binding, and trimming in progress. Folded and collated 'signatures' move along a conveyor of saddles in the shape of inverted 'V's. Wire staples are inserted along the fold of the spine. The three remaining edges are then trimmed by a series of guillotine blades prior to packing.**

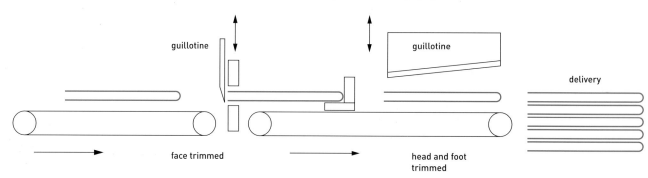

guillotine

guillotine

delivery

face trimmed

head and foot trimmed

part 02. surface design

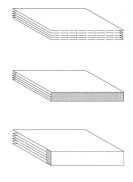

Right: **Perfect binding. The sections are collated and the spines then trimmed off. The edges are roughened and glue is applied to attach the wrap-around covers.**

Binding may be performed by several methods. Booklets, and magazines up to about 96 pages, are commonly bound by saddle-stitching (stapling), while unsewn or 'perfect' binding can be used for almost unlimited numbers of pages. Gathered and collated sections are placed in the binding machine, spine down; the edge is roughened and an adhesive applied. The cover is folded, scored, and wrapped around the pages. The adhesive is cured by heat and the pages are trimmed. In large perfect-bound books, the designer must use a generous gutter to avoid text and pictures disappearing into it, as the spine is less flexible than sewn titles and some fold is lost in trimming.

Case-bound or hardback books have a separately made cover. The page sections are sewn through the spine with thread and gathered together to form a 'book-block'. The cover and book-block are assembled with tipped-in endpapers, usually of a heavier stock. Finally a separate 'dust' jacket is wrapped around the cased book.

Above: **Multi-folded concertina brochure commissioned by Photo '98: Year of Photography and Electronic image.**
Design by Eg.G, UK

Right: **Promotional Brochure for 'The Lightbox' property development. By using a plastic cover and ring-binding mechanism, this brochure could be economically updated by inserting or removing pages as the project progressed.**
Design by Foundation, UK

Above: **Kenneth Grange Design Identity. A monochromatic two-dimensional logo has been given a three-dimensional quality with thoughtful use of embossing.**
Design by Lippa Pearce Design, UK

Right: **Case-bound books are assembled with a 'book block' made up of sewn sections or 'signatures', endpapers, and a heavy board cover or 'case'.**

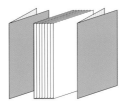

CHOOSING PAPER The choice of paper is the foundation of a successful print job. The designer must consider carefully what the finished item is trying to achieve and select a stock that will not only convey the right message but also fit within the print budget.

A huge range of papers and boards is available – machine-made, handmade, and recycled. For some jobs, the type of paper will be determined by the method of printing employed. Offset litho presses require papers with good surface strength and dimensional stability, preferably with a low water content. The finish is a less important factor, as offset ink will adhere both to glossy coated and to matt uncoated surfaces. For gravure, the paper must be smooth but absorbent enough to collect the ink.

The paper must fit the brief for the job, and the finish should also be appropriate to the content. For good-quality colour halftone reproduction, a coated stock (made with mineral fillers to create a very smooth surface) would normally be used, although some very fine uncoated papers now boast excellent colour quality. The weight of paper is classified by grams per square metre (gsm or gm^2), a standard sheet of copier paper weighing 90 gsm. The impact of a prestigious catalogue could be increased by using 150 or 200 gsm. Generally, heavier papers or art boards are thicker than light ones, but the density and type of fibre will have an effect on thickness (bulk). Glossy art paper can feel thinner than an uncoated stock of the same weight, so it may be necessary to increase the weight when choosing a gloss finish. Be careful of ink

showing through some lightweight papers. If a brochure needs to be mailed, the weight of the stock will affect the cost of postage.

Of course, budget may also limit the choice of paper. Your spending power can be maximized by choosing the size and format wisely, taking into account the sizes of paper the printer can use so that costly wastage can be avoided.

Paper is manufactured in A and B sizes according to an international standard based on the ratio $1:\sqrt{2}$ (the ratio is maintained when sheets are folded in half). If possible, your document should be designed to fit within a standard size. Remember to consult the printer and allow for any bleeds and for sufficient free 'gripper' edge as required by the press. If the brief calls for a special finish, such as varnish or lamination, the printer will advise on suitable stock. Do not overspecify: it is not necessary to use a gloss stock if you are adding a gloss varnish. Types of binding may be influenced by direction of grain (the way the fibres lie), so prior consultation is important.

You or the client may also have strong views on the environmental impact of the chosen stock. An increasingly attractive range and quality of recycled papers is available; new paper from sustainable forests is another option. Even recycled papers are often bleached with chlorine, releasing extremely harmful by-products. But many papers are now 'chlorine-free'.

The printer should be able to supply sample books from paper merchants and mills. It is a good idea to build a library of these – some are inspirational works of design in their own right.

Right: **Paper sample books such as this one for Monadnock Paper will usually include all the weights and colours available from a manufacturer and extend to such items as envelopes if they are available.**
Design by Pollard & Van der Water
Golden, USA

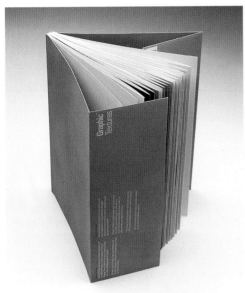

Above: **Paper sample books can be interesting design projects in their own right. Modo Paper Mills Inc, USA, strive to stimulate their target audience – the designers who will specify their product – with strong, colourful photographic imagery and unusual binding.**
Design by SEA, UK

Right: **Rolland Motif Paper Promotional Calendar. Innovative use of print techniques, die cutting and binding, cleverly demonstrate the versatility of the paper samples.**
Design by Époxy, Canada

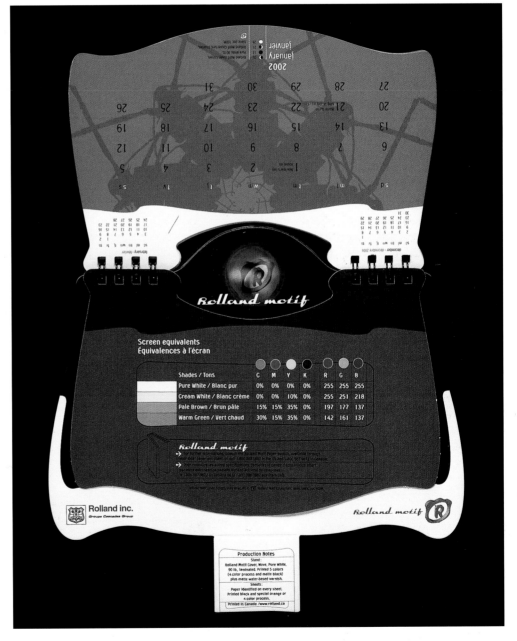

CASE HISTORY   LIVING IN THE CITY

An exhibition to display the results of an international architectural competition organized by the Architecture Foundation in London, to promote the regeneration of derelict inner city sites, and develop innovative models of future urban accommodation. The exhibition was held at the Design Museum in London.

The Architecture Foundation and the Design Museum required a number of printed graphic elements to both promote the exhibition and explain the architectural concepts proposed by the winning entries.

The designer was briefed to produce the exhibition graphics accompanied by a promotional poster, advertising, and various invitations to openings and private views. The initial brief also included a catalogue. However, as the results of the competition arrived from the international architectural practices, it became apparent that a more substantial publication would be required, and a book was proposed.

Although the exhibition was funded through sponsorship supplied by business and charitable trusts, the budget was limited, precluding the use of a photographer or expensive production methods. The graphic and exhibition designers worked closely to ensure the graphic elements would complement both the display stands and the exhibits. An architectural sheet-plastic material was employed to create the stands themselves, and it was decided to use this theme as a basis for the graphic imagery.

The material is translucent and lightly colour-tinted. Cost and practicality ruled out the use of the actual material as an innovative binding concept. Instead, the designer used a digital camera to create close-up images of the material, using light and reflection for architectural effect. To add a further level of transparency, the book was covered with a tracing paper wrap simply printed in one colour. The tracing element was also bound into the publication to create section divisions.

It was deemed part of the designer's brief to liaise with the architects wordwide to collect the illustrative content of the book. These included digital photographs of architectural models, drawings, and three-dimensional renderings. As the time-scale was critical, electronic transmission had to be employed to collate these elements from all points of the globe. The images were supplied in a number of different formats, file types, and resolutions. Most were compressed as JPEGs to speed transmission. All the images had to be re-sampled to TIFF or EPS format to create 300dpi CMYK files suitable for printing. Text was supplied as a digital word-processing file by email and run into the page layouts. The pages were designed entirely on screen and first stage proofs created as PDF files. A set of hard-copy page proofs were also supplied to the client to ensure the 'feel' was balanced and the weights of type sympathetic to the design.

After final corrections were taken in, the digital files were sent on disk to the lithographic printer based in Belgium. The printer ran the files to plate and supplied page proofs so the designer could check there were no file errors or incompatibilities that might cause poor-quality imagery, or font conflicts.

Below: **Page layouts in progress in QuarkXPress. Text was imported from emailed word processing documents. Pictures, emailed as compressed JPEGs, were converted to CMYK TIFF files prior to positioning on the page.**

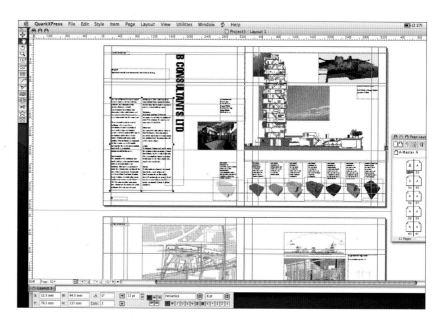

This page: **Some of the elements that made up the printed material designed to promote the exhibition: invitation, poster, and book, with a spread depicting architectural concepts from one of the winning practices.**

The practices of advertising, corporate identity and branding cut across other sections in this book, yet the profession of advertising has a distinct character that connects it closely with corporate identity and branding but sets it apart from other forms of visual and commercial practice. This section therefore looks at advertising, branding, and corporate identity together. Although they used to be billed as separate practices that incorporated graphic expertise, the three aspects became more interconnected, as multimedia agencies, developed in the 1990s, were able to mix graphic and advertising skills and to take on entire promotional projects.

Essentially, advertising aims to produce a campaign – a strategic thought voiced in different ways, to surprise, delight, and inform people. Like advertising, corporate identity aims to coordinate the interpretation of a product or service with a distinct visual or verbal 'look', by which it can be recognized. Branding became prominent in the 1990s

with the rise of multinational companies that wanted to extend their promotions outside the normal territories of conventional advertising. Before any other quality, all three areas require ideas to be expressed with absolute clarity.

THE SIGNIFICANCE OF ADVERTISING IN CONSUMER SOCIETY

In each area, graphic design skills are essential. Branding and corporate identity require typographers to craft letterforms and distinguish brand character; and computer-skilled graphic designers to coordinate the connections between all graphic elements, format material for printers (on disk and over the Internet), and define rules that govern the graphics application to different media. In advertising, a graphic designer's sense of organization is essential in order to ensure the flow of information and consistency of treatment. Word-based advertisements depend on skilled and sensitive typography. Most significantly, establishing a brand and developing its corporate identity in an advertising campaign demands graphics expertise,

PART 02. SURFACE DESIGN

CHAPTER TWO

DESIGN FOR ADVERTISING

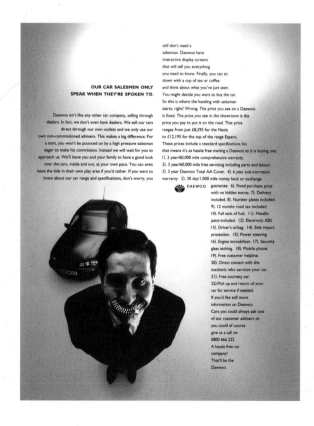

Left: **This ad relies on a tight relationship between the art direction and copy. The organization of props, colour density, and picture space has been carefully arranged with the shape and weight of the text. Note the distinct visual style and placement of brand name and logo. These reinforce the brand name and visual identity.**
Duckworth Finn Grubb Waters, UK

Opposite above: **This Coke campaign drew on the brand's famous marque, effectively reminding the viewer of its established familiarity and uniqueness. The art direction drew on the brand's pre-existing archival imagery, which plays to the strengths of digital image manipulation (scanning, re-editing, segmenting, and enhancing).**
McCann Erickson, UK

Opposite below: **In its location a billboard has to be striking, quickly understood and easy to associate with the product or brand. The layout therefore must be clearly organized while the message must be punchy and succinct.**
Rainey Kelly, UK

because it requires the translation of concepts into images and copy, combined with an acute understanding of visual reference points.

The modes of advertising fall into five categories: warning, informing, reminding, launching, and promotion. The overriding purpose is to provoke awareness by disrupting viewers' routine by grabbing their attention.

Since the beginning of the twentieth century, the usual means of media advertising was in the press and on billboards, and from 1954 this extended to television commercials. From the 1970s, a more direct form of advertising – sometimes called integrated advertising, advertising design, or below-the-line advertising – emerged to counter the over-familiarity of mass advertising. A more recent form – ambient advertising – uses landscape and the placement of brands in situations where their message is most likely to be well received, such as a car manufacturer promoting safety by sponsoring and branding the clothes of a lollipop man.

The expansion of promotional forms has required designers to apply their skills more widely because, in all forms of advertising, the brand and the message have to be applied consistently and understood in the same way.

Life tastes good

Feed your mind [THE TIMES]

SPECIALIST PEOPLE Within the set-up of a media advertising agency, there is typically a creative team that shapes the campaign and feeds ideas to graphic designers and typographers. Designers are usually called when ideas need to be presented at pitches, at review stages and for final artwork. The precise nature of campaign development varies between agencies but one would broadly expect to find the following:

CREATIVES

The creative department is made up of art directors, who construct the artwork, and copywriters, who determine the use and wording of copy. Both are answerable to creative directors, who control the overall direction of campaigns with financial and planning directors. Art directors and copywriters often work as a team, an approach that emerged from New York's Madison Avenue in the 1960s. All three creative jobs require graphic design training, and it is with the creative department – usually called 'the creatives' – that graphic designers, typographers, and brand-design specialists work most closely.

The input required from graphic designers centres on turning rough ideas in the form of scamps (see page 95) into finished digital artwork that brings together all elements – type, image, and corporate branding. Images can be developed digitally and sent via email. Graphic designers need to ensure that the campaign appears consistent with the other applications of branding and corporate identity.

FACILITATORS

The media campaign is usually connected to, and co-ordinated with, other areas of brand-building, such as price promotions and more targeted direct advertising. This is usually negotiated with the client's own marketing department and the project management team, which consists of the creative director along with planners, who translate the client's needs into the creatives' brief, and account handlers, who control the finances of a campaign. In all aspects of advertising freelance work, graphic designers are likely to come into contact with facilitators (often called 'suits'), who employ typographers, illustrators, animators, computer-graphic layout specialists, and production specialists on a project basis. Graphic designers are also likely to come into contact with project time-planners (called 'traffic'); their job is to ensure that deadlines are met. Media-space buyers negotiate with billboard site owners, press, and other media owners to organize the placements of advertisements. In some

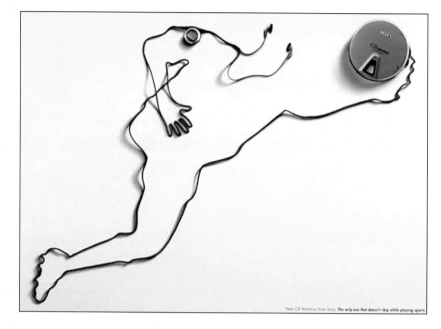

cases, specific advertising sites require designers to tailor their artwork at short notice in liaison with the media-space planning team.

Graphic expertise is usually introduced when the creative direction has been agreed, although the brief on which designers work tends to be established early in the process. Increasingly, because brand-marketing directors move jobs frequently, clients tend to employ their own third party, a 'brand guardian', to oversee their product's long-term development: these people are concerned with all aspects of the brand's development, from campaign direction and corporate identity through to consistency in the development of product packaging. The lines of responsibility often inter-connect, according to the variety of media used in an advertising campaign.

As in other fields of graphic design, work is nearly always produced on an Apple

Above: **Art-direction led advertisement.** The product is clearly central to the artwork, preventing it being confused with another brand, while the negative space emphasizes the simple arrangement. In the past the footballer's crafted outline would have required a skilled model maker and photographic trickery. Today it is more cost-effective to simulate from a sketch model in either Photoshop or Freehand. Tribal DDB, Spain

Right: Copy-led advertisement. The justified copy is easy to read because of the liberal spacing between and around the text. The illustration provides the copy with a distinct visual point of reference, leading the eye into the text. Copy is often written straight into Freehand, therefore careful copy checking beyond electronic spellchecks is essential.
Brook Street, UK

You are your own business. Me PLC doesn't owe its existence to an employer. As chairman and workforce, you supply your services to whoever needs them. And if you want to close the factory down for a couple of months, well that's your business too. What used to be called temping is now called smart. Using your main asset (a very powerful piece of wrinkly grey software) to the best advantage. Brave? Scary? Maybe at first. But not as scary as staying in the wrong job until you hate it. Why not make an executive decision to diversify? Talk to Brook Street. We'll help you make a career of it.

Macintosh. Work is increasingly moved between individuals and groups via the Internet, so computer-skilled graphic designers have in recent years become integral to the advertising process – from the transition of the strategies (in the brief) to visualizing and development stages, and through to the completed artwork ready for production.

In such a busy digital environment, the graphic designer must have a thorough grasp of file management and be conversant with file formats and compression techniques, in the interests of rapid and accurate communication. Producing prototypes is helped enormously by choosing the right software. Final print-quality files can be supplied as PDFs for client approval, and 'one-off' or limited-edition giant posters can be produced on inkjet printers for trial marketing. On a smaller scale, photorealistic proposals for hoardings can be easily photo-montaged in Photoshop. Advertising and branding usually require designs in a wide variety of publications and formats. The ability of software to scale and reassemble design elements in different aspect ratios, and to store multiple document versions in a single file, gives the graphic designer great flexibility.

DESIGN CONSIDERATIONS Within advertising there are many different types of promotion, and agencies tend to specialize. The two most prominent are media advertising and direct advertising. Media agencies produce mass-exposure, high-publicity work through billboard, press, and commercial advertising, while direct advertising – often called one-to-one – is more closely geared to target markets.

MEDIA ADVERTISING

Billboards are usually produced for 48 or 96-sheet sites or single-sheet rectangular format (1 sheet = 15 x 30 inches). On a smaller scale, six- and single-sheet campaigns promote events. In both cases, designers liaise with advertising directors to make images and ideas fit the format.

Press advertising ranges from double- and single-page spreads to column-width ads. Most adverts require graphic judgment from an early stage. Type, colour, and layout are decided before photos and other material are commissioned. Unlike in other media, designers have little control over paper or format, except with inserts, which are printed by the client and dropped in.

Television commercials also require early graphic input. Illustrators are hired to sketch out storyboards, helping the creative team to convey precisely what they require from the director. On-location storyboards are checked constantly to ensure that suitable footage is recorded, timing is met, and material fits the requirements of post-production teams. Digital typographers and graphic designers produce text sequences – added during post-production – to link the film with the end frame. The final connection between product shot, branding, and strapline is often crucial.

DIRECT ADVERTISING

The most common form of direct advertising is direct mail (DM) to potential or existing customers. Graphic design is central, because the work involves presenting offers and information through the design of letters, flyers, brochures, and packaging. So graphic designers work closely with the marketing team. For bigger advertising campaigns using DM, one-off 'interactive' self-liquidating promotions (SLPs) may be commissioned. These are limited-edition branded goods that connect to publicized offers, usually developed from a media campaign.

The Internet is a fast-growing medium for direct marketing. Banners, vertical 'skyscraper' ads, and various forms of pop-up challenge the digital designer to pack a lot of message into a small space, both visually and technically. Using HTML-based email, graphical messages can be sent to large subscriber lists at negligible cost, but technical niceties must be observed to ensure recipients can read them. 'Viral' marketing – releasing a graphic, film clip, or mini-game onto the Web and relying on users to draw each others' attention to it – demands imagination and technical skills as well as a keen awareness of the target audience's mindset.

Point-of-sale requires graphic designers to connect all areas of brand advertising and promotion work. Formats include freestanding boards, dump bins, banners, 'wobblies' (plastic mobiles suspended from shelves), and 'buzz stops' (vertical advertising hoardings between shelves); these are all increasingly quick and cheap to produce using technologies such as large-format inkjet printers. Digital graphics skills are also needed to scan and manipulate environments during concept development.

Right: **Self-liquidating promotions (SLPs) are campaign extensions designed to add to a brand's promotional 'hit'. This megaphone slotted into a press, poster, and TV campaign for a soft drinks company picked up on the colour and branding of the product. The fact that a megaphone was chosen as the SLP reinforced the company's extravagant personality.**
Triangle Communications, UK

THIS MORNING

THEY WERE

AT EACH OTHER'S

THROATS.

FOR YOUR FREE BROCHURE
FREEPHONE 080 80 1000 000

WALES CYMRU
TWO HOURS AND A MILLION MILES AWAY.

WE'VE SQUEEZED
A DESKTOP
INTO A PORTABLE.

No catch. The only difference between a Toshiba portable and a desktop PC is scale.

TOREDUCE When it comes to size and weight the two are oceans apart. And for power, function and features our portables are no small fry. Features like the best chips, Intel MMX, the largest screens, 13.3" and the fastest CD-ROM drives, mean our portables are a good haul. And the PC Card Slots on every Toshiba mean **TOSURPASS** our portables can take the bait of most networks. Whilst our innovative firsts have always created waves amongst desktop and portable manufacturers alike. It's because we would rather lead the shoal than swim with it, that makes us the world leader in portable computing. Our portables have consistently landed **TOACHIEVE** prizes from PC Magazine for Service, Reliability, and Technical Innovation. If you'd like to take the plunge and see why more people are working wherever and whenever they like, call us on 01932 828 828. Hopefully you'll agree, Toshiba really do have portable computing canned.

TOSHIBA

PCD Marketing, PC Division, Toshiba Information Systems (UK) Ltd. Toshiba Court, Weybridge Business Park, Addlestone Road, Surrey KT15 2UJ.

Top: This ad for the Welsh Tourist Board was designed for 48- and 96-sheet billboards, which enabled the small inset image contained in the top left to contrast with the less constrained image representing the free open expanse of Wales.
Impact FCA!, UK

Above: This press ad uses a visual pun as a lead into the body copy. Note that the text is separated from the image so that it does not distract from the image or text's clarity. The text is further simplified with separate headings to make it appear less bulky.
Duckworth Finn Grubb Waters, UK

DESIGN CONSIDERATIONS FOR MEDIA AND DIRECT ADVERTISING:

✳ An advertising campaign must have impact, relevance, and 'connect' simply with the intended audience.

✳ Advertising must not lose sight of its subject – the graphic content is essential in this.

✳ Clarity – in print advertising 80% of the space usually conveys the idea, and 20% the additional information.

✳ Analysis of the brief defines precisely what is required – the ideal is to reduce the proposition to a single sentence – and defines the types of skill required of a graphic designer.

✳ The prominence of the logo or product shot must be considered, remembering that the purpose of the graphic input is to emphasize the advertised goods.

✳ The brand characteristics must be systematically adhered to in terms of layout, tone, and treatment of the copy.

CORPORATE IDENTITY IN ADVERTISING Corporate identity is the commercial face that represents a company, where branding is its commercial application. They often get confused because the term 'brand' is the name given to a company's identity, while 'branding' describes the marque by which a company, product, or service is recognized. Expressed simply, corporate identity is the creation of the brand, while branding is how it is then applied through all areas of communication.

The corporate identity has to represent the values by which a company should be known, but in recent years major brands have turned their products into sub-brands; and consequently advertising activity has diversified. In modern communications agencies, the roles normally associated with branding and corporate identity tend increasingly to cross over.

The most common outlets for corporate identity include journals and in-store magazines, which are typically quarterly publications that show, through their editorial contents, how the company's products and services connect with the presumed lifestyles of consumers. Graphic design considerations include the creation and implementation of the brand's corporate rules regarding layout, and the organization of leader stories, advertorials, and features in a visually stimulating manner.

Clear rules as to how the corporate identity will be used in different media have to be established. These typically range from stationery and advertising to digital applications. Appropriateness and consistency are key considerations. How changes affect the reading of the brand is a significant issue in the development of a corporate identity: does it still retain a connection with earlier brand associations?

Bigger brands have tended to develop and implement corporate identities through their own retail environments – most notably superbrands such as Nike and Disney Stores. Such total branding involves the bringing together of all visual aspects and the development of corporate signature styles to create a brand experience.

Corporate identity, therefore, requires background knowledge of the product's or firm's chief characteristics, the type of market in which the clients want to develop, and the nature of promotions to which they want to commit.

Above left: **Internet search engine Ask Jeeves placed animated ads within many other sites to raise its profile among Web surfers, reportedly attracting large volumes of 'click-through'. In the fast-moving online world, a clear, consistent, and unchanging corporate identity is a great asset.**

Above: **Although the company's primary product is its computers, Apple's iPod was its most successful launch of recent years. The instantly recognizable style of its integrated press, poster and TV advertising campaigns evoked Apple's established brand values of innovation, style and freedom.** Design by TBWA/Chiat/Day, USA

DESIGN CONSIDERATIONS FOR CORPORATE IDENTITY

Graphic consultants typically are involved in key stages of corporate identity work: primary research and recommendation, visualizing (through sketch work and digitally imaged scamps) image concepts, development and detail, then implementation (digital type specifications and media appropriation). It is important for designers to be able to blend traditional and digital skills in order to get the right results in as little time as possible.

Corporate identities need to convey a sense of belonging, must be representative and must be clear. Designers need to ensure that the placement of, and any appropriations to, a brand marque are consistent with core brand values. They should check to see what rules govern its usage. The visual dynamics of a corporate identity must be well measured in terms of appropriateness to market and consistency. This is absolutely essential to the inherent character of the product or firm it represents.

Having extracted key graphic qualities, the designer will need to consider the need for flexibility and assess how these qualities can be effectively reproduced at different scales and in different contexts.

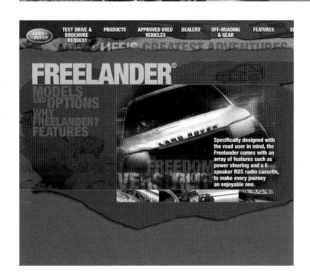

Above: Land Rover's direct mail has been credited with developing their existing customer base. Using data to target established and potential customers, the agency have developed a variety of promotional material that has coordinated user group outings, mailer posters, and small publications. Together it forges a bond between customers and the brand ethos. The range of paraphernalia is connected through strong corporate identity, which underpins the entire range of promotional work including the Land Rover website (left).
Craik Jones, UK

BRANDING Compared with corporate identity, branding is directly connected with raising awareness. It usually involves the development of a brand's identity within the everyday surroundings of its target market, using graphic techniques to ensure that the brand is associated with a particular space and mood. Branding therefore fits between direct advertising and corporate identity, because it commercializes the brand by applying the graphic identity to appropriate contexts.

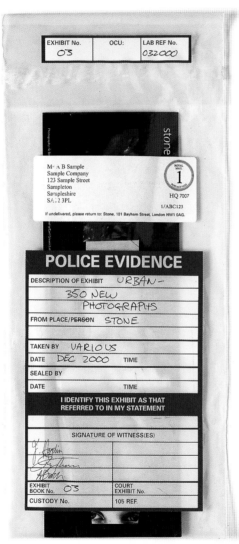

Above: This limited edition business-to-business mailer treats a Tony Stone picture library image as police evidence. The team that designed this as part of the stock archive's re-branding had to develop the total package, linking separate elements such as a flyer, poster, cover letter, and sealed bag. All elements were rendered in Freehand and printed onto the different media.
Tequila, UK

Recently, branding has engaged a wider range of specialist graphic practices so that environments and products – from coasters and clocks to nightclubs and public spaces – have become vehicles for promotion. The role of the designer is to apply the corporate graphic style to situations that, in most cases, require re-thinking of an existing identity. Photoshop is an ideal tool for producing mock-ups showing products and brands in different situations. However, final artwork will usually be produced in FreeHand or Illustrator, vector-based files being more versatile for use at a variety of scales and with printing methods adapted to different materials.

The objective of such ambient or 360-degree advertising may be to engage customers at the moment they are most likely to want the product – for instance, a drinks brand in a bar – or to make a new opportunity to communicate with a hard-to-reach audience. Graphic designers are typically employed to rework graphic elements, taking into account how the branding will be understood in its given context. In online branding, the development of corporate identity rules is essential, and usually involves collaboration between digital graphic designers, copywriters, and web designers.

Branding is also called on to extend direct advertising activity. Branded booklets, collector cards and correspondence may be sent to existing clients to maintain customer dialogue.

Many brands develop their identity by diversifying into other markets. Brand stretching can simply mean a brand name being applied to another product, but more often it involves developing a brand through a new product range – for instance a drinks brand expanding into leisure clothing, where new lines provide links to the brand's main area of operation.

In some instances clients have their own 'brand guardian', who ensures that the advertising strategy and other new ideas fit with the existing brand ethos and the company's other development plans. Digital asset management (DAM) systems may be implemented within the company so that in-house and external designers can store and retrieve logos, graphics, photos, text, and other identity material using a central database, with version control and access restrictions to help ensure items are used correctly.

Right: Even in the design of the Porsche mug, the placement of the marque and copy are key design elements, as is the sourcing of a mug manufacturer with the appropriate surface finish, proportions, and details for Porsche's brand identity. Such qualities may be defined in a corporate identity specification manual.

Right: The Smirnoff Experience – a branded dance event – was a version of 360° advertising, where the landscape was dominated by a single brand. Such sponsorship strategies reinforce the association between a venue and a distinct brand or product. They are coordinated with a range of branded design material including posters, environmental graphics, and self-liquidating promotions.
KLP Euro RSCG, UK

Right: Initially produced as a brand extension of the fashion label Benetton, *Colors* magazine espouses many of the values associated with the brand's established global identity. The magazine added depth and kept the spirit of Benetton's brand ethos, which had been developed through earlier ad campaigns.

DESIGN CONSIDERATIONS FOR BRANDING

Graphic consultants are typically involved in three stages of branding development: primary research and recommendation, visualizing the brand in context, then working out implementation feasibility.

The role of graphic designers in branding involves consultation and recommendation more than re-design. Branding must graphically reflect, in situ, a company's aspirations in a wide variety of contexts, ensuring that the visual distinction of a brand is clearly evident and that its primary function is to condense key characteristics into a 'signature' – a visual typographic or graphic element. This will be the marque by which it is recognized.

With promotional work in mind, the branding should incorporate commercial hooks that suggest how the brand typography and graphic styling could be adapted. This may suggest to a brand's marketers or advertising creatives the key qualities that can be picked out as a selling proposition.

The context in which the brand is placed has to be clearly relevant and easy to associate. It is important, if it is to work effectively, that the branding cannot be misconstrued and that any brand extensions of the work must connect with the core ethos of the brand's other promotions.

PLANNING AND PRODUCTION Careful planning and control of production are key to a successful advertising campaign. With so many creative professionals involved, it is vital that the graphic designer is aware of all the critical stages of the process.

KEY STAGES IN THE PLANNING, DESIGN, AND PRODUCTION OF A PROMOTION CAMPAIGN

Stage 1 is the brief – defining the campaign objectives. The creative brief is broken down in order to interpret statistical evidence, to define a 'hook' as the most suitable selling proposition, and to define appropriate modes of delivery (and appropriate media) to reach the defined target market. The components are translated into a project plan that defines art direction, and suggests tone of voice and the most appropriate types of graphic designer (and illustrator) for the project.

Stage 2 concerns the defined key words and proposition – concepts for advertising. This is the task of thinking through ideas on paper using layout pads and markers to produce scamps – ideas in rough, simply communicated. At this stage, the concepts are shown to the rest of the creative team, then to the planning team (occasionally with client representatives) to ensure that all aspects of the brief have been addressed. At this first visualizing stage, art directors work through and negotiate ideas with copywriters, who will consider the ratio of type to image.

Initially a campaign plan is defined – developing the strongest strategies, and detailing the concept – and a plan for art direction and execution is set out. Ideas are presented in-house (using scamps and mock-ups) and adjustments are made, with graphic specialists employed to tidy the presentation. The agency's project team puts a detailed presentation plan together. This is followed by the external (client) presentation for which key ideas are polished (with external graphic design expertise) to presentation level. By this point graphics software such as FreeHand or Illustrator and photomanipulation tools such as Photoshop will play a vital part in the process. Clients are usually presented with a central campaign plan and a series of alternatives, so that a final direction can be agreed and signed off by the client.

Right: **The stages shown in this diagram are typical of those commonly found in media advertising agencies. Digital graphic designers are mostly called upon in the run-up to the key presentation stages, such as the presentation of strategy, concept, and for the final artwork.**

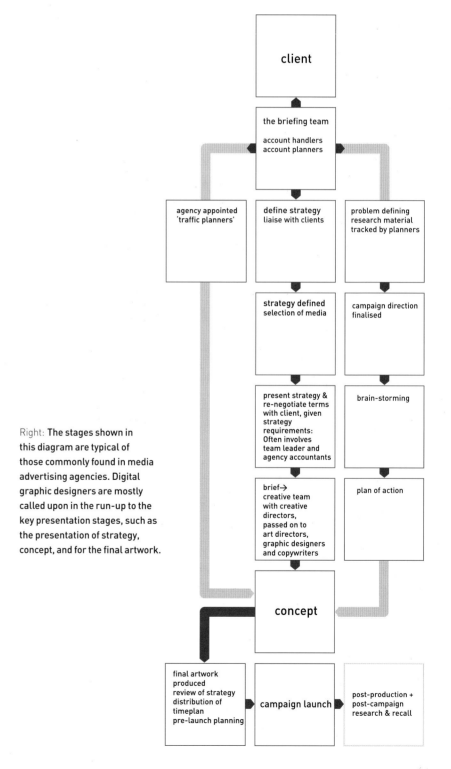

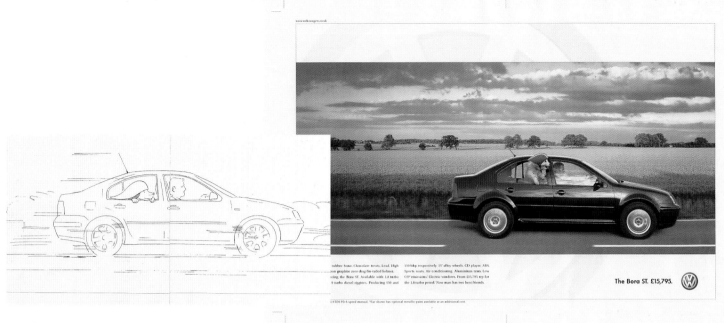

www.volkswagen.co.uk

rubber bone. Chocolate treats. Lead. High
on graphite zero drag fin-tailed helmet.
ncing the Bora ST. Available with 1.8 turbo
9 turbo diesel engines. Producing 150 and

130 bhp respectively. 15" alloy wheels. CD player. ABS.
Sports seats. Air conditioning. Aluminium trim. Low
CO² emissions. Electric windows. From £15,795 rrp for
the 1.8 turbo petrol. Now man has two best friends.

The Bora ST. £15,795.

Stage 3 concerns final concept development –
fine tuning for production. Art direction is
detailed, and specialist typographers,
photographers, film director, illustrators, and
specialist media experts are commissioned.
Any other promotional aspects are also tied
into the overall strategy. Commissioning of
media is then made, and a timetable is set,
with 'traffic planners' controlling the meeting
of deadlines. Printers are booked and media
space buyers negotiate the appropriate venues,
release dates, and length of campaign run with
account planners and media space sellers.

The agency team meets with all the
client representatives for final project
clearance. At this stage follow-on promotions
may be discussed.

Stage 4 is when all printing and production
takes place and the synchronized campaign
is launched.

Above: A detailed scamp, used as
a visual to convey the concept to
clients, and the resulting press ad,
prepared for a double-page spread
in a glossy magazine. The detail of
a crying car (left) was one of a
sequence of 'moodboards',
produced in marker and pencil, to
guide a film crew in the shooting
of a television commercial.
BMP, UK

BASIC REQUIREMENTS FOR GRAPHIC DESIGNERS WORKING IN ADVERTISING

A graphic designer working in contemporary corporate
identity, branding, and the various forms of advertising
promotion will need a 'book' or portfolio of ideas to
demonstrate his or her thinking. It should demonstrate skills as
a visualizer and the ability to generate highly finished detailed
graphic design, layout, and typographic work. It should also
prove ability to use the appropriate graphics software.

Advertising creatives will often have digital skills of
their own, so it is the graphic designer's creative expertise that
is mostly called upon. To work in promotions, you will need
the following basic equipment.

* **Hardware:** Apple Macintosh, colour printer, scanner,
  access to email (preferably broadband Internet for
  transferring large document files)
* **Software:** Adobe Illustrator or Macromedia FreeHand
  (original artwork creation), Adobe Photoshop
  (image manipulation)

You should also consider learning a 3D application, as 3D
effects are increasingly popular in still image work and can
often add depth and gloss to illustrations. Make sure your
portfolio shows your flexibility and competence both with the
software packages and in combining traditional and digital
techniques to produce clear, polished visual work.

02.02

CASE HISTORY   DAEWOO ADVERTISING CAMPAIGN 2001

The agency campaign team, led by their creative director, liaised with Daewoo's marketing director and team. The agency re-presented developed project work to the Daewoo team at interim presentations and final presentation stages.

The first stage of the process was to define the requirements of the brief and the type of finished outcome that was being sought. Agency planners and the creative director constructed a brief for the creative teams, based on consumer research and initial client meetings. The key quality picked out from the brief – Daewoo's service quality – was translated into ideas through roughs and initial scamps.

It was agreed that the agency would develop press, poster, billboard, and self-liquidating promotional material. Such work often has to coordinate with other direct promotions, such as point-of-sale showroom displays. At this first development stage the campaign direction was reappraised, next stages were agreed and a time scale put in place. Daewoo's marketing director signed off the plan of progression for the next phase.

The creative team for the job consisted of graphic designers, a creative director, two creatives (sharing art direction and copywriting roles), and a planner. Scamps of the poster were developed from rough sketches, incorporating many of the corporate layout elements and logo. These are often collaged in Freehand. Freelance graphic designers were briefed at the studio, and then developed the work, corresponding via email and phone. A 'book' of interim solutions were presented to the Daewoo team for approval.

Decisions were made within the agency on the most appropriate solutions to go forward to the final presentation of ideas. Three different versions for each promotion strategy were developed for the presentation, which were presented with detailed scamps. The creative director planned the presentation as a demonstration of how the work addressed the brief, met existing Daewoo objectives and broke new ground. Some ideas were rejected at this last stage before the development of final artwork.

The winning concepts were then refined though scamps and mock-ups, with regular creative team development meetings. Having defined the direction of the final execution, graphic specialists worked on the typography and graphic arrangements for the poster and corresponding promotional material. Production technicians were contracted to work out feasibility and costings with account planners, then the agency's 'space buyers' investigated relevant venues for the campaign duration. Final variants in design detail were presented to the rest of the creative team at an 'internal crit', where graphic treatments were selected for detail design. Final mock-ups were produced for client approval using digital packages.

At the final client presentation, campaign work was presented to Daewoo's project team by the agency's creative and planning directors. The work was approved and signed off for production, pending minor graphic amendments. 'Traffic' planners then co-ordinated final location shoots for the art direction, while typesetters were employed to coordinate the final copy arrangements. Space buyers signed up to poster and billboard sites while printers and manufacturers were contracted to produce the final printed artwork. Simultaneously, call centres were organized to deal with inquiries and coordinated promotion offers. Contractors were hired to install the posters.

All that remained to be done was to print and install the posters and launch the campign.

BRIEF

What is this brand called? What is this campaign/ ad called?
Daewoo Brand Relaunch - Matiz

What is this brand's DNA?

Who do we want to buy it?

Anyone's who's looking to buy a new car who is fed up with the pressures of urban driving.
Whether they're young or old, a businessman or a creative type, they will all share the same
frustrations: congestion, lack of parking spaces and dismal public transport all make urban
driving a nightmare.

The Daewoo Matiz is the perfect urban car, in fact its even won the 'Best City Car' Award to
prove it. It's nippy enough to move though traffic, and small enough to slip into the smallest
of parking spaces.

The Matiz has also won the 'Best Budget Car' and if you have to commute into work, might
well work out annually, as not much more than the cost of your travelcard

Why should people buy this brand?

The award winning Matiz, designed to ease the pain of urban driving

The Daewoo Matiz is small and nippy enough to be the ultimate in urban driving, and it
comes at an affordable price: that's why its won the Best City Car and the Best Budget Car
awards

Requirement		Appearance Date	Budget Guidelines

Signatures	Date	Internal	Present	Creative Team(s)
Plan/ Acc.				
Traffic				
Job Number:				

Left: The agency brief, developed from client meetings.

Below left: Initial sketches, first concepts produced as rough visuals, which are used for in-house discussions and development meetings only.

Below right: Final presentation scamp: text and image elements assembled in Photoshop.

Bottom: The completed poster. The final version was produced as a Photoshop document, and was transferred to Adobe illustrator format for print production.
Duckworth Finn Grubb Waters, UK

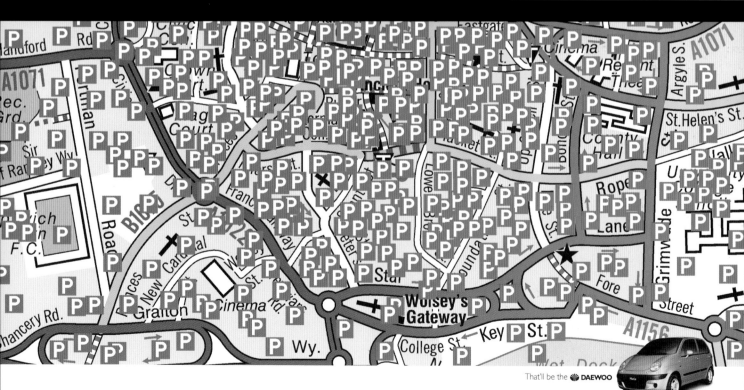

That'll be the 🟊 DAEWOO

Every day, we come into contact with packaging of differing shape, size, and purpose, informing us of the merits, dangers, goodness, or value of the products they contain. Some packs are designed to be discarded immediately after purchase, others are integral to the life of their contents. The graphic designer has to create compelling and attention-grabbing packaging items and take into account the legal requirements, trading rules, and environmental concerns that govern the industry. Packaging must function physically as well as being visually attractive and enticing.

The ability to visualize two-dimensional designs in the round is almost essential to the digital graphic designer, who has to imagine the packaging in its made-up form to determine how text or images will sit in relation to

components such as folds, gluepoints, or lid mechanisms. The scarcity and expense of suitable tools, however, means that simple cartons and folders often have to be designed in an ordinary drawing program, with visualization conducted by means of scissors and glue stick. In many cases, however, the physical design of the package will be of an existing standard form or may have been previously completed. Often manufacturing or cutter guides can be imported from specialist CAD software into a drawing package and used as templates for the graphical content without the designer needing specialist engineering skills.

Where constructing the package is part of the brief, the computer screen can be seductive, so designers must be careful not to be beguiled by the ease with which an initial idea can be worked up in two dimensions. What is seen on the monitor will ultimately have to be translated into a physical, fully functional, three-dimensional product.

It is essential to test a package design at every stage by producing an accurate mock-up and checking that the design itself and the surface graphics work together. Once constructed, a package can dramatically change in appearance. Type, for example, may become distorted, cut-out windows may not align well enough to display the

PART 02. SURFACE DESIGN

CHAPTER THREE

DESIGN FOR PACKAGING

Left: To a consumer, this bag represents style and luxury, but strip away the cosmetic elements of the design and you are left with a simple paper bag. The design is no more practical, despite the extra cost in materials, but is now an effective marketing tool for the brand.
Design by Kenzo, France

product, or the overall design may simply have less impact off-screen. Keep printing out and test assembling work frequently. This can save you much embarassment when it is time to show ideas to the client.

Different pack shapes are continually being developed which can be manufactured from an expanding range of materials. Polyethylene, high-grade plastics, acetates, and many other new materials, have been added to the already extensive range available. These different textures and surfaces provide both creative opportunities and technical challenges.

Branding is essential to packaging design, and goes deeper than a logo. Typography, shape, image, layout, choice of colour, and tactile qualities all contribute to developing product identity.

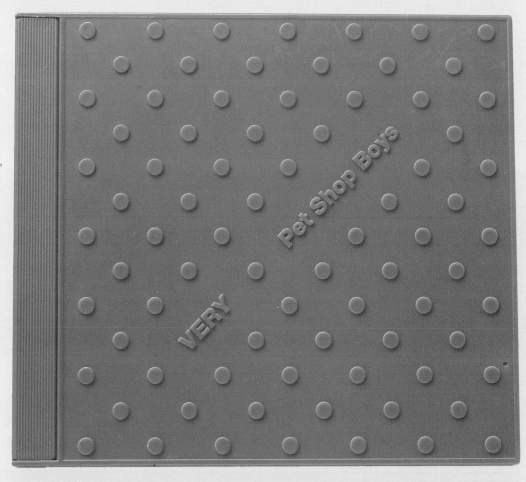

Above right: **This award-winning cover for the Pet Shop Boys'** *Very* **CD stood out in the competitive charts crowd by defying the traditional approach to packaging design. Taking advantage of alternative manufacturing techniques resulted in not only a practical packaging solution, but an effective publicity device. The designer conveyed a message to the consumer of an individual and creative band setting themselves apart from a crowded industry.** Design by Pentagram, UK

Right: **The plastic carrier bag was once an undesirable but very cheap device for carrying shopping home. With advances in printing technology, the colours, texture, and quality in production of this bag means it can now proudly be used to successfully represent a contemporary brand image.** Design by Paul Smith Ltd

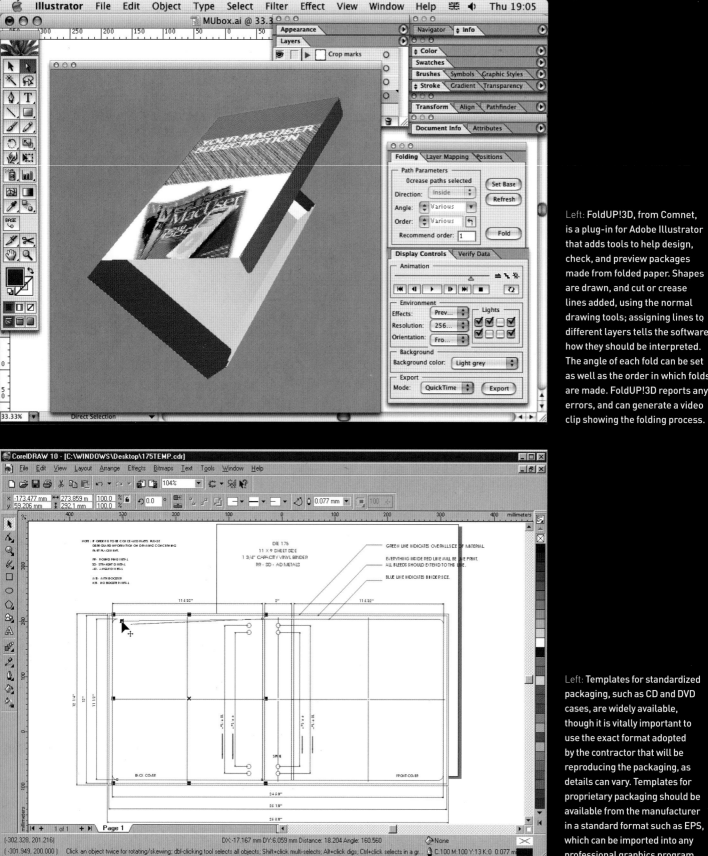

Left: **FoldUP!3D, from Comnet,** is a plug-in for Adobe Illustrator that adds tools to help design, check, and preview packages made from folded paper. Shapes are drawn, and cut or crease lines added, using the normal drawing tools; assigning lines to different layers tells the software how they should be interpreted. The angle of each fold can be set as well as the order in which folds are made. FoldUP!3D reports any errors, and can generate a video clip showing the folding process.

Left: **Templates for standardized** packaging, such as CD and DVD cases, are widely available, though it is vitally important to use the exact format adopted by the contractor that will be reproducing the packaging, as details can vary. Templates for proprietary packaging should be available from the manufacturer in a standard format such as EPS, which can be imported into any professional graphics program.

DESIGN TOOLS Graphic designers should have a good understanding of all the major graphic arts software, ideally including three-dimensional modelling applications, but when working with packaging the most important requirement is probably to be fluent in at least one drawing program.

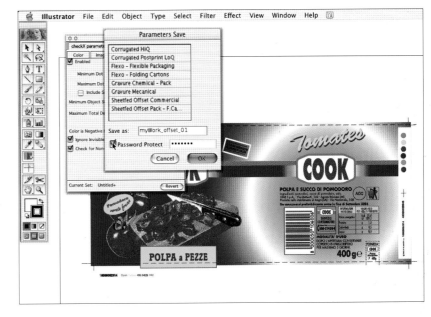

Computer-generated artwork can be extremely accurate, allowing the designer to work to precise tolerances. This has knock-on benefits for the manufacturing processes.

Designers often tend to favour one program over another for reasons of familiarity, but DTP programs – more suited to multi-page work – are less frequently used for packaging design. However, artwork for manufacturer's cutting guides and templates can be imported and locked into these programs and graphic elements used as necessary. Dedicated drawing programs such as Adobe Illustrator and Macromedia FreeHand are widely used, as they have many functions that assist the design development process. Almost infinite scalability and distortion controls, together with lockable layers and guides, give designers greater flexibility for experimentation and for previewing their creations at different stages.

Working with layers, which can be locked and/or hidden, allows numerous permutations and variations of a design to be made on screen without accidental deletion or movement of key elements.

Repetitive transformations, 'click and drag' duplication and knife tools are just some of the highly productive features of drawing programs. As with DTP programs, additional elements – including photographic images, text, and manufacturer's templates – can all be easily imported. Bitmap editing programs are used extensively to modify and prepare images for use on packaging, but the final artwork will always end up in a vector-based application.

An interesting feature of drawing programs is the facility that to assign different output attributes, such as halftone resolutions, to individual elements, thus allowing a high degree of control over differing graphic components when printed onto different surfaces.

While a very small number of dedicated packaging design applications seem to drift in and out of the market,

some useful plug-ins are available for drawing programs (see above and opposite). These range from fairly to very expensive, but may quickly pay for themselves in a busy studio devoted to a particular type of work.

Particular care must be taken when saving finished artwork that it is in a format compatible with the next stage in the production chain. PDF files may not be acceptable, as the contractor may need to manipulate the artwork before outputting it. When asked to supply files in a program's own proprietary format, check which version the contractor is using before starting work: graphics created using advanced tools cannot always be saved for use in earlier versions.

Above: **Esko DeskPack** is a specialist plug-in for Illustrator that addresses the technical and practical challenges of two-dimensional design for packaging, such as this tin-can label. Extra tools make it easier to draw and align objects at irregular angles, allow gradient fills to be edited in situ so that their interaction with type and other elements can be seen immediately, and to combine process and spot colours into multi-colour tints. Document specs can be checked against the requirements of the particular printing process to be used.

MATERIALS Products of most shapes, sizes, and weight generally need some form of packaging. This must be suited to the individual product to ensure adequate protection as well as ease of opening and good customer appeal.

One aspect of packaging design that cannot be dealt with by computer software is the choice of the right material. The substrate's behaviour when folded, bent, stamped, moulded, or blown is crucial to how the final product will look. This is simply something you have to learn from experience and by making or commissioning mock-ups.

Paper and cardboard are widely used in the packaging industry. They are relatively inexpensive and have a versatility that makes for simple and quick processing. Additionally, they are materials that designers can also use easily for constructing presentation mock-ups. Embossing, creasing, cutting, folding, slitting, gluing, and the printing of inks, varnishes, and other finishes are all straightforward processes suitable for use with paper and cardboard.

Recycled cardboard is used for many forms of packaging. This lowers unit costs and also carries the added bonus of being 'environmentally friendly', a quality that is exploited by manufacturers of 'wholesome' or 'green' products. Inexpensive card can be treated with a range of coatings to enhance its performance. Water - and oil-resistant laminates, for instance, can be applied for effective food packaging or other moisture-producing goods. Card is often coated purely to resist marking that can occur from frequent handling.

Other materials are regularly used in conjunction with card packaging to provide strength or to give extra visibility of the product. Acetate windows, for example, can be glued into position over an area that has been die-cut from the card sheet.

Intricate or fluid shapes cannot be easily constructed from card, so many of these designs are produced by using plastics and films. Injection moulding, in which melted plastic is forced into a mould, is widely used, though set-up costs can be high and only large production runs bring the unit cost down to acceptable levels. A popular type of plastic for packaging is PET (polyethylene terephtalate), which is easy to shape and good looking.

Plastics use numerous chemicals in their manufacture and do not degrade quickly, making them difficult to use for products that in themselves are considered environmentally friendly. Designers need to be aware that materials can 'speak' to the audience as clearly as graphic imagery does.

Glass, once a popular packaging material, has seen a decline in use. It is more temperamental than plastics such as PET, shatters easily, and cannot withstand extreme temperatures. However, its transparency, moulding capabilities and self-colouring, together with its suitability for frosting and engraving, give it a tactile and aesthetic appeal, appropriate for giving products an unusually luxurious feel.

Metal, as a packaging material, accommodates extremes in packaging price points. At the lower end of the market it is used in great volume for tinned foods, aerosols, and oil containers, as well as being used for luxury goods, such as gift-set tins printed with interesting graphics – making them collectable once the contents have been used. Metal is also suitable for recycling as it is easy to melt down and re-form. Recent advances in manufacturing techniques enable steel, for example, to be used in surprisingly creative ways, whether for mass-market packaging or limited edition promotional items.

This page: **Packing different food types demands various solutions depending on the nature of the contents. The breakfast cereal (below) needs to be sealed in airtight containers to avoid spoiling. Heat sealing, plastic zip sealers, and foil packing help the longevity of the product. Eggs (far right, below) have always been awkward to package. This effective solution is created from one sheet of card making it easier to manufacture as opposed to more common moulded designs used today.**

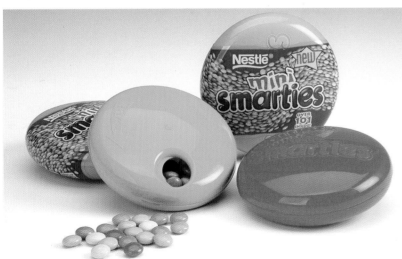

A simple cardboard tube used to be the only pack you could buy Smarties in. But market forces demand interesting and novel approaches to retailing, and so this toy-like pack (above) was created for Mini Smarties – a very similar product that was judged to need a very different approach to packaging design.

The glass bottle for Coca-Cola (top) has remained a favourite, indeed a classic design. Essentially unchanged since 1915, the shape is a registered trademark and proves that innovation in packaging is not always the best approach. The filter coffee pack (top right) makes use of foil wrapping and vacuum packing to retain freshness.

All materials have their own unique qualities and behavioural properties. A lot of packaging incorporates several materials that have to combine successfully. It is a good idea for designers to take the time to familiarize themselves with the manufacturing capabilities and performance of each of the materials they intend using.

Understanding the purpose and function of a package design is of prime importance to the graphic designer. The major consideration for large, bulky items such as, for example, computers, microwave ovens, and washing machines, is ensuring the packaging provides adequate protection and has prominent instructions for lifting and storage. In a retail environment large items are usually displayed unpacked, suggesting that compelling, marketing graphics play a subordinate role in these instances. Despite this, there are manufacturers who use every opportunity to advertise their products and recognize that even large cardboard boxes offer a chance to promote the qualities of the product within.

KEY KNOWLEDGE So diverse are the methods of packaging and materials used, that designers are constantly having to up-date their technical knowledge both in terms of production, digital software upgrades, and new applications designed both to facilitate and expand conceptual work and to create digital artwork.

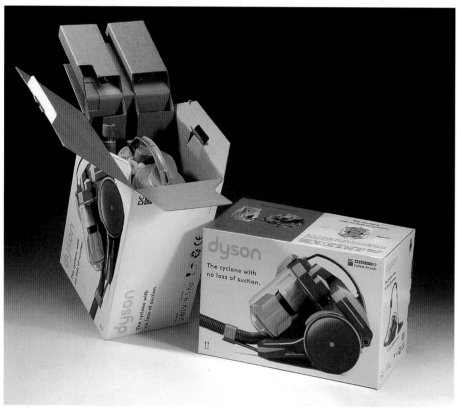

Above: **Packaging for large domestic appliances** usually makes use of basic corrugated cardboard with a single colour application of type and virtually no coated finishes. Here the experience of buying a innovatively designed product such as this is enhanced by the pack design. The four-colour image on coated stock and the intricate and environmentally friendly card inserts all point to attention to detail, encouraging confidence in the product.
Design by SCA Packaging, UK

Right: **'Squeezable' bottles** formed from flexible plastics are cheaper than metal or glass alternatives and are more convenient for the consumer. This innovative tube incorporates a small silicone valve that self-closes immediately after use. The graphics are printed on a soft, flexible, transparent sleeve that is then shrink-wrapped around the tube.
Design by Fuji Seal Europe

Cutter guides are used frequently in the manufacture of card packaging. Printing card packaging is usually done by offset lithography and the steps taken by the graphic designer to create graphic files for reproduction are similar to those for any general design for a print job (see Design for Print section). However, once the sheet is printed, it will then be cut, creased, and perforated in order to form a three-dimensional pack. The printed graphic work has to fit accurately within the physical shape to be cut in order to display as intended. For this reason, cutter guides are supplied to designers (usually as EPS files) from which to work. These guides accurately show where the cuts, folds, and creases will be made, thus providing an accurate template to show the designer where to place the surface graphics.

Cutting and creasing equipment runs at high speeds so can have plus and minus tolerances and specific 'bleed' allowances that have to be taken into account when graphic artwork files are prepared.

Different materials and packaging shapes may require a number of alternative methods of printing and/or have properties that might affect the overall design. For example, corrugated card has a coarse surface which, if uncoated, soaks up ink, and the fluting on the reverse side acts as a cushion, making printing flat areas or delicate halftone work difficult.

Flexographic printing (see page 76) is used to print onto rounded or curved surfaces, as on washing-up liquid bottles, although precise registration of colours is difficult to achieve. Fine text and hairlines also tend to suffer, breaking up and distorting as a matter of course. Transparent stickers are

Above: **Packaging of crisps never took any interesting forms until the Phileas Fogg Tortilla crisps pack was created. To create this eye-catching design required the commitment of the client and the technical know-how of the designer and manufacturer.**
Design by Lawson Mardon Packaging, UK

Above right: **Cartons of juice and milk used to be a challenge to open without spillage. The latest packages from companies such as Tetra Pak use combinations of materials and forms to deliver greater convenience for the consumer. Products supplied in these generic packages rely on graphic design to differentiate them from rivals on the shelf.**
Design by Pemberton & Whitefoord, UK

increasingly being used as a more accurate alternative with assured, high-quality, printed results – but at an increased cost.

Most metal packaging design is printed as flat sheets that are subsequently pressed or stamped into the required shape or component.

Unit cost is critical in the packaging industry. Print runs are usually very high compared to general publishing work. The number of colours, gluepoints, and separate processes in a pack design affect the production costs, so the designer's ingenuity and creative skills will often be exercised to the full when working with low-level budgets. Safety in packaging demands care and consideration and can impose significant restrictions on design. Packaging must protect toxic or sharp objects from being accessible to children, or piercing the pack, and all food products must have tamper-proof devices such as protective films, ring pulls, and pressure buttons on jar lids, incorporated into the pack design. Additionally, adequate warning or directional texts (also in braille) have to be prominently displayed on packaging that contains any form of hazardous product.

DESIGN CONSIDERATIONS The average pack on the store shelf has a tough job to do. It has to attract the customer by promoting its contents in competition with many other similar products around it and without making false promises. It must also be highly functional so that it can be safely and efficiently stacked, and be easy to use for the consumer.

In creating or re-designing a package, the graphic designer has to weigh up the advantages of following trends in typography, colour, imagery, and layout against the fact that these can date quickly. Although we constantly see new packs appearing on the supermarket shelves, it is surprising how long branded items keep their identity, and in many cases, packaging designs have to be created to be durable and outlive transitory fashions.

Designers need to develop a strong visual language and understand the effect of colour and be sensitive to the way in which the consumer is influenced by different styles of design. Illustration and photography can play an important role in packaging design, evoking aspirational lifestyles and ambience. Specialist image makers should be commissioned for this purpose.

Making one product more desirable, so that it is chosen in preference to another brand, is a challenging task. A considerable amount of packaging design is direct and focuses fully on the virtues of the product, although other designs are deliberately created to appeal, obliquely, to lifestyle values so that the virtues of the packaging content are relegated to second place. This is seen clearly in the worldwide use of popular 'designer' labels and logos, subliminally suggesting that, by purchasing these products, the consumer will automatically adopt an enhanced lifestyle. Some packaging shapes have adopted their own branding characteristics in their own right, as in the triangular pack for Toblerone chocolate and the Coca-Cola bottle shape, now registered as a trademark.

Above right: **Kodak** have successfully used colour to brand their products. This particular shade of yellow has become synonymous with Kodak film. It is not the name but the colour the consumer looks out for on the shelf.

BRANDING AND COLOUR

Recognition plays an important role in branding, particularly in supermarkets and other self-serve environments where shopping time can be limited. It is so much easier to reach out and pick up a familiar item or scan the shelves for products identified by colour association (see Designing with Colour). There are, however, occasions when powerful branding transcends traditional colour association. The turquoise colour used on the Heinz Baked Bean labels is so well embedded in the minds of most consumers, that the more usual association of blue/green in food with mould is not automatically made. Selecting colours appropriate to a product that also forms part of a design that will stand out from other competitive brands, many of which display similar colourways, is an interesting challenge for the graphic designer.

In packaging, typography acts as the voice of the product. Appropriate choice of typeface can help to evoke the right mood, suggest authority, and generate confidence. When working three-dimensionally, it is important to ensure that information is displayed on the correct surface and presented in a logical order. Contents, weight, size, colour, style, or model number must be clear and easy to read.

Below: This is where the designers work will compete with the rest. The object of the task becomes apparent when faced with this wall of colour, type, and image. Surface graphics are relied on totally in a display of this kind as all pack formats are the same. The most successful design will have communicated a great deal of information such as the merits of the contents and the brand value, in the notoriously short attention span of the passing customer.

Left: Visualizing a pack's design, before committing to paper or card mock-ups, is made easier with specialist software, available as standalone applications or, more often, as plug-ins for drawing, DTP, or CAD programs. The latter option has the advantage that familiar creative tools can be used alongside the packaging-specific features. A useful function is the ability to create a 3D 'walkthrough' of the finished package, including an animation of the steps involved in folding it, and to export this in a standard format such as QuickTime for client approval.

INFORMATION REQUIREMENTS

Pack designs need to communicate information about their contents as well as persuade the consumer to make a purchase. There are a considerable number of elements that have to be incorporated into a pack design – some seemingly excessive but usually necessary for safety reasons or legal requirements. Barcodes; ingredients; instructions for preparation, use or assembly; warnings; sell-by dates (usually overprinted separately, but sometimes incorporated into the artwork

for long-life products); technical data and promotional advice; all have to be accommodated, and ultimately to be typeset with unerring accuracy. Many of these elements are fixed in terms of size, position, and colour, and cannot be ignored or visually relegated simply because they might degrade the overall appearance of the pack design. Due to concerns raised by the aging population and legislation enforcing consideration of consumers with disabilities, the minimum size of type may be restricted.

The graphic designer should also consider that FMCG (fast-moving consumer goods) packaging is normally first seen as a collection: row upon row of the product. A stylish design with powerful impact viewed in isolation, either on screen or as a physical mock-up, may look less successful in a general display context and viewed from a variety of heights, distances, and angles. A 3D modelling program or dedicated packaging software will produce realistic renderings of packs from various viewpoints; Photoshop or 'virtual reality' software can then be used to visualize the pack in its in-store context, merging it into photos or interactive panoramas of store interiors.

PLANNING AND PRODUCTION Packaging briefs are usually more comprehensive than those for other areas of graphic design. In large retail organizations, the brief is usually drawn up by senior buyers after consultation with the manufacturer's marketing department. Marketing departments and manufacturers themselves may also commission designers directly. The product is often already in existence and the target consumer, retail outlets and a unit price for the packaging (as a proportion of the selling price) are already known.

Designers need to obtain as much of this information as possible and also consider potential modification and application of the design to future range extensions or different consumer markets. Clients are increasingly likely to use the same basic branding and packaging in different territories, particularly within Europe, meaning that the design must appeal equally to diverse groups of consumers and be capable of accommodating varying amounts and formats of text in the relevant languages.

Unit costs will determine the number of colours and construction methods that can be used, but inventively simplifying one aspect of a design allows elaboration of another.

If the product in question can be accommodated in a standard pack design, the creative process can begin straight away using the relevant templates from the manufacturer. Like brands themselves, packaging manufacturers are increasingly

Below: Cardboard engineering plays an important role in the design of protective cartons for fragile products such as this Wedgwood china. Die-cut corrugated board inserts fit both the box and lid to securely hold individually shaped items. Inserts can be stamped and creased from a single sheet, or cut and slotted together for extra strength.

consolidated and global in outlook, and can offer a wide range of versatile ready-made designs with proven functionality and standards compliance. If the pack has to be purpose made, the designer will usually need to confer with specialists in paper engineering, mould-making, die-stamping, or other manufacturing techniques. Glues, inks, materials, and assembly techniques are so varied that collaboration and research is essential. Many respected design companies now specialize in packaging, and employ both graphic and three-dimensional designers side by side to tackle bespoke projects. A broad range of skills will be an asset to any graphic designer competing in this marketplace.

Designs for two-dimensional or folded artwork can be created in a drawing program, with images imported from Photoshop. For more complex packaging, a CAD package – perhaps linking directly to manufacturing systems – will be more appropriate. Mock-ups can be generated on screen, or models can be exported to dedicated 3D rendering software for higher-quality visuals, putting off the need for a physical mock-up or prototype at least until the final stages of approval. Flat artwork can be sent as PDF files (see page 70) to the client, who can add comments on screen. As a final check, colour contact proofs should always be obtained and hand-cut samples made up to check for constructional errors.

Final digital files should be prepared with great attention to dimensional accuracy and colour specification before being sent to the production contractor.

CASE HISTORY   MISCHIEF – PULL-ALONG TOY

The brief was to design packaging for a range of 'own brand' wooden, pre-school toys, to compete against well-established brands. The client wished to avoid brash and garish designs associated with cheaper, plastic toy packaging. The packaging was to represent accurately a higher-quality product with a potentially long life-span.

The products were aimed at children aged between twelve months and three years. However, as the purchase would be made by an adult, the packaging had to appeal to their perception of quality and value for money. It was considered important to allow access through the packaging, to the toys inside, so that potential customers could feel the texture and quality of the wood used. This need for accessibility involved cutting a panel from the main pack, which could weaken the overall package structure, so minimum guidelines were drawn up to ensure optimum strength and durability.

A packaging engineer was commissioned to develop the structure of the packs for this range, taking into account the client's requests for accessibility. To ensure the mock-ups created were accurate, a drawing program (Macromedia Freehand) was used to produce scaled line drawings of each toy. This provided accurate information to help the engineer create precise dimensions for each of the proposed packs.

After evaluating the full range of toys to be marketed, the engineer designed a range of ten boxes to accommodate a total of twenty products. The number of boxes could have been further rationalized by constructing a range of more evenly sized boxes, however, this ran the risk of criticism of 'over packaging' as the customer could be left feeling cheated after finding a small toy in an oversized box.

The packaging engineer then tailored each pack to ensure that the toy was secured within it. Simple but effective strengthening techniques, including double-folded handles, were designed to ensure the product could be safely carried. Problems, such as ripping at stress points, could occur during handling if such details were overlooked. The intention was to have as few tie or glue-points as possible to help reduce

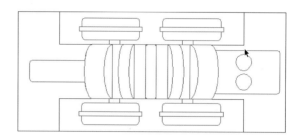

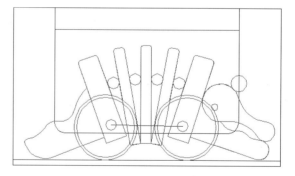

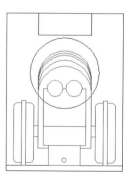

Above: **The packaging engineer supplied these scaled drawings of the product to establish how much space was required by each item. An outline of a possible box shape was placed around each item to determine the minimum number of boxes capable of packaging the entire range.**

Above right: **The mock-up helped to illustrate the validity of a box shape to the client's manufacturer. This starting point answers initial questions such as cost or shelf area required. Once approved, the progression to further mock-ups and the final design can continue.**

Pull along toy which click-clacks
when pulled along.

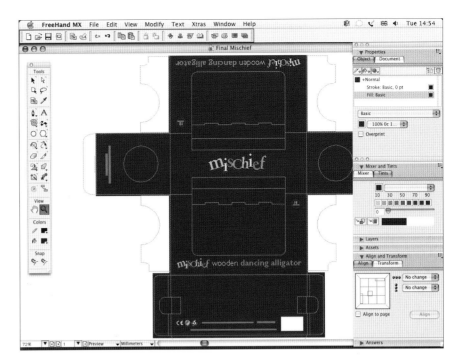

costs. This was achieved by creating supports and grooves within the cardboard to enable the pack to be created efficiently from one piece. Minor adjustments were easily made, redrawn, and quickly re-presented using the drawing program. Finished, physical mock-ups were then constructed.

The design of the packaging structure was subsequently passed to the graphic designer, who created surface graphics in the same drawing program, developing three options for a client presentation.

The selected design used a rich, earthy terracotta colour to represent both the toys' natural origins and quality. The colour had a traditional quality which contrasted well with the strong, lowercase Gill Sans typeface that was used. Cutter guides were supplied via email to the graphic designer and were transferred to layers in Freehand. Other layers were placed underneath for text, colour panels, and logos to manage the origination of digital artwork efficiently.

Once the final artwork was approved, the files were emailed to suppliers in Korea, Thailand, and Taiwan for manufacture. Printer's proofs were received and colour corrections to match those of the client-approved mock-ups were requested before the job was finally approved for production.

Below: **The final printed product with an insert structure holding the product in place during transit and on the shelf. Sales of this range have been very successful with a like-for-like increase of 54% within two months of being launched.**

Above: **The final artwork is ready to email to the various Far Eastern countries who will produce the designs. Finishing details such as age warnings, barcode spaces, and colour specifications were checked and signed off by the client. Die-cutting details such as the circular window were incorporated to not only add interest to the pack, but to enable the customer to see and feel the product more readily. This was a request made at the briefing stage.**

Even hanging a small sign outside the local shop will need some thought. Will it be seen from the end of the street? What will it look like at night? How can it be cleaned? Will it need planning permission? Larger sign projects are even more involved. An ordered mind is needed to pull the complex threads of a signage system together.

Anyone who has ever taken a wrong turn, got lost, and asked for directions from a passer-by will know how confusing verbal directions can be. As the Chinese proverb goes, 'one hundred tellings are not as good as one seeing.'

This is the reason we have signs; to help us travel independently. Signs distil information to the absolute minimum, they speak to you just at the right moment, they keep us moving. Seeing one good sign is better than a whole crowd of helpful locals.

Signs are often considered as merely two-dimensional directional aids – as arrows on posts or lists fixed to walls. A lot of this type of signing surrounds us: construction sites use basic, temporary signs, hospitals need rigorously functional signs, and department stores rely on floor-by-floor directories to list each sales area. These are all good, conventional signs, with each serving different, but important roles.

But there are many opportunities to branch out into three dimensions, where signs can become an integral part of a company's identity and embody the spirit of their brand. On a larger scale, signs can also be landmarks or even advertisements. If the purpose of a sign is to help you identify your destination, then sculptures or even an icon such as the Statue of Liberty can also act as a sign – after all, the statue unmistakably proclaims 'America' even without carrying the name. So signing can take many different forms. While conventional signs quietly go about their business directing you from point A, there are many other ways of announcing your arrival at point B.

PART 02. SURFACE DESIGN

CHAPTER FOUR

DESIGN FOR SIGNAGE

Left: These directional arrows are large-scale sculptures, each weighing two tons and reaching nearly six metres high. With signposts this size the designers can be confident that nobody is going to get lost.
Design by Pentagram, UK

Right: How large can you get? This sign just can't be missed - it not only signs Warner Bros flagship New York store but alos keeps you up-to-date with the latest company successes. Cleverly, the sign is presented by one of the company's most important assets, Bugs Bunny. A perfect mix of information and brand experience.
Design by The Partners, USA

GRAPHIC DESIGN AND SIGN DESIGN The graphic designer draws together creative expression and analytical problem solving. Sign design demands that the analytical problem solving must come first, in order to inform creative expression appropriately.

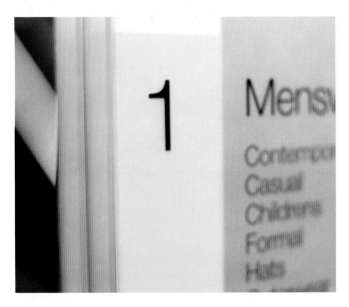

Left: **Tall, thin monoliths made of frosted polycarbonate sleeves allow ambient light through and make the dark type stand out in a crowded retail environment. Vinyl cut lettering is applied to the hollow inner surface. This can be peeled off and updated when the store layout is changed.**
Design by North Design, UK

Below: **This museum orientation map uses silkscreen printing and vinyl frosting on the reverse side of a large sheet of glass. When secured with heavy duty stainless steel fixings it seems to float away from the wall.**
Design by Atelier, UK

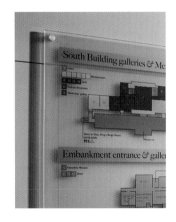

Designers have to consider that many who momentarily glance at their signs will be on their way to somewhere else, wrapped up in their own worlds, engrossed in the exhibition they've come to see, finding their way to the train, or simply on the way to the toilet. In this sense, sign design can be a straightforward occupation – merely guiding a fellow human being from one place to another, without fuss or bother. That is when signs really work in the real world. However, to be able to achieve this functionality together with style, panache and wit is the designer's creative challenge.

Sign design is a distinct area of graphic design in that signs take longer to plan, develop, make, and install than many other graphic design projects, with perhaps the exception of permanent exhibition projects (see Exhibition and Display). They are also around for a lot longer – making mistakes painfully lasting for the client (and the designer) involved. Signage is a design area that can be very rewarding for the graphic designer in that it can make a significant contribution to a visitor's experience of a building or space.

DIGITAL TOOLS FOR SIGN DESIGN
Although sign design demands a different approach f rom many other areas of design, the tools a signage designer needs can be found in virtually any properly equipped design studio. Signage design is requires strong type and graphics, so the key digital tools of this trade are either FreeHand or Illustrator – used for design, graphics production, and typesetting – and a good range of typefaces. QuarkXPress is sometimes used, but it isn't really useful as a true drawing tool. Photoshop can be invaluable for creating mock-ups of signs montaged into photographs, but is generally not that useful for actual artwork production. Similarly, three-dimensional modelling and CAD tools can be an asset for creating more effective presentations of work and might be used extensively by architects involved in the project, but aren't used for core design and production tasks.

Many signs are produced using cut-vinyl lettering and shapes. These are produced on vinyl-cutter machines, most of which can work happily with vector-based EPS graphic files exported from any professional drawing program. However, some less-common production tools, such as computer-controlled milling machinery for cutting and routing metal or wood items, may require other file formats. DXF is likely to be the format required in these cases. This format is more commonly used by CAD software, but FreeHand and Illustrator can export 2D DXF graphics when required.

Right: This sign system for the Bristol Legible City Project was built of component parts that could also be used for street furniture and bus shelters. Made from stainless steel supports and vitreous enamel panels, in the street scene these kindred elements provide a coherence and sense of identity for the city.
Design by MetaDesign, UK

Note that type may need to be converted to editable shapes first to preserve the desired look and feel, and plan with the machinery operators to make some test runs before committing to a production schedule.

Silkscreen printing is a common print process, and lends itself to the reproduction of strong line artwork with flat colours. It is ideal for signs that have to withstand temperature and weather extremes, and exposure to public abuse. For more temporary uses large-format digital printing is becoming increasingly popular. Digital printers can handle complex imagery with graduated tones and vignetting. These graphic techniques are very difficult to achieve using more traditional sign production processes. It is very cost-effective for short runs and one-off signs and posters, but the drawback is the fragility of the medium. Results are easily damaged, and in particular are prone to fading even when protected by lamination or encapsulation. More lightfast inks are being developed to address this problem, but be careful when considering this production method for anything but temporary signs.

Below left: British Airports Authority, London VIP lounge, internal signs. In keeping with the calm atmosphere of a VIP lounge, these signs were treated like pieces of art – made from embossed leather, simply framed and hung like works of art. They present a contemporary British feel to business travellers on a stop-over between flights.
Design by Pentagram, UK

SPECIALIST PROCESSES NEEDED FOR SIGNS

The environment in which signs are placed and the roles they play influence their physical construction and form. Only then does the designer have a surface upon which to work.

The signs shown on these and following pages have all been influenced by their environment. They differ in a range of ways: visually, in the use of materials, and in manufacturing processes. Specialist processes for sign-making are almost limitless. The lifespan of signs lends itself to a wide range of durable materials including metal, glass, plastic, wood, stone, slate, woven fabric, and even leather. Lettering and images can be etched, cut out, routed, carved, or moulded.

New technologies also encourage experimentation with less permanent but more exciting media. Electroluminescent strips (a low-voltage alternative to neon) and panels can add an eye-catching glow or even constantly changing patterns to graphics on a variety of substrates. Bright, efficient LED lights allow focused and controllable illumination in a broader range of contexts. Large-format inkjet devices can print cheaply and in excellent quality on to paper, plastic, and fabric. Almost all of these diverse processes can now be driven directly from the designer's digital artwork files.

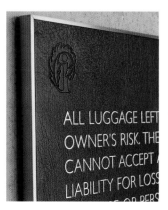

Left: These signs for a listed 1950s theatre are simple elliptical 'blades' with a period typeface screen printed onto powder-coated trays. They are finished with stained hardwood trim.
Design by CDT, UK

DESIGN CONSIDERATIONS The start of the sign creation process is to take an in-depth look at both the signage problem in hand and the client's brief. Once the designer is fully informed about the project, there are a few guiding principles that can help the design development.

AntyeeA

1   2   3   4   5   6   7

It is good design practice to make signs simple, understandable, and to the point, as well as inventive where appropriate. The site is all-important and signs should be designed to integrate into, and function in, this environment. What might look eye-catching on screen in the studio might be lost in the vastness of a building space or when erected outdoors and placed on the horizon. It is imperative to be consistent throughout a scheme, remembering that one sign always follows another. Signs need to engender trust in the user by being both clear and consistent.

Signs must work for as many groups of people as possible, not just the average, but the tall, the short, the less sprightly and able, as well as those confined to wheelchairs. A surprising number of people have trouble with their eyesight. In some contexts multiple-language signs might be required. Signs obviously have to cater for everyone.

There are few rules covering colours, type sizes, and pictograms. However, the experienced graphic designer will know that colour can be used effectively as a coding device and also that colour choice and combinations are affected by different lighting conditions and any dominant colours within the sign system environment. Pictograms need to be unambiguous; they may entertain, but primarily they must inform, and the type size must be legible at the correct reading distances. Special-access groups often provide guidelines for designers; these may be incorporated into signage contracts. Common sense should always prevail, and the designer who focuses on selecting a robust typeface, an appropriate colour palette, and using it in a creative but consistent way, will usually succeed.

CHOOSING A TYPEFACE

It is important to note that most of the typefaces available to designers today originate from letterforms developed for printing. Certain letterforms were drawn for use with particular printing processes, paper, or for a specific purpose such as for books or newspapers. Few letterforms have been specifically drawn for display and signing purposes, so designers should rigorously test their selected typeface at different sizes.

Any letter enlarged above 72pt will take on a new persona. Choosing a typeface for a sign system can therefore be rather difficult. When selecting a typeface for signage purposes you should take into account the following:

1. Cap height	Should be high in proportion to width of letter
2. X-height	Should be large (see Designing with Type, page 38)
3. Ascenders	Should ideally be same as cap height
4. Descender	Should be as short as possible
5. Counter shapes	Should be as open as possible
6. Type design	Should be as strong as possible, with a selection of weights for emphasis
7. Serifs (if used)	Should be strong – bracketed or slab

Sometimes the available range of typefaces, although vast, simply doesn't offer what a job needs. It is perfectly permissible to turn some type into editable drawn shapes in FreeHand or Illustrator, and then to tweak and modify shapes to get the letterforms you want. But remember that these won't be real editable typefaces, just letter shapes you can arrange by hand.

Letter spacing and individual letter pair kerning need particular attention in sign work. As signs carry relatively few words the structure of each word needs to be visually correct to ensure clarity and legibility (see Design Basics).

CHOOSING COLOURS

Being able to read large text on a contrasting background is normally sufficient, but locating the sign in the first place can be a challenge. When considering a colour scheme, the colour of the sign itself should contrast with its environment. If colours are pre-determined – such as those of a corporate identity – it may be difficult to achieve a good contrast. In such instances, adding a distinctive but simple border round the sign, or using rules to break up text or inserting a special design feature for the visitor to look for may be a solution (see Rules, Design Basics). Working with most graphic arts software will enable the designer to sample numerous colourways quickly and simply. A coordinated colour palette can be achieved using the HSB (Hue, Saturation, Brightness) features. Select colours to emphasize information or to colour-code areas.

Before picking a suitable set of colours, however, consult those involved with the final signage production. If, for instance, you're planning to use cut vinyl, your choices of colour will be limited to those available in the material. This is also a production process that doesn't lend itself to the use of many overlapping colours. Learn as much about your intended sign-production process as possible, preferably from those who will be responsible for creating the actual signs, before committing to a particular set of designs.

Right: A freestanding museum sign that can be removed when the space is needed for functions. The clear information is presented at eye level downwards, allowing for wheelchair users to read the information in comfort.
Design by Atelier, UK

POSITIONING

The designer's family of sign types (see The Design Process, page 120) will need to develop from the environment in which they are to be placed. So a typical sign family may comprise a free-standing structure, a wall-mounted or hanging sign, a statutory sign, and perhaps one or two individual variations for particularly tricky areas. Working with this family of sign types, a walk through the site (physically, electronically, or mentally) is needed to establish the earliest points at which a visitor needs to see each aspect of information.

Motorway signs are a good illustration of this principle. Users are usually travelling at great speeds so these signs are provided well before a turn-off – allowing time to get into the correct lane, slow down, and prepare for exiting. Placing signs ahead of the exit means that drivers remain calm, make no sudden movements and are able to get to where they want to go with relative ease. The same principles apply to all signs even at the comparatively gentle pace of walking through the foyer of an exhibition hall or strolling through a park. Repetition of information is not a problem – remember that visitors often enter environments from many different directions and the repetition of information will help nurture trust in the sign system.

Naturally signs need to be positioned where they can be seen. The ideal is to locate signs so that information is presented just above normal eye level for general ease of reading, which will also accommodate wheelchair users – with tactile signs appropriately located for the partially sighted (which may be additional to the general sign system). However, the concentration of visitors in that particular area should always be considered. If signs are to be located in crowded areas there may be no other option but to place the signs higher so they can be read by everyone at all times – even though this may be at a distance.

Right: Whether above a motorway or in a hallway the principles of signage positioning remain the same. In the 1970s French designer Jean Widmer worked with a team of specialists to examine the legibility and positioning of motorway signs. One of his recommendations was to position exit signs at 2 km and 1.5 km ahead of the slip road as well as on it.

Lighting is a factor to consider when positioning a sign. What looks good on a screen presentation, doesn't always work in situ with the harsh glare from sunlight hitting a reflective sign surface. This glare may become a dark shadow later in the day – with the sign disappearing altogether at night if not illuminated. Avoid reflective materials, keep to matt finishes and ensure that signs are properly illuminated.

IMPLEMENTATION

Digital artwork can be prepared using a standard drawing application. Sign manufacturers may use their own specialist software for certain processes, so the designer's digital files will need to provide accurate information regarding type, spacing and typeface. In some instances it may only be necessary to produce 'master' artwork for a typical sign from each member of the sign family to serve as a control model. From these control models prototypes can be made and in turn used as the final controls for the complete system. A visit to the factory to check manufacture and fine detail is worthwhile as errors can be difficult to rectify at a later stage.

Sign manufacturers will usually be contracted to install the signs and during this crucial stage it is worth making daily visits to the site. On completion there will be a walk-around tour with the client to pick up on outstanding issues. Identifying these issues is known as 'snagging'.

Once the project is complete it is important that the client receives 'as built' records for future maintenance. Meticulous filing, data back-up, and recording of the design drawings during the development of the project can be transformed into a handover manual comprising instructions on maintenance, repair, and updating. This should also include all the final sign schedules; their positions set against floorplan journey routes, technical drawings, and fixing instructions.

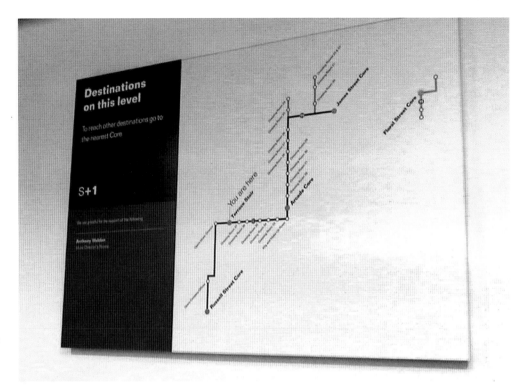

The Royal Opera House, London, backstage sign. This sign has an integrated tray into which slots a digitally printed route map of the back-of-house area. With constantly changing accommodation in this part of the building, it was essential that the signs could be updated by the client themselves. Digital maps held on system provide a cheap and simple self-maintenance solution.
Design by CDT, UK

MAINTENANCE

Good sign systems should last for many years since they are generally serious capital investments. Designers have to rely heavily on the professional expertise of sign manufacturers for advice on the practicalities of appropriate materials, paint finishes, fixing solutions, and other production processes.

It is important to convince the client that materials and build quality should never be cost driven – skimping on a second protective paint coating, initially to save on production costs, may result in rapid fading from the sun's ultraviolet rays after a few years. It is more expensive to replace a whole sign system earlier than normal, than it is to prepare more robust signs to begin with.

Vandal-proofing is an important factor in sign design. Signs should be strong enough to support physical abuse and their surfaces may have to withstand 'tagging' with spray paint, marker pens, and relentless flyposting. Signs are a magnet for vandals so surfaces must be easy to clean and signs should be designed to enable quick replacement of component parts.

Such components need to be simple enough to order and to fit – ideally by the client's own maintenance teams. This is where the 'as built' handover documentation becomes essential to the client. All final design solutions should detail each component part and provide ordering and fitting instructions. Self management is important to many clients, as their site activities may change in line with their business. Signs therefore may need to be frequently amended, taken down, or added to by the clients themselves.

PLANNING AND PRODUCTION On large signing projects it is essential to become involved as early as possible. This involvement helps the designer understand an architect's vision for a building or space and this should influence the final signage solutions. It also provides the opportunity to integrate signs into the fabric of a site; thereby reducing the number of signs needed to be applied to wall surfaces.

DESIGN TEAM

If the project is a large one, there will be a number of parties involved. First, the client, who should outline the extent of the project and provide any corporate guidelines that may be applicable. Second, the architect, who should provide the brief on the thinking behind their design, the purpose of each space, and the materials to be used. The architect will be closely shadowed by a construction manager and a quantity surveyor who will supply delivery schedules, budgets, and liaise with other contractors on the designer's behalf. Additionally, there will be a selection of interested parties including local planning authorities, fire and safety officers, access groups and possibly heritage organizations. And don't forget the users – they will need to be consulted, for instance through focus groups.

RESEARCH

The designer should start by studying the site plans thoroughly – not forgetting all the external approaches. Signs should be seen by the users before they arrive on site. The design team members should then be consulted individually and sounded out for their concerns for the project.

A site visit by the designer is important particularly for observing how people move through the space. If the environment is not yet built, designers should visualize themselves as visitors and walk their way through the plans. Journey routes and all possible destinations should be mapped. This process will indicate the points with the greatest number of intersections and decision-making points for visitors. These points are key sign positions. Lists of all the information a visitor may need to know at these points should be made. In preparing these lists it will be found that some are quite short, others long. The amount of information a sign has to carry and its position should dictate its physical form. For example, an extensive list of information might result in a large freestanding sign, whereas small amounts of information may necessitate a small, wall-fixed, or perhaps suspended sign. By examining the site, a family of signs will emerge. It is best to keep the family numbers to a minimum, as numerous sign variations will be not only more costly in manufacturing and future maintenance but also potentially confusing for the user.

THE DESIGN PROCESS

When the site has been fully researched, the designer should begin by designing a representative example of each member of the sign family. This can be achieved using most page-layout or drawing programs. These initial concepts should then be presented to the project team. It is best to make paper prints at full scale and stick them onto walls in situ if possible. Only then will the project team understand the full impact of the concepts.

After client approval, the graphic designer will prepare a design specification for each sign type. Talking directly with the sign manufacturer is vital at this point. It will help with any necessary design refinement for production and costing, and the manufacturers should be willing to prepare early prototypes.

Below: Typical floorplan with journey routes and sign points identified. Each sign point will be numbered and a sign schedule prepared (see opposite).

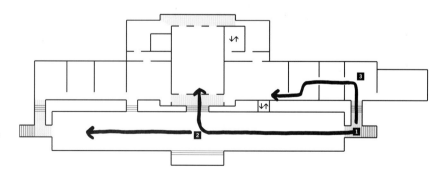

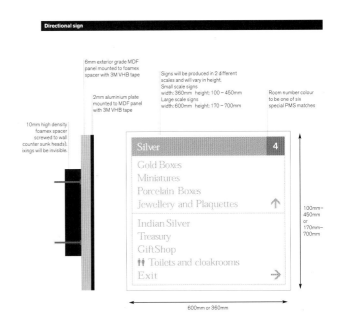

Below: An extract from a sign schedule showing sign identification number, sign type, what it has to carry, how it is to be fixed, and how many needed.

Right: An extract from a sign specification tender package showing the level of detail needed for a prototype.

Left: A finished sign from the same project.
Design by Atelier, UK

6mm exterior grade MDF panel mounted to foamex spacer with 3M VHB tape

2mm aluminium plate mounted to MDF panel with 3M VHB tape

10mm high density foamex spacer screwed to wall (with counter sunk heads). Fixings will be invisible.

Signs will be produced in 2 different scales and will vary in height.
Small scale signs
width: 360mm height: 100 – 450mm
Large scale signs
width: 600mm height: 170 – 700mm

Room number colour to be one of six special PMS matches

100mm– 450mm or 170mm– 700mm

600mm or 360mm

Mid basement

number	area	code	legend	Fixing/Construction	quantity
1	B	Direct	Silver + Gilt/Gold Boxes Micro Mosaics	screened or vinyls on glass wall/wall mounted	1
2	4	Room	Room 4	wall mounted	4
3	4	Info	lift access details/In event of fire do not use lift	wall mounted	1
4	4	Direct	Room 4 – Silver Gold Boxes/Miniatures/Porcelain Boxes/Jewellery + Plaquettes Indian Silver/Treasury/Shop/Toilets/Exit	wall mounted	1
5	C	Direct	Micro Mosaics/Jewellery + Plaquettes Indian Silver/Treasury/Toilets/Shop/Exit	screened or vinyls on glass wall/wall mounted	1
6	5	Room	Room 5	wall mounted	1
7	5	Info	Research room about Research room appointments	wall mounted/door mounted	1

It is important for the graphic designer to be fully involved in the preparation of prototypes, the tender documents and in reviewing the tender submissions. In cost-driven projects, designers often find themselves being the sole champion for quality. Accepting the lowest tender for a sign system can be a false economy as quality may suffer, resulting in a higher incidence of damage, repair, or replacement. A close working relationship between the designer and the sign manufacturer is essential if the preparation of artwork is to be trouble-free.

DEVELOPING A HIERARCHY OF INFORMATION

Who will be the main users of the signs and what information should they carry at what point? This information should be ordered according to its level of importance. For example, in a public building such as a performance venue the main user will be a member of the audience. First they will want to know where the box office is in order to pick up their tickets, then where the auditorium is, which side of the auditorium to enter to get to their seat, and how much time they have before they have to take their seat. They may want refreshments and to sit down while they wait or they may want to find the cloakroom.

Understanding the user's requirements helps the designer organize the placing of elements on a sign and determines the level of emphasis. By taking on the role of a member of the audience, the designer will probably arrive at the following hierarchy: box office, auditorium, seat numbers, clock, café, and cloakroom. Obviously the box office is a key source of information and will be in large type along with directions to the auditorium. The clock needs to be nearby and easily readable from the sign point. Seat numbers are another level of detail and can be smaller. Facilities such as the café and cloakrooms can be indicated using pictograms. Thus, an information hierarchy emerges directly from identifying the needs of the user.

THE ROYAL NATIONAL THEATRE

The extensive refurbishment of the Royal National Theatre, London, introduced more facilities and new entrances to the building. It had been a common complaint that visitors found it difficult to find their way around and so the new sign scheme was an important part of the refurbishment. CDT Design was commisioned to develop a new signage system.

STAGE 1

A number of problems were faced. The structure itself is a protected building, is multi-levelled and has many entrances on many floors. To make things even more confusing, where traditionally there is just one main auditorium at a theatre, the Royal National Theatre has three.

To win planning consent for a new sign system in a listed building there has to be an improvement upon the existing signs, in sympathy with the architectural features of the building. The whole site was carefully studied, noting the raw shuttered finish to the concrete, the chamfered corners, and the recessed holes in the walls left when the tie bars holding the shuttering together were removed after the concrete had hardened. These details affected the form and detailing of the final sign solution. This was composed of modular slats with chamfered edges, which when stacked together echoed the wall shuttering. The signs wrapped themselves around columns which also had chamfered corners. As an interesting finishing detail some signs had subtle recessed holes that matched the tie bar holes in the walls. The building was built on a 45- and 90-degree grid, with all the walls, supporting columns and even the floor tiles conforming to the grid. This determined the choice of Ehrhardt as a suitable typeface – with bracketed serifs set at 45- and 90-degree angles it echoed the spirit of the building.

Above: **The three theatres at the RNT are clearly identified and the colour associations are established well before a visitor enters the building. Here, the signs act as both a draw to the main box office from the outside and serve as a sun blind for the box office staff on the inside.**

STAGE 2

Making sense of the building required more analytical thinking. While each theatre had its own catering facilities there had previously been instances where visitors took pre-performance refreshments in the wrong bars and then found themselves trying to enter the wrong theatre for the wrong performance! After studying the floor plan, the whole theatre was divided into zones to ensure that every sign within each theatre area was prefixed with the theatre name, and then colour coded to each zone. This colour coding was adopted by the architects during the interior refit. Wall coverings and furniture were selected to match the zoning system.

The multi-level nature of the building meant every entrance had to have a complete directory of facilities available at each theatre and (particularly important for latecomers), directions for getting directly to each theatre quickly. With its imposing concrete, steel detailing and dark tiled floors the RNT is quite a monotone building, so the signs introduced 'spots' of colour acting as a trail to each theatre.

STAGE 3

With the introduction of new entrances and new facilities, the way in which visitors used the building was going to change. Schedules of information were compiled that listed every possible visitor requirement for key points around the whole of the building. The information listed dictated the type, size, position, and fixing for every individual sign. In the early stages many of the signs were designed then printed out full size and pasted on the walls in situ. Three-dimensional prototypes were also tested in the same way, this time in conjunction with the lighting designers who tested the readability during day and evening light conditions. Some fixing tests were also carried out to accommodate the irregularities of the wall surface. These early prototypes acted as control samples against which the complete sign package was checked for quality during production and installation.

Left: The main internal signs wrap around supporting walls so that they could be seen from an otherwise hidden angle.

Below: Visitors are greeted by large directory panels detailing all facilities available at each theatre. Each theatre was zoned with a different colour.

Above: To avoid any confusion, all facilities relating to a particular theatre were prefixed with its name.

Top: Large external banners were designed to be seen from the other side of the River Thames and from the flyover bridge nearby.

Early design work was produced in QuarkXPress and the final artwork was prepared using Adobe Illustrator so the manufacturers had outline paths for printing purposes. The signs themselves were manufactured from extruded aluminium, sprayed with several protective paint layers, and the type and pictograms were screen-printed on top. All fixing screws holding the signs together and onto the wall were concealed for security reasons.

This entire signing project took a little over two years to complete from early concepts to the final installation. All of the work – schedules, flow routes, tender package, engineering drawings, final typographic proofs and fixing details – was then compiled into one 'as built' handover document for RNT's maintenance department.

Graphic designers working on exhibitions face the challenge of creating a thematic design for viewing in large spaces at a human scale and in a variety of different dimensions. They must be able to think three-dimensionally, often having to visualize the exhibition space from architectural drawings and consider the general themes, atmosphere, tone, and messages that need to be communicated to the audience.

The overall visual identity, the display panels, and the accompanying publicity material – the two-dimensional aspects of an exhibition – are the main responsibility of the graphic designer. Digital technology makes for imaginative and flexible design and production, and also allows for easy sharing and exchanging of files by email or ISDN – a great advantage in exhibition design, which can involve designers from many different disciplines working together towards a common goal.

The three-dimensional aspect of exhibition design is produced by specialized exhibition designers, who may have had architectural or interior-design training but can equally come from a variety of backgrounds. Spatial awareness, developing themes with a narrative, interpreting subject matter effectively, working closely with the graphic designer, communicating to the target audience, and producing detailed working drawings (on AutoCAD) for contractors are all paramount to the exhibition designer.

Although it is not absolutely necessary for the graphic designer to be familiar with CAD drafting programs or packages such as form•Z, which are used to create walk-through vistas, both of these tools are often integral components of the exhibition design process. It is also useful for members of the design team to be able to exchange and understand each other's digital files. Graphic designers working on exhibitions normally produce flat artwork for panels using vector-based software, such as Adobe Illustrator, FreeHand, InDesign, or QuarkXPress, which allows for scaling up without loss of quality. Images scanned or created in Photoshop, perhaps at high resolutions, can be imported into all these programs along with text files.

PART 02. SURFACE DESIGN

CHAPTER FIVE

DESIGN FOR EXHIBITION

Above: **Pearling and fishing in the Arabian Gulf, from the National Museum of Dubai's Underwater Gallery. The underwater effect is achieved using reflections and floating glass panels. Clear and full-strength images are mounted onto glass, and projected water images complete the picture.**
Design by Event Communications, UK

Left: **The entrance to the Fondation Folon exhibition in Brussels, a permanent exhibition on the work of the artist Jean Michel Folon. Euroculture, the designers, have perfectly captured the poetic, dreamlike qualities of the artist's work in the design of the exhibition space, which starts off by allowing the visitor to enter through a giant book that slowly opens as the visitor moves past the admission desk.**
Design by Euroculture, Belgium

Left: Guggenheim Museum exhibition on the work of the architect Frank Gehry. Gehry's drawings, enlarged and printed onto the walls, show his fascination with capturing a sense of motion in his work. To produce this effect, the artwork was printed onto the maximum width of paper available, (virtually any length is possible, but widths are dependent upon the size of the roll of paper the printer takes), mounted onto MDF and heat-sealed or wrapped for installation. Alternatively, laser cut vinyl can be applied to painted walls, and again heat-sealed if it is in danger of being damaged.
Design by Guggenheim Museum, USA

Below: The Science Museum in London is committed to making itself attractive and exciting to younger visitors. Nowhere is this more evident than in the Wellcome Wing, a multi-gallery annexe completed at the turn of the Millennium and deliberately designed to extract the maximum 'wow factor' from new technology. Futuristic materials and giant illuminated displays of type and image make the building's interior as much of an exhibit as the interactive displays it houses.
Design by Casson Mann, UK

THE NATURE OF EXHIBITION DESIGN

Exhibitions vary widely in their nature and complexity, and so can assume a variety of shapes, sizes, and forms. However, conveying the message appropriately is key to every situation, whether the context is a simple panel system or a full-blown major exhibition.

EXHIBITION OPTIONS

The simplest cost-effective way to communicate a message to an exhibition audience is to use portable panel systems. These can take the form of multiple, flat-panel, and fascia configurations, pop-up, telescopic wire-framed structures or pull-up, single canvas panels. These modular exhibition systems allow simple, digital graphic panels to be economically produced on a wide range of materials including paper, PVC, gauze, cotton, and canvas. Graphics designed for these systems need to be durable and light. This type of exhibition or display is used wherever portability is an important consideration.

Shell schemes are a cost-effective solution to exhibiting at trade shows. Supplied by the organizers, they consist of standardized units that feature power and lighting, to which individual company fascia and wall panels can be attached. They form part of the overall trade show personality.

Above: Visuals of large graphic panels used for The Eaton Group's Five Year Business Plan – 4th Year, Management Briefing. The final digital prints were mounted onto 10mm Foamex and heat-wrapped for durability. JPEGs and EPS files of design work produced for the company's advertising campaigns, brochures, and signing is brought together in a series of three two-metre-high graphic panels.
Design by Perks Willis Design, UK

Alternatives to shell schemes consist of three-dimensional designs built by specialist contractors and are much more expensive.

Purpose-built exhibitions are usually complex, high-budget design concepts built for a specified time span ranging from a two- to four-week-long trade show to a temporary year-long exhibition or permanent museum gallery. These exhibitions are built to a design created by a specialist exhibition designer and, whether long or short term, are built to last for only a designated period. The graphic designer's role involves designing and overseeing the production of the exhibition identity and related design publicity material, often in the form of oversized, digitally printed banners and introductory vinyl cutout lettering. It is the responsibility of the designer to specify the correct materials for mounting, sealing, and finishing graphic panels. The durability of materials used is dictated by the size of the budget and is directly proportionate to the lifespan of the exhibition.

Permanent exhibitions may have a lifespan of ten years, sometimes more, and tend to be located in museums or galleries. The planning stage of such exhibitions can spread over several years. Large budgets and maintenance programmes are necessary to keep them in pristine condition, and to support areas within the exhibition that have to be reworked due to changes in science or popular thinking. The designer's role, however, normally ends when the completed design is 'handed over' to the client.

Educational exhibitions, which may be long or short term, are concerned with

Below: Screen grab showing the use of form•Z software, as used in the Arte Povera exhibition in Tate Modern, London. Once the process of feeding in dimensions, thicknesses, and other data has been completed, it is possible to produce vistas of gallery spaces from many different angles and get a very accurate impression of the intended design scheme.
Design by Philip Miles Graphic Design, UK

communicating complex concepts in an effective and inspirational way. Subject specialists liaise with educationalists and designers to ensure that teaching points can be clearly interpreted by the audience. Interactive devices, although expensive, can significantly enhance these key teaching points, encouraging audience participation and adding greatly to the educational experience.

In situations where a purpose-built exhibition needs to travel, a whole new set of criteria has to be taken into account in the design approach. Durability, packing, weight, and possible language issues need to be addressed, particularly if the exhibition is touring abroad, and a successful travelling exhibition will, wherever possible, make inventive use of panel stands as packing cases. The graphic designer normally designs accompanying touring manuals, giving clear instructions on installation and dismantling.

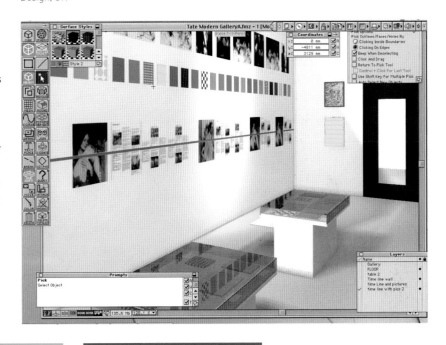

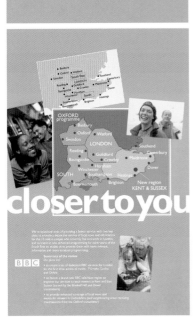

Left: Visuals showing a set of panels designed to fit into a travelling modular system for use in the BBC's public consultation on proposed changes to regional services in London and the South East. A simple, eye-catching design, this had to be instantly accessible using stock photography, striking colours, and simplified maps.
Design by Perks Willis Design, UK

chapter 05. design for exhibition 127

Below: Oversized display banner, Times Square, New York. Banners can now be printed onto an extensive variety of materials, in huge sizes, sometimes covering whole sides of buildings. In Times Square, waterproof banners such as these provide an alternative to neon, LCD and lenticular displays.

Left: Detail of multimedia wall in the Finney Gallery, National Museum of Football, Preston. The wall is formed through a complex layering of information, which has produced a 'reportage' style integration of film, sound, lighting, objects, photography, and text. Many different materials have been used to create this exhibit – wood fibreboard, glass, galvanized steel, and plywood, together with 3D lettering, floor lightboxes and object cases wrapped in supergraphics, all interspersed with monitors and speakers. These are all mounted on a steel support frame.
Design by Land Design Studios and The Chase, UK

Above left: Multi-layered map showing the social order of Europe after WWI, screenprinted in three colours and fired onto ceramic tiles.
Above right: Detail of metal lettering, Holocaust Exhibition, Imperial War Museum. The font used is Bell Centennial, produced in 5 mm thick fret-cut mild steel. It is constrained by welds of steel. The steel wall outlines the aims of the exhibition, and also functions as a projection screen for war film footage.
Design by DEGW, UK

EXHIBITION GRAPHICS PROCESSES Digital technology has radically changed the labour-intensive and limited production of exhibition graphics. This once depended on photo enlargements and photo techniques as the core origination media. Designers can now be much more ambitious. As technology develops, the creation of digital artwork and digital production becomes a more comprehensive and integrated procedure.

The extensive capabilities of giant ink-jet (or bubble-jet) printers allow for artwork files to be run out at virtually any size and on a variety of substrates. Transparencies are scanned to produce high-resolution digital files, and the designer combines these with text and other images. Retouching and manipulating images in Photoshop allows total freedom. Areas of interest or special significance can be highlighted or played down by modifying colour and contrast.

Laser-cut type output from digitized artwork allows for great flexibility – virtually any design can be converted into a path for the laser-cutting program. Matt and gloss vinyls are available in a wide choice of colours, and self-adhesive, frosted films can be used to give the illusion of sandblasting onto clear surfaces. Raised type can also be laser-cut using polystyrene or metallic finishes – almost anything is possible. Spacers mounted between wall and lettering can create the illusion of depth and shadow. Different surfaces can be built up to provide a three-dimensional finish.

Silkscreen printing (see page 76) panels and graphic surfaces is a far more labour-intensive, high-budget process than producing prints digitally. It does, however, produce a sharp image in beautifully flat, hard and durable inks that can be matched to the PANTONE system, unlike digital output, which can only simulate PANTONE colours with varying results. Silkscreening also makes it possible to print directly onto glossy, curved surfaces. The use of 'tough inks' eliminates the need for protective sealing, and allows matt and gloss finishes to be mixed.

Below: **Designs for metal gobos, From The Beginning, Natural History Museum, London. Lasers are used to cut intricate designs from metal discs. When installed into a projector system, coloured lights can be shone through, and the resulting image made to move through gallery spaces, giving another dimension to the exhibition design.**
Design by Exhibition Plus and Perks Willis Design, UK

MULTIMEDIA EXHIBITIONS

The use of multimedia adds an exciting dimension to exhibition design and provides almost limitless opportunities to feed the designer's imagination. Multimedia productions can be projected onto panels or played either on freestanding monitors or on screens set into part of the exhibition structure.

Lenticular panels, created from a high-tech photographic process, provide a low-tech form of animation, with images changing as the viewer walks past. Touch screens – now typically based on flat LCD screens – can be used at a range of sizes to show animated or interactive programs, increasing audience involvement with few moving parts to go wrong. Whatever the interactive designers and engineers may come up with, it will be the job of the graphic designer to integrate its look and feel into the exhibition as a whole.

Lighting is a vitally important part of exhibition design. Gobos – small metal or glass discs with either cut or printed designs – can be added to electronically controlled lamps or projectors to create visual patterns that move slowly, in preset sequences, or in dramatic swooping movements. Projected onto floors, ceilings, and walls or thrown along gallery spaces, these can reinforce themes or individual exhibits, attract attention to awkward corners and highlight entrances and exits. Coloured gels can be added to match colourways.

LED lights are more attractive, versatile, and energy-efficient than conventional tungsten or fluorescent lamps, and can be incorporated into almost any display. Fibre-optic systems use a single light source to drive multiple illumination points with sweeping, rippling, or twinkling colour effects.

DESIGN CONSIDERATIONS The graphic designer is responsible for providing visuals and digital artwork for all the graphic panels, labels, and interactive exhibit components throughout the exhibition. These are produced at a convenient scale that is compatible with the size of the panels.

Viewing ergonomics are particularly important, and it is essential to produce a full-size mock-up of a typical panel before spending time developing a design too far. This enables you to check the effectiveness of size and height of titles, text, and captions. Lighting conditions also need to be taken into account, as they can radically affect legibility. As a general guide, unless you are designing for very young children, the average eye-level should be set at 1.5 m with the majority of the text not falling much below hip-height.

The spacing and arrangement of panels should facilitate overall understanding of the subject matter. Visitor flow and avoidance of bottlenecks is usually the responsibility of the specialized three-dimensional designer, but the graphic designer also needs to be aware of these aspects in considering the arrangement of information.

The design of the exhibition identity, including a versatile logo and a related family of associated elements, is of prime importance since it has to carry the visitor through the entire exhibition. Where the brief is to design an exhibition for an organization that has its own distinct and well-structured corporate identity, the implementation of the scheme needs to be faithful and accurate in every rendition – a detailed manual may be available from the company for guidance on this.

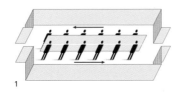

1

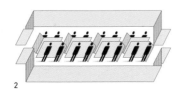

2

1. Partitioning the space creates an orderly flow of visitors around centrally placed exhibits.
2. Dividing the space into smaller manageable areas aids comprehension and allows the subject matter to be broken down into logical units.

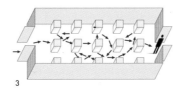

3

4

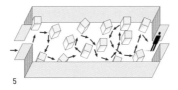

5

3. Regimented positioning of exhibits, allowing random circulation .
4. Regimented positioning of exhibits with regimented circulation.
5. Random positioning of exhibits allowing random circulation.
The solution you choose should be dictated by the subject matter.

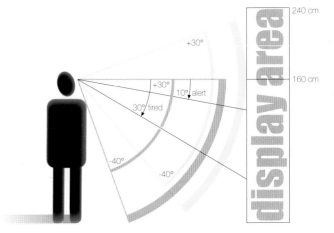

240 cm
160 cm
+30°
+30°
10° alert
30° tired
-40°
-40°
display area

Above: **Ergonomic data showing natural viewing heights and angles, and areas of optimum visibility. The upper segment of the display should be viewed from about 2 metres away to successfully scan the information.**

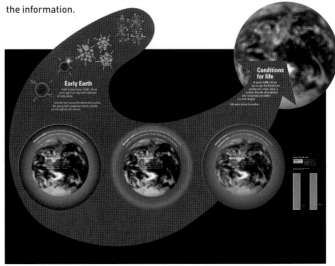

Above: **From The Beginning, The Natural History Museum, London** – an exhibition about the last 600 million years of Earth's history. This visual is from 'Early Earth', a huge exhibit with a large laminate arrow, and doors that visitors can open. The laminate arrow was silkscreened, and the outside of the doors made from digitally produced artwork illustrating the cooling earth. The doors had a heavy-duty coating for maximum durability to withstand extensive handling. Inside the doors were a few simple exhibits behind glass with backlit Duratrans.
Design by Exhibition Plus and Perks Willis Design, UK

PLANNING AND PRODUCTION Planning an exhibition can be a lengthy process. Agreeing budgets, research, finding locations, and checking cost effectiveness must be completed before the design team is appointed. In practice this means that the graphic designer has to be flexible enough to work with restricted budgets and accommodate (or tactfully challenge) preconceived ideas.

The graphic designer's initial role is to formulate the overall design concepts and produce preliminary designs for key panels and related elements for client approval. The style of typography, illustration, and photography, and the processes needed to realize them, must be clearly identified. Illustrators, photographers, and picture researchers have to be commissioned as well as any other experts including lighting designers or multimedia specialists.

Once a writer has supplied a cohesive script for the exhibition, the specialized three-dimensional designer produces detailed plans and elevations. The graphic designer, in turn, has to produce a comprehensive panel specification document to enable contractors to see and understand the full extent of the job. Estimates are then sought to ensure that the intended scheme is feasible within the allocated budget, and the project goes out to tender. When budgetary requirements are met and contractors appointed, design production can begin. The graphic designer then produces digital printouts of single flat-panel designs and views of key sections of the exhibition, using a combination of graphic arts software to simulate realistically the three-dimensional environment. As colours vary dramatically from screen to printer, and from the desktop to the press, constant monitoring is essential to ensure consistency. In order to minimize expensive mistakes, individual components of each exhibit are turned into artwork that needs to be approved and signed off by the client before it is sent away for production.

A graphics issue sheet should be designed to tie in with the specification document, to detail and track each component of the artwork. This sheet should accompany every piece of artwork, together with annotated colour visuals,

Above: **From The Beginning, The Natural History Museum, London.** This photograph shows a view down the gallery featuring a giant mural with a timed sequence of different fluorescent light effects. An etched stainless steel time line runs the length of the gallery, introducing the arrival of different creatures to the planet, and a second layer of smaller exhibits and models run above this in a series of showcases tracing the development of life on earth in more detailed form. Larger exhibits stand behind, and vinyl wall graphics complete the picture. Design by Exhibition Plus and Perks Willis Design, UK

TIFF and EPS files, fonts, etc. Unlike other areas of graphic design, the exhibition graphic designer may well be providing artwork to a number of different contractors (in different digital formats) for a range of different specialized components, including multimedia, animation, or video editing.

Before panel artwork is mounted and sealed to its substrate, a visit with the client to the photographic contractor for the final approval should be planned. Delivery to the site can take place when the finished design is mounted and sealed, but panels will need to be checked again for possible damage, on site, prior to installation.

The exhibition involved a large team of three-dimensional designers, graphic designers, illustrators, model-makers, video producers, interactive exhibit designers, lighting designers, building contractors, photographic contractors, picture researchers, and a composer, all working with the Natural History Museum's in-house writer and project manager.

Initially, the specialized 3D design company, Exhibition Plus, worked with the in-house team, developing ideas and extending the brief. Only then did Perks Willis Design (PWD) start work on the overall graphic scheme and identity. Because 'Rhythms of Life' was to be a travelling exhibition, Exhibition Plus designed flexible structures in bamboo and timber (to illustrate slow and fast growth) and kite-like graphics encapsulated with a matt finish that could be replaced cheaply when the exhibition was translated for touring. It could also be easily dismantled and packed into large oil-cans, which served as some of the bases for the graphic panels and exhibits.

The exhibition was aimed at families with young children. It had to be clear, bright, fun, and animated, and flexible enough to be reproduced in several European languages. PWD's first job was to try to capture the essence of what the Natural History Museum was trying to achieve – to communicate how humans and animals are affected by rhythms around them, primarily day and night, and the seasons – and then produce some key exhibits. Early influences were Keith Haring, *The Beano* comic and Hergé's *Tin Tin* – cartoon-like images with lots of natural movement. The colour scheme consisted of seasonal leaf colours, sunshine yellow, midnight blue, and rich red. Starting with a set of rhythmic symbols of falling leaves, suns, moons, and beating hearts, these naturally led on to the exhibition identity.

After producing an initial graphic panel, a full-sized mock-up was made to ascertain legibility, contrast (in varying lighting conditions), reading heights and distances. Illustrators were then commissioned to work on the kite-shaped graphic panels, with a brief to produce amusing and whimsical images for children aged six to twelve with added 'street cred'. The final panels were to have a mix of photography and illustration.

As an opening piece, large-scale cut-out themed figures of a 'clock boy', tree and dog were designed, to reinforce the concept of time. These were produced as digital prints, mounted onto MDF and then finished with a heavy-duty seal. Type panels were applied as overmounts. Interactive devices were designed, and specifications given to PWD to design graphics for the component parts.

After extensive tendering processes had taken place, PWD started to produce artwork for the exhibition. Transparencies and line illustrations were scanned to produce 'paths' that could be coloured up in Adobe Illustrator. Most of the exhibition was designed in Adobe Illustrator, with Photoshop used for re-touching and superimposition.

Above: Banner showing the exhibition identity and use of related corporate elements. The image needed to be vibrant, appealing to children, and above all seen as having 'street cred'. This banner shows the use of the composite elements of the logo that were used as a background image.

Left: Designs for glass gobos, used to send images shooting up and down the gallery. Glass gobos, although not as durable as the metal variety, allow for more flexible use of colours. These gobo images formed moving markers for various sections of the exhibition.

You have malaria.

You're in bed with a fever.

But why is your fever worse in the afternoon every other day?

Sleep – why bother?

We sleep every day because it's very useful.

Dreaming probably helps sort out the day's memories.

While the body's resting, muscle, bone and the brain are repaired and replenished with energy.

We make the most of our food if we save energy by sleeping.

Right: Artwork for kite-shaped graphic panels. The original artwork was produced traditionally using ink on lineboard. This was then scanned, and turned into Adobe Illustrator paths that had colour added to them. Illustration Debbie Cook and Colin Mier.

Above and right: The matt-laminated kite-shaped graphics and side banners were fixed to the bamboo poles using coloured ties. Interactive exhibits were attached to thick horizontal poles arranged around oil cans or trestle units. Coloured vinyl symbols were applied to the lower surfaces to further enhance the themes.

Artwork was then sent to the exhibition contractor, who produced high-resolution digital prints onto paper, encapsulated them with a matt finish, and finished them with eyelets so that they could be attached to the bamboo frames. The interactive devices also used digital prints and, where necessary, were finished with a heavy-duty seal. Artwork was also produced for converting into gobos. Elements from the logo, leaves, suns, moons, and hearts were all used to highlight different areas of the exhibition. Baggage labels, and clipboards with additional information and facts, were applied to the bamboo and other surfaces to provide low-cost interactive devices.

Below right: Detail of small half life-size lenticular panel, which flips between open and closed eyes using a stock photographic image with illustrated overlay. (This small panel was mounted onto a metronome arm). Lenticular panels provide simple low-tech animation, and can either flip from left to right, or top to bottom, depending on the effect required. More complicated lenticular panelscan have several images incorporated within them.

DESIGN
FOR SCREEN

03.01

The impact of the Internet revolution upon our lives is undisputed. The growth of websites continues at an unprecedented rate, and the challenge for the graphic designer to apply traditional design practices in this digital environment is an exciting and sometimes daunting one.

In the early days of the Internet, Web page construction was a relatively simple process. The constraints of the medium meant that technical and design considerations amounted to little more than positioning small images in relation to text. Today, the role of the Web designer has expanded considerably. New technology and improved functionality on the Web has meant that designers can now employ movies , sound and animation to enhance the user's experience. With technologies such as Macromedia Flash, now supported by most personal computers, dynamic, highly interactive Web content has become commonplace. One result of this progress is that the gap between the early programmers of the Internet revolution and the pure graphic designer has narrowed to the point where the two disciplines are now inextricably linked. The designer has far more scope for creativity, but in return must learn new technical skills.

It is in this rapidly changing arena that designers can make their mark, using the powerful tools at their disposal to create successful designs and solutions that communicate to a universal audience. They must take stock of emerging technologies and strike a balance between applying proven design principles and exploring technology-driven possibilities. At the same time, success is increasingly dependent on adherence to a range of technical standards.

The range of websites on which designers might be called to work is as varied as the Web itself, from educational, cultural and non-profit organisations to ambitious commercial and financial ventures. Re-branding of existing corporate identities forms a major proportion of Web design work, and many companies who entered the online marketplace early have discovered the need to rethink their Web presence every couple of years. As new tools make activities such as e-commerce easier to realize, there is an ever-growing need for effective visual interfaces. In all, the graphic designer is sure to find challenging and varied prospects within the world of Internet design.

PART 03. DESIGN FOR SCREEN

CHAPTER ONE

DESIGN FOR THE INTERNET

Above: **www.2advanced.com**
Aimed at the Internet cognoscenti, the website of California-based designers 2advanced Studios is shamelessly bandwidth-hungry, using Flash to pack typeset text, incredibly detailed user interface graphics, sounds and movie clips into a generously sized window.
Design by 2advanced Studios, USA

DIGITAL TOOLS FOR INTERNET DESIGN

Internet design is done with a mixture of general-purpose design tools and software specific to Web work. Web page editors include Macromedia Dreamweaver, Adobe GoLive, Microsoft FrontPage, NetObjects Fusion and SoftPress Freeway. Of these, Dreamweaver and GoLive are the most popular choices among professionals. GoLive integrates especially well with Photoshop, while Dreamweaver is regarded as the most mature solution, capable of generating highly compatible and standards-compliant pages. Freeway – available only for Macintosh computers – lacks technical credibility, but offers layout tools familiar to graphic designers.

Graphic content is produced using Photoshop, which includes ImageReady, a program dedicated to optimizing images for web use. Macromedia Fireworks is a similar tool. Flash content is best created using Macromedia Flash, although simple animations can be generated from within FreeHand or Adobe Illustrator. (Flash is the only commonly used format that delivers scalable vector graphics on the Web, although drawing programs can be used to create graphics which are then rasterized at the required size.) QuickTime movie content is made with anything from Apple iMovie through to Final Cut or Adobe Premiere.

Left: www.empireonline.co.uk
Much ingenuity and technical skill goes into the design of website navigation systems. Inevitably, though, users will sometimes be unsure where to look, and a simple site map – no more than a plain-text list of pages grouped under headings – is usually included as a navigation aid of last resort. In this example the colour coding used to identify topics throughout the site is echoed in the site map.
Design by Emap East, UK

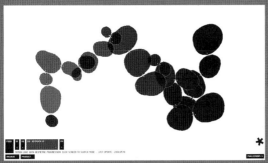

Above: www.yugop.com
Yugo Nakamura applies a rich design aesthetic to all aspects of his site. The level of Flash programming required to create such complex interactive tableaux is very advanced – a successful blend of technical know-how and visual craft.
Design by Yugo Nakamura, Japan

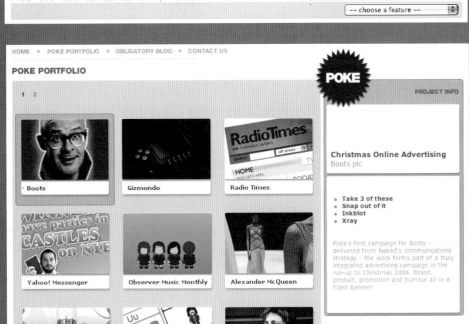

Left: www.pokelondon.com
Today's leading Web design agencies continue to market their creativity and innovation, but stress their technical credentials and commercial savvy more than was the case in the years before the dotcom crash. Poke's portfolio is straightforwardly presented and demonstrates a client-focused problem-solving approach rather than a narrow 'house style'.
Design by Poke, UK

THE INTERNET Computers all over the world are connected by many different means, from copper telephone lines to high-capacity fibre optic cables. What binds them together into the Internet is the use of common 'protocols' to transmit and receive information. The idea of a network that could share information over great distances was conceived in the USA in the 1960s for military communications. It rose to public attention with the invention in the early 1990s of the World Wide Web, which allowed delivery of pages of text and images using a relatively simple programming code.

THE GRAPHIC DESIGNER'S ROLE ON THE WEB

In so far as it can be separated from the general process of constructing a site, the graphic designer's role is to produce an appropriate visual structure for Web pages. The fundamentals of design – layout, colour, type and imagery – remain the same as in other media, but the nature of on-screen delivery and the technicalities of the Web add many unique concerns.

To some extent, a graphic designer can play a useful part in the conception of a site without the need to learn new tools. The basic appearance of a page can be worked out in Photoshop or other graphics software, for example, before being reconstructed as a functioning entity by Web designers. In practice, however, it will normally prove essential to take into account the precise possibilities and limitations of the medium before attempting to visualize the design. These possibilities and limitations will depend on the technologies chosen to drive the site, which in turn will be selected according to its purpose, nature, and target audience.

Nonetheless, a grasp of the core graphic design software is as good a starting point as in any area of digital design. You will need to build on this with some knowledge of one or more key Web design packages. How far you take this depends on whether you plan to deliver mock-ups and guidelines to teams of code writers, create the complete site yourself, or strike some balance between the two. Graphic designers employed within Web design companies are best placed to develop the necessary skills, as they will quickly discover which aspects need to be learned in depth and which can be left to other roles.

Interactivity and user interface design are the other key skills you will need to develop. The Web's 'non-linear' navigation, where users can jump around a site by clicking links, makes clear navigation an essential feature of every site.

HOW THE INTERNET WORKS

Everything that forms part of a Web page is contained in packets of digital data that must be transferred from the site's server to the user's computer. The server, usually operated by

Above: **www.tate.org.uk**
All websites, no matter what their content or appearance, are underpinned by HTML code, which may also incorporate JavaScript (see page 158). This 'source code' can be viewed in any Web browser, allowing HTML-savvy users to see how the site works. Items in non-HTML formats such as Flash are not revealed in the source window.
Design by Nykris Digital Design, UK

a service company rather than by the owner of the site, will be a powerful array of computers with a high-bandwidth connection to the Internet, so any limitation in speed is imposed by the user's system. An Internet service provider (ISP) operates the link between the individual computer and the World Wide Web, enabling two-way transmission at speeds dictated by the user's connection, which may range from an ageing modem on an analogue telephone line to a cable or DSL 'broadband' service working up to around 50 times faster.

Web pages are created using HTML (hypertext markup language), which is received by the user's computer and deciphered by 'browser' software that renders the page on screen according to standards devised by the World Wide Web Consortium (www.w3.org). Images, Flash animations and other content are received and rendered as part of the process.

Left: Connecting to a cable or DSL 'broadband Internet' service is as simple as plugging the digital modem into the computer's Ethernet port; your computer is usually allocated an Internet address automatically. 'Dial-up' connections, made via analogue phone lines, are slow but remain an option for occasional users and those in remote areas.

Below: www.google.com Search engines are an essential tool for Internet users, helping to sift through literally billions of pages to find the required material. Sophisticated algorithms are used to find and rank search results, and modifying a site's code so as to encourage higher rankings is a specialist skill in Web design.

Right: www.apple.com/ukstore Apple's website is constructed to work correctly in as many browsers as possible using standard HTML code. Font tags tell the browser to display the text in Geneva, a font installed on all Macs, but specifies Arial and Helvetica – standard on PCs – as alternatives. While the format of the product listings (centre) is necessarily fixed, ensuring that images and captions fit neatly, the navigation text down either side can be resized using browser options, allowing partially sighted users to magnify it.

BROWSERS – THE WINDOW ON THE WEB
Internet browsers are exactly what they say they are – a means to 'browse' (or 'surf') the World Wide Web, not unlike browsing the pages of a magazine or book. The browser is not responsible for making the connection to the Internet – this is done by the connnection utility built into the computer's operating system (Mac OS or Windows).

A browser, then, is just a tool for reading and displaying files found on other computers that are connected to the Internet. Entering a Web address (usually beginning 'http://www', for 'hypertext transfer protocol, World Wide Web') tells your computer where to look for a page; the letters and numbers in the address are translated into the actual location of the page data using look-up tables maintained by ISPs. The browser sends a request to the machine identified by this process, and – if that machine responds as expected – obtains Web page data by way of reply. It then displays the page according to the formatting instructions received. When the browser finds references to graphics or other 'rich media' content, it returns to the remote computer and requests those items. The results of all this are rendered on screen to the best of the browser's ability. Error messages, blank pages and 'broken link' symbols represent problems finding or interpreting the Web page data.

THE HIDDEN CODE
In most pages, the text carries the majority of the information. HTML-formatted text is certainly not the most flexible or exciting form of typesetting; the choices of style, fonts and spacing are limited, although CSS (cascading style sheets), a relatively recent but now standard enhancement, provides some typographic control. Text can be set using Flash, or delivered as an image of the pre-typeset words; these may be effective

solutions for headlines and navigation elements, but are unsatisfactory for the main text of a site, since search engines cannot read the text and users with disabilities may be unable to see it comfortably or process it using assistive tools.

Browsers can render text and images without help, but require additional software to cope with other media such as QuickTime video or Flash animations. This extra help is provided via browser 'plug-ins' – add-on software that extends the browser's capabilities. Plug-ins are either provided as part of the standard browser package, installed along with purchased applications, or can be found on magazine cover discs or downloaded from software manufacturers' websites. Most are free, because manufacturers want their technologies to become as widely used as possible. Popular plug-ins include Macromedia Flash and Shockwave (for interactive animated content), RealPlayer (for video and audio clips), and Apple QuickTime (for a variety of video and audio content).

MODERN BROWSERS
Today's browsers are vastly more capable than the simple tools that started off the Web. The market is heavily dominated by Microsoft's Internet Explorer, which successfully saw off its chief rival, Netscape. On the Mac, however, Apple's own browser, Safari, has proved so effective that Microsoft has

Above: **Microsoft Internet Explorer comes installed on almost all PCs, and Safari on all Apple Macs. Inevitably, these browsers dominate their platforms – a situation that may not always be in users' best interests , particularly in the case of Microsoft, which on occasion prefers to define its own standards rather than adopting those ratified by the rest of the industry. A small but significant minority of users choose alternative browsers such as Opera and Firefox.**

| Macintosh OS X | | | | | | | | | | | | | |
browsers	java	frames	tables	plug-ins	font size	font color	java script	style sheets	gif89	dhtml	I-Frames	Table color	XML
Explorer 5.5	X	X	X	X	X	X	X	X	X	X	X	X	X
Mozilla 1.3.1	X	X	X	X	X	X	X	X	X	X	X	X	X
Mozilla 1.0	X	X	X	X	X	X	X	X	X	X	X	X	X
Firebird	X	X	X	s	X	X	X	X	X	X	s	X	X
Camino	X	X	X	s	X	X	X	X	X	X	X	X	X
Safari	X	X	X	X	X	X	X	s	X	X	s	X	X
Netscape 7.0	X	X	X	X	X	X	X	X	X	X	X	X	X
Netscape 6.2	X	X	X	X	X	X	X	X	X	X	X	X	X
Netscape 6.1	X	X	X	X	X	X	X	X	X	X	X	X	X
Opera 6	X	X	X	X	X	X	X	X	X	X	X	X	X
Opera 5	X	X	X	X	X	X	X	X	X	X	X	X	X
OmniWeb 4.2.1	X	X	X	X	X	X	X	s	X	s	s	X	X
iCab	X	X	X	X	X	X	X	X	X	X	s	X	X
Lynx		X	X										

Left: **www.webmonkey.com Web Monkey, maintained by industry enthusiasts, provides a vital resource for Web developers and designers. The site offers useful statistics and advice on common Web design problems, including which browsers support which features. For example, this table compares the browsers commonly used under Mac OS X. Similar tables cover Windows, Unix and other computer platforms.**

Apple – Safari

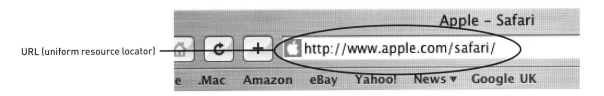

URL (uniform resource locator) http://www.apple.com/safari/

Right: All browsers employ an identical method of locating websites by prompting the user to input a Web address or 'URL' (uniform resource locator) in a box at the top of the window. Hitting the Return key prompts the browser to locate the address on the Internet. Some other functions – including Forward, Backward, Stop and Reload buttons, and 'bookmarks' (or 'favourites') to store URLs you want to remember – are also common to all browsers. Each then has its own special features, such as Safari's tabs, which allow multiple Web pages to be kept open without cluttering the screen.

Below right: Microsoft Internet Explorer is bundled free with virtually every new PC sold. Apple provides its own browser, Safari, with Macs. Neither is available for the other computer format. Alternative browsers are available for both platforms.

discontinued Explorer for Mac. Other browsers currently vying for market share include Opera and Firefox. Each browser has its own strengths and weaknesses, and users will have their own personal preferences, but a fundamental principle is that every correctly coded Web page should display correctly – although not necessarily identically – in all browsers. Naturally, this excludes any content elements that use technologies that post-date the browser version being used, or require plug-ins that the user has not installed.

In practice, browser makers have sometimes stepped outside the agreed standards set by the W3C, whether deliberately or accidentally, so it has been a headache for Web designers to check the way pages behave in different browsers and make any necessary adjustments. The emphasis is now very much on adherence to standards, and if the designer is confident that a site's code is compliant, browsers can reasonably be expected to handle it correctly. Any tweaks introduced to overcome specific problems with particular browsers should be kept to a minimum.

This page: There are many
contrasting views about what the
Web should be used for and how
content should be conveyed. Jakob
Nielsen (www.useit.com) is a
staunch believer in keeping the Web
firmly rooted in functionality, while
those at www.typographic.com
want the Web to be as visually rich
and engaging as possible.
What matters most for any site
is that it adheres to certain
elementary design principles and is
suited to the content and the needs
of the audience. In this respect, both
these sites are well designed.

THE CHALLENGE FOR THE PRINT DESIGNER There are some fundamental differences between design for print and design for the Web. All Web publishing is intended to be viewed on screen. This means the 'end-user' will determine the precise output of the design by the particular set-up or preferences they may choose for their computer. The challenge for the Web designer is to adapt and learn to make the best of this environment.

Unlike print design, the Web designer has to come to terms with their work being seen in different viewing tools and on different screens, and even with different sizes of text. The most common factors that affect the way a page is seen are monitor resolution and browser window size, Web browser preference settings, and display differences between Macs and PCs. (Remember that although most designers work on Macs, the vast majority of Web surfers use a PC.)

In Web design, unless steps are taken to lock things down, everything in a layout can move. This is very different from the immutable layout of a printed publication, and can be disconcerting. Some designers do their best to take control by locking down elements to preserve the design's intended appearance. Others try to produce pages that take this issue into account, retaining a measure of the intended appearance ('degrading gracefully') as items shift in the browser's window. This form of design, sometimes called fluid or liquid design, can ensure layouts fit browser windows regardless of window size, but it does impose aesthetic constraints on the designer.

The most common orientation of print design, whether a book, a magazine or an annual report, is portrait. However, computer monitors are landscape-oriented devices, so many existing print designs don't directly translate into good Web page designs. Pages that are too tall to be seen in one go can be scrolled, but this is a poor answer to the design problem. Good design, careful planning and a structured page-navigation system are all an asset. Fluid page design techniques can also be a strong asset, where it suits the desired design structure.

To work effectively, a Web designer should understand the needs and limitations of their work's intended audience, not just the possibilities.

DESIGN DECISIONS

Some Web designers prefer to work to the lowest common denominator in order to maximise compatibility for users, no matter which browser version or platform they have. This precludes use of the latest technologies, however, and is something of a red herring, because outdated technologies often fail to render accurately in any case.

Instead, it makes more sense to take advantage of enhanced Web standards such as XHTML and CSS, and then take measures so that the site either degrades gracefully in old browsers, or offers only the content, often consisting mainly of text. Only a small percentage of users do run obsolete browsers, and that figure is continually dropping.

ACCESSIBILITY ISSUES

Users with disabilities can face particular problems in accessing websites. Those with poor sight, for example, may use 'screen reader' software which reads out the text of Web pages. This will only work with HTML text, not type set as an image or in Flash or other proprietary formats, and of course will ignore pictures and video clips. A simple way to help is to ensure images and other non-text content have an HTML 'alt' tag containing a text description. Navigation is another issue, especially where buttons and menus, created using JavaScript or Flash, are used in place of hyperlinks. There are now comprehensive W3C guidelines on accessibility, and sites should aim to comply with these to avoid infringing anti-discrimination legislation such as the UK's Disability Discrimination Act.

MONITOR RESOLUTION The variable nature of how a Web page is displayed on an end-user's computer can be particularly vexing for a designer. One of the most hotly debated aspects of this is the problem of varying monitor resolutions. A page that holds together well on the designer's screen may completely break on another.

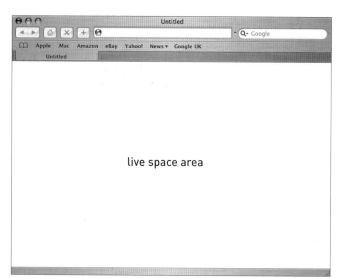

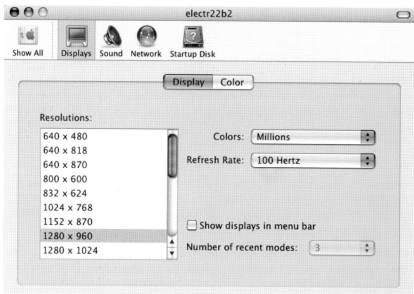

DESIGNING FOR VARIABLES

The greater the number of pixels in the screen display (or, more specifically, in the browser window), the greater the detail that can be displayed. This factor alone is crucial in deciding upon the optimum size for images and text for a Web page.

Early monitors could only display 640 x 480 pixels on a 14-inch screen. Today's monitors are capable of displaying a wide range of resolutions, depending not only on the size of the screen but on the graphics card installed in the computer and the wishes of the user. So it is vital to design pages that either fit into a minimum size or flex to accommodate varying sizes. The majority of computer users now have at least a 17-inch screen set to 1024 x 768 pixels, or a similar size in widescreen format; 19-inch CRTs and 17-inch LCDs offering higher resolutions are increasingly common. But this assumption may not hold for your site's intended audience; some users, for example, access the Web through TV-based

services with much lower resolutions. A very common mistake is to produce pages that are too large, simply because designers tend to work on bigger monitors than average.

More important than the overall monitor size and resolution is the smaller space where your pages will appear. Browsers take up a proportion of the screen with their menus, toolbars, tabs and side bars. The area where the Web page is actually displayed is referred to as the 'live space'. Of course, users can turn browser features on and off, or resize the whole browser window at will, but you can only assume a standard configuration.

If you choose to design to a fixed size, there are published charts that specify live space dimensions for the various browser versions, operating systems and monitor

Above left: The user can rearrange the space where a Web page is actually displayed by adjusting the parameters built into modern browsers and changing monitor resolutions. Even a simple act such as resizing a window can radically alter the 'live space' view of a page. Designers have to equip themselves with all the relevant information to produce a design that will hold up on the audience's system under these conditions.

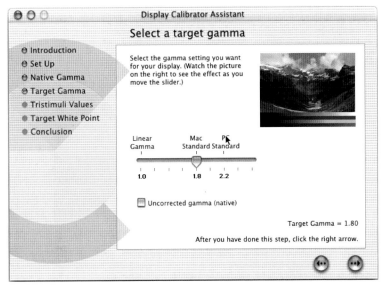

Below: The default gamma setting for Apple Macintosh displays is different from that of Windows PCs, so images that look natural on a Mac may appear dark on a PC. Mac users are provided with the tools to adjust and calibrate their monitors, so in practice each may vary. PC users are unlikely to pay any attention to colour management, but the variable quality of basic PC monitors brings its own problems.

Opposite right and above: **Both Macintosh and Windows operating systems now allow your monitor resolution to be changed 'on the fly', without having to restart the computer. This is particularly useful for designers who need to be aware of variable end-user monitor settings that can throw a Web page layout out of whack.**

resolutions. Alternatively, you can create pages that scale according to the dimensions of the browser window. This is particularly useful in situations where the user prefers to work in a smaller (not maximised) browser window, regardless of the screen resolution. Technically, this can be achieved by not specifying a set width for the content's container, which may be a table or a 'div' (division). Each element within is then aligned left, centrally, or to the right of the screen. As the browser window is resized – or the page is viewed at various screen resolutions – the layout elements 're-flow' to fit the width of the page.

Web page measurements are specified in pixels, not physical dimensions such as centimetres or inches. This means that,

having decided on the number of pixels you expect to be available in your live space, you can make sure your design fits. On the other hand, it means you have no control over the actual size of visual content. Text set in a specially designed typeface less than ten pixels high, for example, may look crisp and legible on a monitor set to a relatively low resolution, yet be all but invisible on another screen.

Similarly, you can specify colours with great accuracy, and see exactly how they appear on your own screen (which may be fully calibrated and colour managed), but this tells you little or nothing about how those colours will appear on a user's monitor. Differences between the standard set-ups of Macs and PCs mean that the same image will tend to vary in 'gamma' (midtone balance) between platforms, and the differences between individual machines can be just as significant. Testing your designs on several different computers, as well as in different browsers, is a good way to ensure any potential problems are within acceptable bounds.

FILE SIZES No matter how stunning a website design might be, if it takes too long to download (and anything much over ten seconds is too long) then it cannot be counted a success. Until broadband cable Internet connections become universal, the Web designer must still cater for the user with a 56k modem and a copper phone line designed for the comparatively low demands of voice transmission. In practice, this means getting the most out of small files.

IS YOUR WEB PAGE SLIM ENOUGH?

Usability and efficiency are the currency of popular websites, therefore page download time is critical. The speed at which a page is displayed in a browser window is directly related to its file size, so the drive to minimize the total file size of a given page has been fanatically pursued by Web designers. Now that many users have broadband connections, however, it may be tempting to assume that all but the heaviest pages will load almost instantaneously. In fact, however, pages are increasingly content-rich, and a basic 512K broadband link may not perform stunningly. Meanwhile, the number of users with slow dial-up connections may be very significant.

A fast-loading page will greatly enhance the first impression of a visited site, and hopefully attract the viewer back for repeat visits. For the dial-up user, no page is going to appear instantly, and frustration is inevitable; the aim should be to minimize it. The way in which a page is rendered by a browser follows Western text reading, moving from left to right and top to bottom, so content will be revealed in this order. Place something simple at the top left, and the user will at least have the impression of progress.

To understand the impact of page file sizes, it is useful to outline how data is measured. File size is calculated in bytes, sets of eight bits. 1024 bytes is a kilobyte, or 1K. Bandwidth is measured in bits per second, so, allowing for a few extra bits that have to be transmitted for technical reasons, the maximum number of kilobytes received per second will be around a tenth of the modem's

Below: One way to cater for dial-up users without compromising the full-blown broadband experience is to offer alternative versions of your site. An HTML version without multimedia content will suit slow connections as well as users who may lack the latest software. 'Sniffer' code can be used to detect browser versions and the presence of plug-ins, but the results are not entirely reliable. Asking the user explicitly is safer, but delays the initial experience of the site.

Kbits/sec rating. Most modems still in use are 56Kbits/sec, so they'll pull down no more than about 5K per second. In practice, the norm is between 38K and 44K, depending on the quality of the telephone line connection.

So how big should your Web page be? One rule sometimes quoted is that an entire page should not exceed 20K in total. This is often highly impractical: even the basic graphics required for branding could push you over that threshold. A more realistic guide is 50K, which should take no more than 15–20 seconds for modem users to download. Even this will require deft planning and tight compression for JPEG graphics. If part of the point of your site is to impress and entertain users, aiming for such a small size could make the whole exercise counter-productive; sometimes the harsh reality has to be faced that not everyone can be catered for, and dial-up users must be left to wait or go somewhere else.

Text file sizes are smallest, followed by images, with sound, Flash, Shockwave and video content requiring the most data. Video content can be 'streamed', however, so that a clip begins to play as soon as a small proportion has loaded, with the rest continuing to load during playback. With Flash and Shockwave, a small animation can play during loading.

DESIGN MUSEUM
London by Tower Bridge

Enter **Flash** Version (Full Content)

Enter **HTML** Version (Reduced Content)

CLICK HERE FOR
DESIGN MUSEUM SHOP

Colour and Form
Design: Peter Saville Studio

five programmes. tv guide. competitions. milkshake! news and weather. register/login.

napster FREE TRIAL visit4info on five ads

Above: **www.five.tv**
The eye-catching home page of Britain's fifth terrestrial television station uses a moving video clip as a full-bleed background. A movie of this size would normally have even broadband users twiddling their thumbs, but Five gets away with it by running a short clip with extreme compression. The quality is poor, but this in itself adds something to the effect.
Design by Lateral /NeoWorks, UK

An approximate guide to various Internet connection options and their throughput:

Connection	is rated at	typical throughput	to be safe, assume
28.8K modem	28.8 Kbits/sec	2.4 Kbytes/sec	1.8 Kbytes/sec
56K modem	53 Kbits/sec	4 Kbytes/sec	3 Kbytes/sec
Single ISDN line	64 Kbits/sec	6 Kbytes/sec	5 Kbytes/sec
Dual ISDN line	128 Kbits/sec	12 Kbytes/sec	10 Kbytes/sec
Budget cable/DSL	256 Kbits/sec	20 Kbytes/sec	15 Kbytes/sec
Standard cable/DSL	512 Kbits/sec	40 Kbytes/sec	35 Kbytes/sec
Fast cable/DSL	1024Kbits/sec	80 Kbytes/sec	70 Kbytes/sec

COLOUR AND TYPOGRAPHY Print-based designers making the switch to Web design must be aware of various differences and limitations involved in file output. One major difference is the expanded, yet unpredictable, RGB colour space; another is the typographical limitations of HTML and Web browsers.

WEB COLOUR

To those familiar with designing for print, the Web environment offers some new concepts and practices in using colour. In general, the Web designer has to think of colour in very specific technical terms. Traditional rules and techniques involving CMYK and PANTONE colours do not apply.

By mixing red, green and blue light additively (see page 190), today's computer monitors can display millions of different colours. This was not always the case: a few years ago, many computers could only manage a palette of 256 colours, and even colours within this range could sometimes be rendered incorrectly by a Web browser. Mac and Windows systems each had their own standard palette of 256 colours, but they were not the same. This gave rise to the 216-color 'Web-safe' palette, consisting of colors that ought to appear correctly on both Macs and

Right: Photoshop's colour management functions can be used to get an idea of how images will appear on different systems. Here, working on the Mac, the image on the left is displayed as-is, while the copy on the right is shown using the Proof Colors option with Proof Setup set to Windows RGB.

Below: www.mundidesign.com Although the Web-safe palette is no longer a real concern for most online designers, its limited number of tones can still provide a useful simplification of the RGB spectrum. Mundi Design's Web Colour Theory resource presents the palette in a tonal arrangement devised by Bob Stein of Visibone, and allows you to experiment with combinations of swatches.

PCs. With the demise of 8-bit (256-colour) monitors, the Web-safe palette became largely obsolete – although the idea is now relevant to some designers again thanks to the less capable colour screens fitted to mobile devices, such as phones and PDAs, which include basic Web browsing facilities.

When working on Web pages, most designers now choose colours freely from their graphics application's usual colour picker. To help ensure colours look roughly the same on the user's monitor, they work in the sRGB colour space (see page 195), the standard to which consumer systems are increasingly likely to conform. Note, however, that you should still test your content on a range of platforms to see the effects of the display differences already mentioned. Detail in shadow areas is especially likely to be lost on a PC monitor, while very light tones visible under Windows may be too subtle to see clearly on a Mac screen.

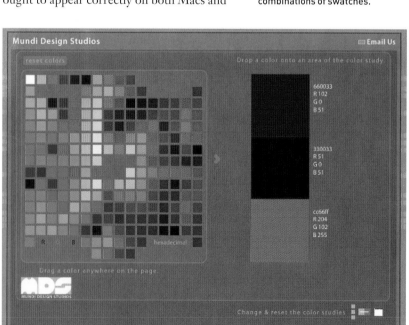

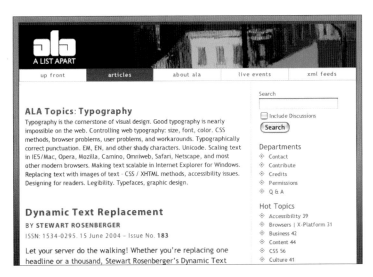

WEB TYPE

HTML is a proficient tool for coding basic formatting instructions. Its original purpose was semantic mark-up, providing structure to information. Later, it gained presentation-oriented tags that provided a modicum of typographic control, including the ability to define the colour, font family and size of a piece of text. Cascading style sheets (CSS) has removed many of the limitations of these basic tags, but designers are only gradually using this standard to its fullest.

Although it is well known that CSS enables you to set the colour, font family and size of a piece of text, often by defining a rule applied to a specific HTML tag, it also provides control over leading, kerning, word spacing and case (upper, lower, capitalized or normal). Text can be emboldened or italicized, and alignments can be set to suit. The level of freedom may not be on a par with type in QuarkXPress or InDesign, but it is a far cry from the limitations that Web designers were stuck with in the late 1990s.

One critical restriction remains, however: the lack of available fonts. In the same way that a bureau usually requires a copy of a font in a document sent for print, so too must a Web surfer have your chosen fonts installed before type within your site will appear correctly. In practice, this restricts you to fonts common to Windows and Mac: Verdana, Trebuchet MS and Arial for sans serif; Georgia and Times New Roman for serif; Courier New for monospace; Arial

Above: **The array of available fonts for print publishing is vast; the choice in Web publishing is not. Any attempt at decent typographic style will depend on some deft compromises. Advice can be found in a number of online resources, including www.alistapart.com/ topics/typography/.**

Below: **Although nowhere near as flexible as the typographic formatting supported by print-oriented DTP software, CSS does give you a fair amount of control over Web typography, including kerning, leading, font family, size, colour, case, and other attributes.**

Black, Impact and the inexplicably over-used Comic Sans MS for display type. Although it is possible to define 'fall-back' fonts (these are listed one after the other, separated by commas, and the browser moves to the next choice if the previous one isn't installed), it is pointless to set a first choice that the vast majority of your audience will not see, so you will have to get used to these 'Web-safe' fonts. Note that, like images, Web fonts should be sized in pixels (or percentages), not measurements such as points and millimetres.

Of course, there are times when corporate style guides or creative impulses demand sometimes more esoteric at least for headings. In this case you can render each piece of typeset text as an image file – GIF is the most suitable file format for this purpose – and ensure that it is marked up correctly on your page: set the image as a heading, and include alt text for non-visual browsers.

As with images, there are some slight cross-platform differences with Web type. The Mac operating system anti-aliases text by default, but Windows does not (although some laptops and TFT monitors do). This means body text may appear a fraction wider on Mac, while characters may not look completely smooth under Windows. At least one major discrepancy has been resolved, however: by default, both Mac and Windows browsers now generally display text at 96ppi, so fonts no longer appear smaller in Mac browsers.

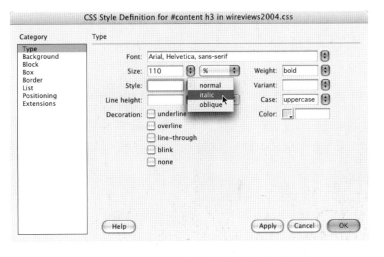

OPTIMIZING WEB GRAPHICS Designers face a new set of constraints when working with images on the Web. The need to keep file sizes as small as possible means efficient storage is paramount, so file formats that incorporate data compression must be used and settings tweaked for optimum results. The two dominant image file formats on the Web at present are JPEG and GIF.

The production methods employed to create graphics are similar to print in so far as images are created or sourced, drawn or scanned, manipulated, then saved for output. The main differences lie at the start of the process, with decisions about resolution, and at the end, with the saving of a file.

To develop a more proficient working practice, it must always be borne in mind that everything happens on the screen. The high resolutions necessary for magazine-quality printed output would be useless here, since everything will be delivered at 96ppi on screen. Even then, a further amount of image information must be sacrificed in order to create file sizes small enough for Web delivery. Aggressive data compression methods will do further damage to image quality, but this is something that Web designers just have to accept.

Production of Web-ready images is generally done in Photoshop (with ImageReady), Fireworks, or relatively low-cost image editing applications such as Paint Shop Pro (Windows only). All provide some form of preview to help find the right trade-off between high compression with reduced quality and low compression with large file size.

Below: **The importance of experimenting with file format compression settings cannot be overstated for Web graphics. Even the basic rules can be misleading depending on the specific nature of the graphic being used. A good practice for the Web designer is to always keep the original prepared graphic. Then, export a range of compressed files to view comparatively within the most popular browsers, ideally also over a number of monitor types.**

IMAGE FILE FORMATS

GIF (Graphic Interchange Format) was the first file format to be supported by Web browsers. It remains the most widely used graphics format on the Web today, partly because of its use to deliver large numbers of workaday graphical elements such as rules, buttons and background tints. GIF files use their own fixed colour palette, not unlike older monitors, with a maximum of 256 colours; the exact colours are set at the time of creating the file, usually in such a way as to include as many as possible of the shades within the original image. Compression is achieved by rationalizing rows of pixels of similar colour, so the smallest files are obtained from graphics with flat areas of colour, such as text and logos.

JPEG (Joint Photographic Experts Group) files contain 24-bit colour information, allowing up to 16.7 million

Original image

jpeg

gif

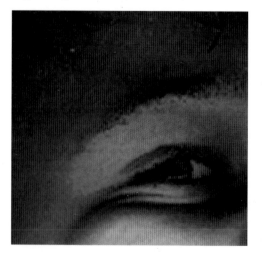
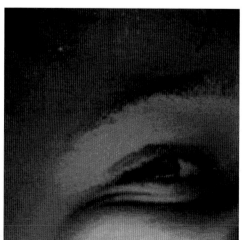
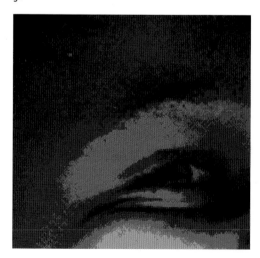

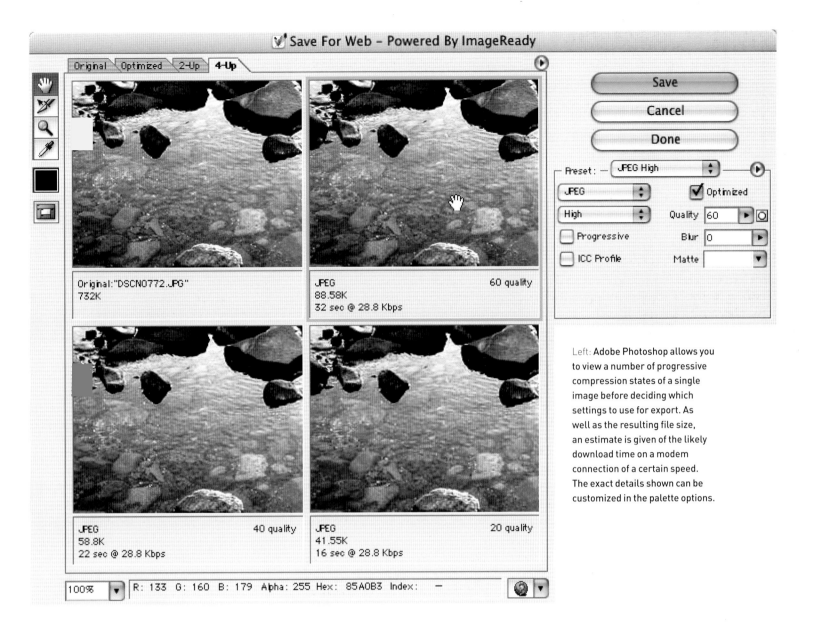

Left: **Adobe Photoshop** allows you to view a number of progressive compression states of a single image before deciding which settings to use for export. As well as the resulting file size, an estimate is given of the likely download time on a modem connection of a certain speed. The exact details shown can be customized in the palette options.

colours. They use a 'lossy' compression method, where some image information is thrown away rather than just being stored more efficiently. A sliding scale is used to choose the level of compression; medium or high settings should avoid visible degradation. JPEG files are ideal for photographic images, but not for flat colour, as unwanted mottling can occur. Because some data is lost with each save, you should keep uncompressed copies of images that you save as JPEGs.

PNG (Portable Network Graphics) allows lossless compression with 8-bit indexed and 24-bit true colour, but this format has never been very widely adopted.

Right: **GIF** is an excellent format for bitmapped text, since it allows file size to be reduced by limiting the total number of colours used, and in most cases very few will be required. Here, black text on a white background has been converted using a palette of eight shades of grey, including the solid black of the lettering and pure white of the background plus sufficient intermediate shades for anti-aliasing (edge smoothing). The 100K image is reduced to 2.5K.

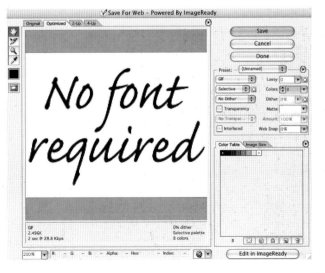

HTML – THE SECRET CODE HTML code is the framework of the Internet upon which the visual interface hangs. It sits behind every Web page giving instructions to the browser on where to place images, render text and manage assorted media. It is the foundational building block upon which all Web development has been built. Its principal function of 'hyperlinking' – the ability to jump between pages and addresses on the Internet by clicking on a word or image – remains one of the most potent tools on the Web today.

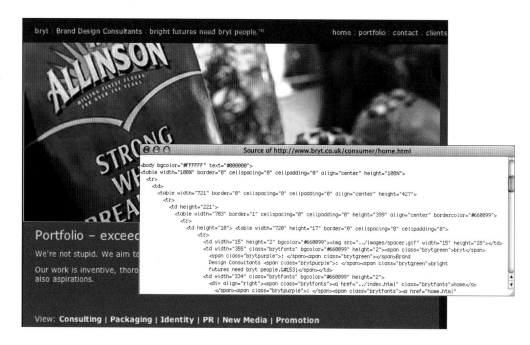

HTML consists of a number of elements that are used to semantically structure a web page, providing the web browser with instructions about how to display things like headings, body text, tables and images. For designers not used to looking at programming code, it can appear daunting, but it's actually quite logical. Although HTML does have some presentation-oriented tags and attributes, such things are better taken care of in CSS.

HTML TAGS

An HTML element consists of a start tag, content, and an end tag. For instance, a paragraph starts with <p> (the start tag), has content (whatever the paragraph text is), and ends with </p> (the end tag). Notice the slash that distinguishes an end tag. HTML content should always sit within the <html></html> element, while anything you wish to be displayed in the browser as text, rather than interpreted as an HTML instruction, should be within the <body></body> element. The <head></head> section of a page houses information describing the page. This can include its title, character set information, and keywords intended to assist search engines when indexing the site.

HTML KNOWLEDGE

Designers need to understand HTML to a reasonable degree in order to work with specialists such as database programmers,

even if they will never actually hand-code a page themselves. The HTML files that browsers read are ordinary text files, so you can edit them and create new pages from scratch using nothing more than a text editor, making sure to save the file as plain text.

Building Web pages by hand using text editors used to be the only option, and many experienced Web programmers still do it. Fortunately, today's professional Web design programs let you build a page visually, then generate working code automatically without ever having to key a tag at all. So while it is important to understand the structure and principles of HTML, you should not believe the myth that you are not a Web designer until you can build a site by hand.

HTML is a language that continues to evolve. New standards are released on a fairly regular basis to address various issues raised by industry and technology groups. Elements of the language can be added or marked as 'deprecated'. The latter kind are due for removal from the specifications, and should therfore be avoided. For instance, most presentation-oriented HTML is deprecated, and you should now use CSS (cascading style sheets) instead.

Above: **It is a very handy skill to be able to look at a page of HTML and 'decode' it. 'Hand coding' is no longer an essential skill for the designer using a WYSIWYG page design program, but when code is generated by applications such as Dreamweaver it can sometimes contain glitches such as unused tags which may disrupt the page. To understand and be able to edit the tags will save time and trouble and enable professional results.**

WHAT YOU SEE IS WHAT YOU GET There is a huge variety of Web design or 'authoring' tools to choose from. At the professional level, WYSIWYG ('what you see is what you get') programs, such as Macromedia Dreamweaver and Adobe GoLive, offer a work environment bearing some similarity to the DTP programs favoured by designers. With precision tools for layout, image placement and text editing, these packages are ideal for print designers wishing to enter Web publishing.

The consumer market for Web design is catered for by low-end programs that provide basic formatting options but lack the flexibility and control of professional tools, often forcing the user either to adopt a predefined template or to edit code manually. They can provide a useful introduction, but designers will imediately feel frustrated by their limited abilities.

PROFESSIONAL AUTHORING TOOLS

Professional visual website design packages are the best choice, as they offer methods of working that straddle the divide between the WYSIWYG approach of DTP software and the technical needs of Web design. The designer arranges the elements on the page, and the software writes the code required to recreate the layout in a browser. Dreamweaver and GoLive prefer everything apart from text to be prepared for the Web beforehand, and can provide 'smart links' with Fireworks or Photoshop/ImageReady for image optimizing.

SoftPress Freeway aligns itself more closely to the DTP side, and can work with print graphics formats such as TIFF and EPS as well as JPEG and GIF, then create and optimize Web graphics along with the page code. Using

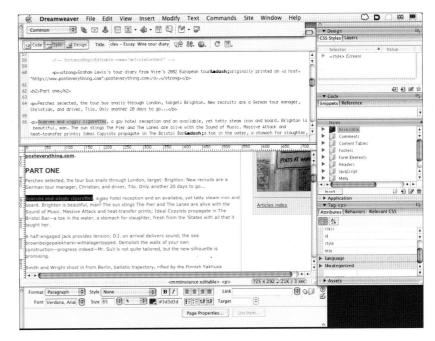

Above: **Macromedia Dreamweaver's interface** simultaneously enables you to work visually and edit the HTML code. This level of flexibility is useful, because it provides you with greater control of the output.

Left: **Freeway's approach to** layout is based on traditional DTP behaviour, scaling graphics and styling text on the page. Guides can be dragged onto pages manually or set up as regular design grid structures.

Freeway, a basic site can be produced fairly quickly by a designer without specialist assistance. It is not a particularly useful first step, however, towards building something more complex.

Web design applications such as Dreamweaver and GoLive can be mastered by both designer and programmer, and there are benefits to be gained from exploiting this to run an integrated workflow. Many designers feel more at home creating layouts using QuarkXPress, FreeHand or Photoshop, but by getting involved with Web production tools they can keep control of the design further into the process – and have a better chance of understanding what coders are talking about.

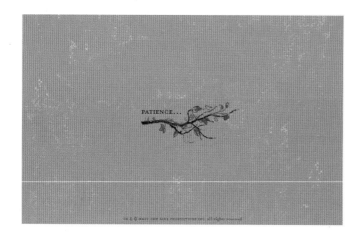

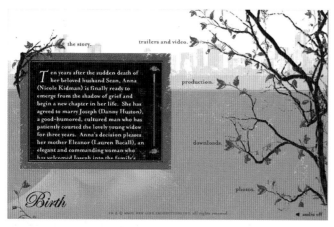

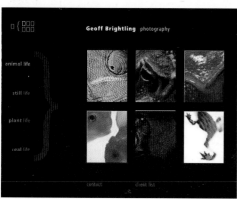

WYSIWYG

Entire sites can be constructed and edited with WYSIWYG tools; hyperlinks can be made and tested, interactive forms, buttons and rollovers created and pages uploaded to the hosting Internet Service Provider. Flash and Shockwave files can be included as elements on a page, but often they are used to create stand-alone pages or sets of pages. They both use a traditional, time-line format for creating animation with the capability to script links to other pages, movies, Internet addresses or for sending mail. The advantage of using Flash and Shockwave for Web design is that they can be treated as 'embedded' files, or objects, within HTML. This means that they cannot be altered when displayed in a browser, assuring design fidelity. Flash, in particular, is favoured by Web designers for this fact alone.

SHOCKWAVE

Shockwave is the Web export format of Director (see page 72), Macromedia's multimedia authoring software. It is used extensively for on-line gaming because of its powerful Lingo scripting language, which facilitates versatile interactivity. Shockwave can contain sound, animation, graphics and 3D components. However, it is far more complex to work with than Flash, which offers many of the same features.

FLASH

Macromedia Flash (the name applies both to the delivery medium and the program used to create content) can be used for anything from simple animations to entire sites with interactive navigation. Flash uses vector technology, similar to Illustrator and FreeHand, which is ideal for the Web because of its small file sizes and scalable qualities. It compresses sound using in MP3 format, contributing to efficient download times. The Flash plug-in is already installed in millions of the world's Web browsers. However, this doesn't mean that all these browsers will have the latest version of the plug-in, or may not have had it disabled for some reason. It is good practice not to design sites that require Flash unless you are confident that enough of your target market will have the necessary version installed.

Left: **www.brightlingphoto.com**
Carefully prepared photos are combined with subtle rollovers and a neat graphical representation of the user's current location within the site (top left). The result is an elegant site that is foolproof to navigate.
Design by Biggles, UK

Above left: **www.birthmovie.com**
This promotional site for New Line's 'Birth' uses Flash to create a tightly controlled atmosphere. Colour, type and imagery evoke the mood of the film. In a touch of wry humour, the initial loading screen enigmatically bears the single word: 'patience'.

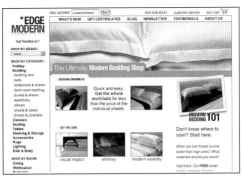

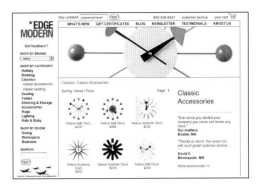

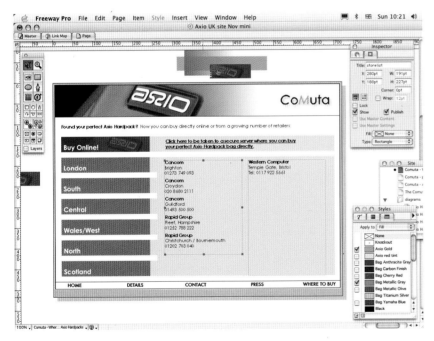

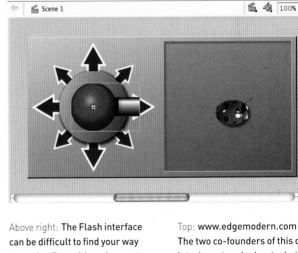

Above left: **Freeway enables graphic designers with little Web experience to hit the ground running and create a working site, with the exact appearance they want, in a far shorter time than would be possible with Dreamweaver or GoLive.**

Above right: **The Flash interface can be difficult to find your way around at first, although recent versions look a little more like a DTP application. For those new to multimedia design, numerous tutorials and sample files are provided to give an immediate idea of what can be achieved and how.**

Top: www.edgemodern.com **The two co-founders of this online interiors store had no technical experience, but with Dreamweaver were able to create a fully working ecommerce site. Thanks to CSS, any changes to the design are easy and quick to implement.**

INTERACTIVITY To interact with a computer is the fundamental principle of communication in the digital world. Almost without exception every type of content on the screen requires some level of user interaction. Websites are designed exclusively for this purpose – to encourage the visitor to explore and access areas of the site that offer up information. Web designers have to fully understand the concepts of interaction in order to use them appropriately.

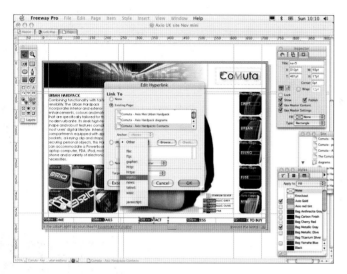

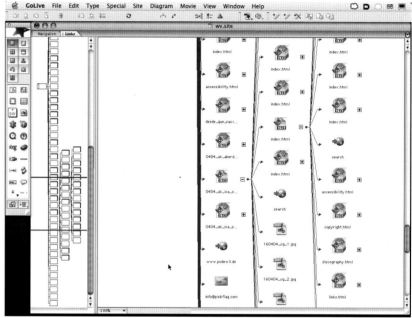

CREATING HYPERLINKS

Interactivity is a key element of any website, making the design dynamic and encouraging the user to stay and look around. The simplest form of interaction is clickable hypertext links. These provide links to other pages via clickable text items. Visually, graphic buttons and image maps are a more sophisticated form of link, but the technical aspect of the link is produced in exactly the same way.

The process of producing links varies slightly from one website layout tool to another (Freeway is shown above), but the principle is the same. The process begins by selecting a graphic or piece of text on the page. You then opt to add a link to it, and set up the link by typing a complete URL or choosing one of the other pages within the site you are creating. When the page is tested in a web browser, clicking the linked item will take the user to the specified page.

Above left: The principle of text hyperlinking can be applied to any graphic element on a page as well. It is always important to check for broken links when publishing a site. Trying to navigate your way around a site with over a thousand links can be a very arduous task! Most WYSIWYG applications offer a fast and efficient method to check the integrity of all links within a page as well as an entire site.

Above: Mapping the links from a page can be a tedious business, but with complex sites it will be vital to keep track of your overall site navigation structure. Look for site and link mapping features in your web design application so that you can keep on top of this when handling large projects.

ROLLOVERS AND IMAGE MAPS

Rollovers are used to make link items (whether icons or buttons, 'hot' areas within imagery, or even pieces of text) more eye-catching and to provide feedback to the user, so that they know an item is a clickable link and can be sure when the cursor is correctly positioned to activate it. Rollovers can use a different graphic for each of several 'link states': link (indicating the item can be clicked), visited (when the item has previously been clicked), hover (while the cursor is over the link), and active (responding to a click), although link and hover are the most commonly used. For instance, a button may 'light up' when the cursor is over it, then appear to depress when clicked. Rollovers traditionally require JavaScript for the interactive element, but can be created using CSS alone. Likewise, CSS can apply effects to HTML-based links (see opposite).

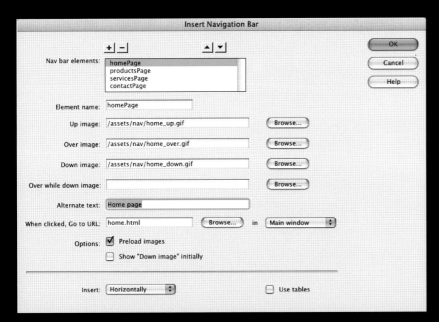

Below: **Four possible states of a clickable hypertext link.**
Plain Text: This is plain black HTML text, here set in Verdana.
Linked Text: This text is hyperlinked and bold; hyperlinks are set to dark red on this page.
Visited Link: This text is hyperlinked and bold, but has already been visited; visited links are set to brown on this page.

Hover (CSS): Using cascading style sheets, this link has been given a 'hover' state. When the mouse pointer is left over it, it turns bright red to indicate that it can be clicked.
Active Link (CSS): Using cascading style sheets, this link is made to turn orange when clicked.

Image maps work by plotting separate areas of a larger image and linking each area to a separate URL. This creates 'hot spots' within the graphic that take the user to different destinations when clicked. The graphic itself is an ordinary image file, and the map coordinates, which plot out the hot spot areas, are listed within the HTML code. Image maps allow a very visual design method and don't demand that the designer slice their image up into multiple parts to create each graphic link. There are two forms of image map; client-side and server-side. Client-side image maps hold everything to do with the map, including all the URLs, within the HTML page code. Server-side image maps send custom messages to a remote Web server that passes back the final destination URLs. This latter method is now practically obsolete.

Above: **Like most web design packages, Dreamweaver makes it relatively easy to create graphical rollover navigation bars. Images and links are defined in the dialog box seen here, and the application itself outputs the relevant JavaScript and HTML code without the designer needing to worry about the technicalities.**

Plain Text

Linked Text

Visited Link

Hover (CSS)

Active Link (CSS)

Below: **Graphic buttons and rollovers serve exactly the same purpose as hypertext links, but offer the designer infinite scope for creativity.**

JAVA AND JAVASCRIPT Java and JavaScript are two distinctive coding languages used to add interactivity to webpages. Java is an object-orientated 'full' programming language that can be used to create complete applications. The manifestation of Java on the Web is in the form of Java applets – independent, executable programs placed on a page like an image. JavaScript is a client-side scripting language that allows the creation of rollover effects, the opening of pop-up windows, and many other interactive page functions.

Above: **Just like regular TV, Apple's QuickTime home page offers the viewer a choice of 'channels' delivering movie trailers, music videos, and educational content. With a broadband Internet connection, high-quality clips download with little delay.**

JavaScript and Java are actually two entirely different things. JavaScript is a scripting language that is used to give specific instructions to browsers. These are placed into regular webpages alongside the HTML code, or attached as external documents, and read and acted upon as required. Designers working in visual web software will frequently use JavaScript without even realizing it, as part of rollover effects and similar tricks that the software codes behind the scenes.

Java, on the other hand, is a complete programming language used to make self-contained miniature applications, or 'applets', which can be embedded into webpages but are actually very much separate from the browser. The major browsers support Java applets but can be unreliable in handling them. Applets provide an array of functions from games to numerical computations. They are practical for sites that require fast response from user input, because they can make calculations on-the-fly using the host computer's processing power. Designers who are not conversant with programming can download ready-made Java applets from sites such as http://javaboutique.internet.com and add them directly to their HTML pages.

JavaScript is generally very stable, as long as it is written competently and in compliance with current standards; if not, browser compatibility can be a problem. It can perform rollovers, randomly display content on a page, or load content into new browser windows, as well as a host of other functions, many offered as part of the feature set of the leading web design applications.

SOUNDS AND MOVIES
Sound and movies (audio and video) are commonplace on the Web, but handling these weighty files can be a testing experience for the designer. Both formats require specialist applications to prepare them for webpage use, and the user browsing your site will need a fast connection to allow quick download and uninterrupted playback.

Left: RealPlayer is the leading independent alternative to the QuickTime and Windows Media players provided by Apple and Microsoft on Macs and PCs respectively. The Mac version of the software can also play video files in QuickTime format.
Film 'Ambush' by John Frankenheimer, US / BMW

Below: When video footage is included in a webpage, it is generally played back within the same window, with the playback application represented only by a toolbar. Here, the same movie is being played in RealMedia (left) and Windows Media Player – the user may not even know which.
Film 'Battle of the Sexes' by Eric Kripke, US / Atomfilms.com

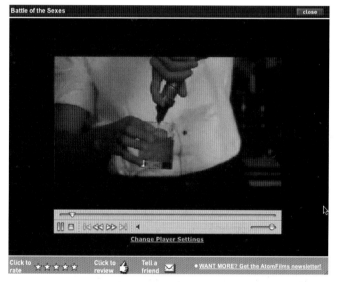

SOUND FORMATS AND CHARACTERISTICS

The most commonly used formats for audio and video on the Web are MP3, QuickTime, and RealAudio. These all use forms of 'streaming' technologies which allow playback to begin without having a complete file downloaded, thus avoiding the user having to wait for a lengthy download before hearing anything. Sound quality is directly related to file size, so CD-quality sound is not best suited to the Web. Sound files are compressed to reduce download time, thus sacrificing the full tonal range and fidelity. Speech is acceptable at 11KHz sampling rate, whereas music is better at 22KHz, both in mono. Macromedia Flash uses sound very efficiently.

VIDEO FORMATS AND CHARACTERISTICS

Both Apple QuickTime ('.mov' file extension) and Microsoft Windows Media Player ('.avi' or '.wmv' file extension) can be received and played back on either computer platform, but only if the recipient has the necessary software installed, so it is safest to offer a choice of formats. As with other types of content, larger file sizes give better quality. RealVideo is a common cross-platform format on the Web, although not only is a plug-in required on the end user's side, but a dedicated RealMedia server is also needed to host the video content. Some form of streaming, plus a relatively low frame rate and small window size – depending on the likely connection bandwidth of your target audience – is the only way to deliver video smoothly.

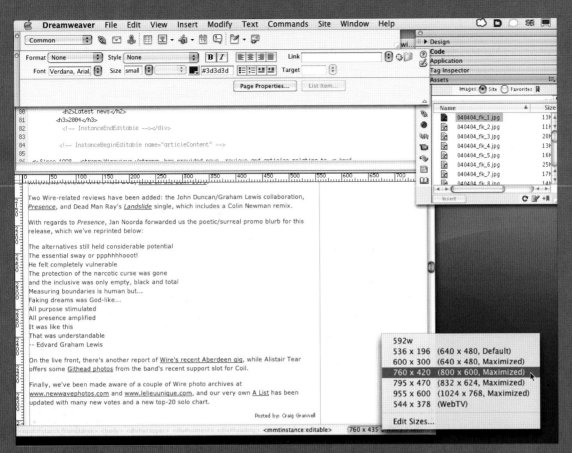

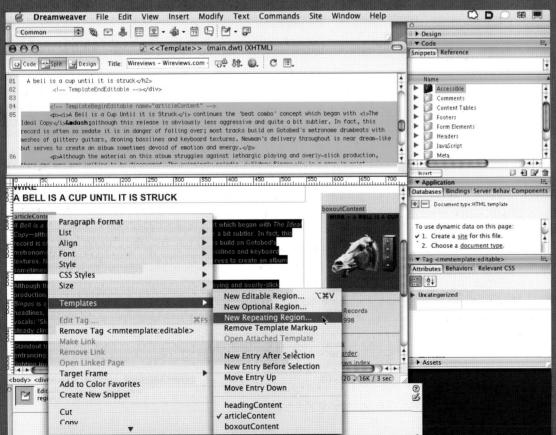

Left: Like master pages in DTP software, web design tools allow you to set up templates, ensuring certain aspects of a page remain consistent throughout the site. Dreamweaver takes things a step further, enabling you to 'nest' templates, so you can use a master template as the basis of templates for individual site subsections.

DEVELOPING A WEB DESIGN STRATEGY Web design has become an industry in its own right with its own unique workflow, structures, and ethics, and digital designers have had to develop strategies that work in this field. Websites are not just marketing tools for the corporate world – they are focal points that enable businesses to stay at the cutting edge in highly competitive markets.

Traditional designers will be pleased to note that it is good practice to start a website design on paper. After all, we read screens more slowly than paper, and even today's software isn't as quick and flexible as pencil-and-paper sketches. Even if you are comfortable with digital drawing tools, the client may not be. In most cases it will be best to visualize ideas, work out navigational structures, and sketch site maps on paper before going to the computer. To design the navigation of a site is a creative process in its own right, involving considerable planning and, with complex sites, teamwork.

Set yourself a clear brief with well defined objectives that can be articulated to the client, bearing in mind that many clients will not be familiar with the norms, limitations, and possibilities of web media. Build in a time scale, as this will help to deter clients from adding more and more content as the job progresses, which is all too tempting given the open-endedness of this particular medium. Unlike a printed brochure, a website may never be pronounced 'finished'.

When moving onto the computer, don't be diverted from your original plans. Keeping an eye on the overall project is vital. Webpages contain many ingredients that can quickly evolve from the original conception. Bear in mind the very real limitations of current web technologies in areas such as typography, and the necessity of ensuring that pages will be received promptly and successfully by all target users, and avoid being talked into promising what cannot be delivered.

Consider the number of graphics you are using, and assess their file size and download times. If you are using other applications, such as Flash, ensure that you output the movie for the oldest version of the plug-in that you can, to maximise compatibility. Remember that a Flash movie will take much longer to create than the page on which it resides.

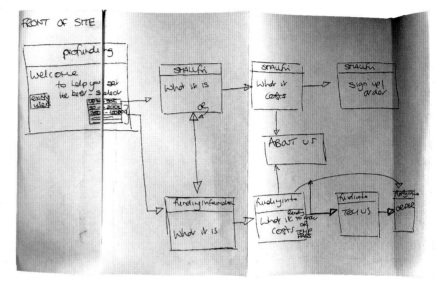

An overriding factor in your design strategy is an understanding of the audience's computer capabilities. Designers usually work on well-equipped computers; it is easy to overlook this and produce a design that is too unwieldy for the average user. Consider browser versions as well as the possible age (and thus processing speed) of hardware. Although all but the oldest machines in current use support sound and video, not all will handle it well enough to be worthwhile.

Finally, do seriously consider the need to study accessibility guidelines and check your site for compliance. If you understand the principles of accessible design when you start out, then there need be little or no extra work in applying them; converting a non-compliant site, however, can be a very large and time-consuming job.

Above: **Many a high-tech project begins on the back of an envelope. Brainstorming with the client may initially produce a confused and confusing plan for the website, but it is at this stage that the big issues need to be thrashed out. What information goes together? Should the structure be broad or deep? Will users already know what they want, or must they be led to it? It will soon start to make more sense.** Client: Profunding, UK

PLANNING AND PRODUCTION The planning and production of web design are different from those of traditional desktop publishing. The technical and development aspects of the medium should always be capitalized on, but never allowed to override the design concept.

A diverse range of roles are needed to design and produce a successful, large-scale website. These could include graphic designer, market researcher, project manager, programmer, production manager, picture editor, sound production manager, or video editor. This covers such a broad set of skills that no individual is likely to have them all, so in practice, freelance designers will sub-contract work to other specialists for specific tasks. Sub-contracting can be expensive, so it is important to be aware of the scope of the project and adjust the overall design fees accordingly. For example, when a site requires a lot of expensive scripting for e-commerce or on-line booking, this could form the major financial part of the job, with the design costs being relatively modest.

A fundamental planning consideration is deciding whether a site is linear or non-linear in its navigation structure. More than likely it will be the latter, in which case a legible site map should be created, clearly indicating all the possible linking routes for the user to explore. Refer to this often during the production process to avoid becoming confused when tying pages and sections together.

It is advisable to mock up key pages in graphics tools, such as Photoshop or Fireworks, and get them approved by the

Below: **www.tate.org.uk**
A clear and simple layout can never be underestimated. Keeping an eye on the actual problem to solve and giving the audience something accessible is a prime objective in web design. Information should be easily retrievable without many layers of navigation to wade through. The alphabet is one of the oldest ways of organising information and is still one of the best, as seen in this page from the Tate Gallery website.
Design by Nykris Digital Design, UK

client before moving over to your website design package. Or, if your package is sufficiently DTP-like, you can move straight to it from paper sketches.

With the exception of GoLive, few web design programs allow you to zoom in on page elements or images, so you will need to inspect and test the quality of your graphical content in an image editor before importing it.

Testing is absolutely critical and should not be compromised in any way. The designer is well advised to use both a Macintosh and a PC for this purpose, although using Virtual PC on a Mac is an acceptable solution for sites that do not use Flash or Shockwave. Remember that colours and fonts may appear slightly different between PCs and Macs. It can be useful to set up a private testing folder on a remote web server so that the client can monitor progress and view 'live' pages. It will also help you, because testing work without first uploading to a remote server gives a false impression of download times. Remember to build in enough time for exhaustive testing and keep the client updated with 'milestones' as things progress.

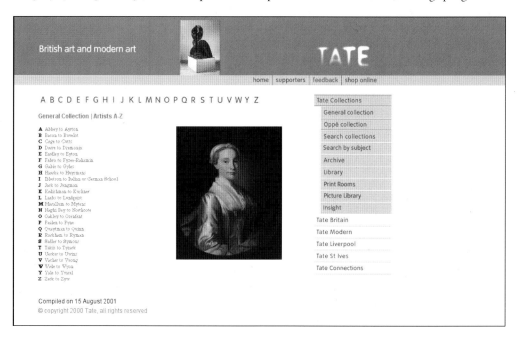

When a site design works properly, there is a place for everything, and everything is in its place. Content is found, neatly presented, where users would expect it, not shoehorned into unused spaces or mangled to fit formats that were never intended for it. A feeling of consistency and openness ensures browsing never feels like a chore.
Design by Domani Studios, US

The World Wide Web Consortium is the industry body responsible for web design standards. Although few legal cases concerning the Internet have been brought under the disability discrimination laws, the W3C guidelines on accessibility could be used as a benchmark if owners of commercial sites are accused of failing to serve disabled users. Clients are well advised to insist that all site designs comply with these standards.

W3C®

Checklist of Checkpoints for Web Content Accessibility Guidelines 1.0

This version:
http://www.w3.org/TR/1999/WAI-WEBCONTENT-19990505/full-checklist
(plain text, postscript, pdf)
This document is an appendix to:
http://www.w3.org/TR/1999/WAI-WEBCONTENT-19990505
Latest version of Web Content Accessibility Guidelines 1.0:
http://www.w3.org/TR/WAI-WEBCONTENT
Editors:
Wendy Chisholm, Trace R & D Center, University of Wisconsin -- Madison
Gregg Vanderheiden, Trace R & D Center, University of Wisconsin -- Madison
Ian Jacobs, W3C

Copyright © 1999 W3C (MIT, INRIA, Keio), All Rights Reserved. W3C liability, trademark, document use and software licensing rules apply.

1. Pages	max file size (inc graphics), max active area
2. Text	minimum size, consistent font specs
3. Graphics	all RGB format; titles as transparent GIFs;
	all other graphics as JPEGs within max page size
4. Background	common to all pages
5. Hyperlinks	check internal and external links plus mailto: contacts
6. Accessibility	alt tags on all graphical content; passes agreed checks
7. Test	all pages, content and links tested on all platforms that
	are to be supported

Left: A simple checklist is useful when a project gets under way. Web projects can exceed their intended scope, and team members may forget what has previously been decided or agreed. Paper plans are invaluable to refer back to when the screen becomes too cluttered, and have the advantage that the previous version is probably still there, rather than adrift on a hard disk.

03.01
CASE HISTORY

WENDY CAULES CERAMICS

Wendy Caules is a ceramicist who lives and works in the UK. Designer Phil Taylor was commissioned to produce a website that would provide a showcase for her work as well as a contact point for customers. The emphasis was on simplicity of layout in order to allow the work itself to breathe and stand out. The client specifically requested that the navigation should be 'straightforward' yet 'intuitive'.

The website would comprise a home page with links to pages with samples of work, a live email contact and a curriculum vitae page. Within the sample pages it was suggested that a QTVR (QuickTime Virtual Reality) movie could be used to show a 360-degree view of an individual piece.

THE FIRST STAGES

After the brief was agreed and the launch date set (to coincide with an exhibition of the artist's work) the next stage was to capture images of the work. Most examples of the work tended to be in 35mm transparency format, which is not ideal for high-quality reproduction. It was, therefore, decided that Headprecious Design would photograph the work using a digital camera to obtain a suitable format for web publishing. An extra day was added to the schedule for photographing the work in a studio. The resulting images were used as a starting point for the initial design ideas and mock-ups. Samples of four

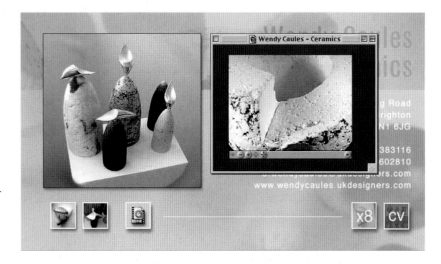

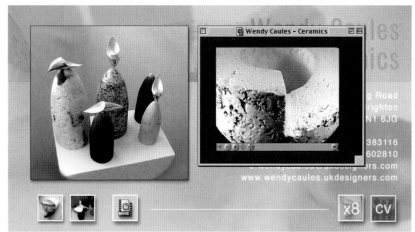

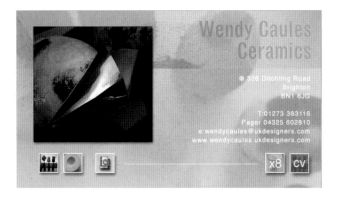

This page: QuickTime Virtual Reality was used to offer a 360-degree view of a ceramics piece, accessed via a pop-up window from the main portfolio page. Relying upon the intended audience's recognition of visual symbols as navigational devices (buttons) relieved the need for a large amount of HTML text to be included in the site.

different design concepts were presented, each incorporating the photographic images with varied options for type, layout, and navigation structures. The artist chose a design that had a bold, clear look and feel with a dominant photographic element, large-scale type heading, and three visual (non-text) navigation buttons. The background graphic on the home page was chosen to run throughout the site to help maintain consistency. It was agreed that the only section that would use HTML text would be the curriculum vitae page.

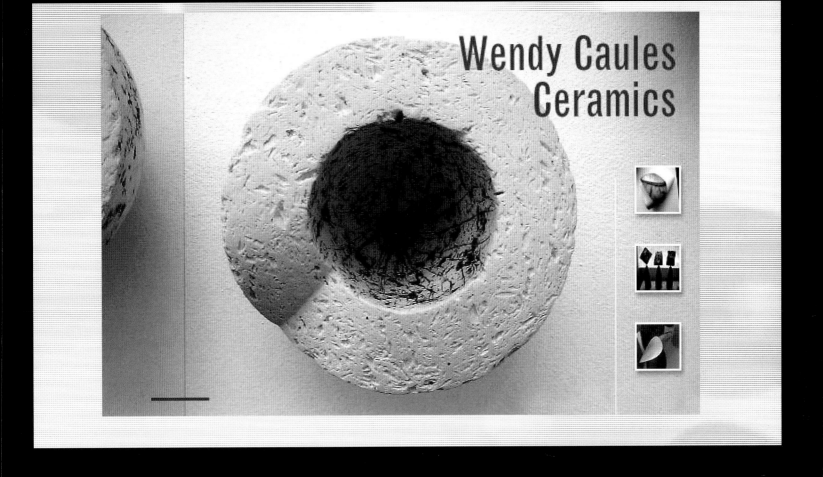

Wendy Caules Ceramics

The background image was constructed in Photoshop using a technique that maintained the image quality but allowed for a small file size, allowing a shorter download time. The technique employed a screen of alternating 50 per cent transparent horizontal white lines, two pixels apart, placed over a subdued montage of photographed ceramics pieces scaled to a 'live space' area measuring 800 x 466 pixels.

OPTIMIZING THE SITE

To achieve a smooth screen rendering, the home page graphic was sliced into three vertical sections, taking up 22, 35, and 10K respectively. Although this still constituted a large file, each image would download progressively and simultaneously, presenting a fluid screen draw. To ensure visual content would be present on the screen immediately, low-resolution, grey-scale versions of the three large graphics were created to render quickly followed by the full-colour versions overlaying them as they downloaded. The same technique was applied to all the images on the work sample pages.

Buttons were made as rollovers, incorporating simple graphic symbols to indicate their function in the rollover state, with small-scale images of ceramics pieces indicating

Above: By slicing the main graphic on the home page, a relatively large-scale image could be employed to create visual presence. As well as the design considerations, an equally important aspect of the project was to ensure successful indexing for search engines. The timescale involved for this should not be underestimated, and correct Meta-tagging on the home page itself is the first step. Pointing search engines at the site can be a lengthy process.

the static state. The buttons were subsequently placed in layers on top of the main graphic, and scaled to match precisely.

THE FINAL RESULT

The entire home page totalled 97K, resulting in an approximate download time of 20 seconds on a 56Kbps modem. This was within the acceptable timeframe for the intended specialist audience group. The brief, to create a highly visual site with detailed graphics while at the same time maintaining a fluid rendering of pages, was achieved.

Multimedia is the broad term that encompasses any communication medium that combines the use of sound, graphics, moving image, video, and animation. It generally involves some form of interactivity, which distinguishes it from simple video productions. It is fast becoming integral to our daily lives, with the advent of interactive digital TV, advanced mobile phones, wireless PDAs, touch-screen information kiosks, Internet-enabled pay-phones, DVD Video, and DVD-ROM. Designers are increasingly involved with the continuing growth of interactive technology.

The CD-ROM, once hailed as the replacement for the printed book, introduced the concept of interactive multimedia products for the mass market. Publishing houses ventured into this new medium with re-workings of existing texts, but after a brief honeymoon found little success. It became obvious that reading on screen was not the 'killer application' for the technology. DVD has secured a much stronger market identity partly due to its focus on entertainment – although it doesn't hurt that the disc goes in a box under the TV rather than a personal computer. Unlike CD-ROM, DVD is a truly rich medium that provides high-quality playback of video and music, with extra features such as user interaction as standard.

The most widespread, but currently least interactive, form of multimedia is television graphics (advertising, trailers, title sequences, and weather charts), produced using digital technology but at present mainly delivered by analog transmission while digital TV services catch up. The ubiquity and diversity of television gives the digital graphic designer a wide range of creative opportunities, and by its transitory nature also encourages experimentation and innovation. Design has flourished in the information screens and kiosks found in banks, airports, museums, in-store points, stations, and public spaces. Unlike their hard-copy counterparts, information kiosks can be updated easily, and hold large amounts of information. Moving images and animation add to their interest and entertain the viewer.

Artists have adopted multimedia as a new medium for self-expression, from on-site exhibition installations to Internet delivery. The internationally acclaimed video artist Bill Viola has a respected 'tradition' of

PART 03. DESIGN FOR SCREEN

CHAPTER TWO

DESIGN FOR MULTIMEDIA

Right: **Touch-screen information kiosks, such as this example from the National Portrait Gallery in London, can offer a plentiful choice of media for the viewer. Illustrations, graphics, and video can be rendered quickly and efficiently with dedicated hardware. The constraints for the multimedia designer are far fewer in number than they are for those in web publishing.**
Design by Cognitive Applications, UK

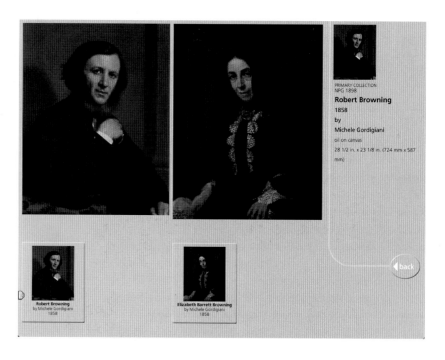

PRIMARY COLLECTION
NPG 1898
Robert Browning
1858
by
Michele Gordigiani
oil on canvas
28 1/2 in. x 23 1/8 in. (724 mm x 587 mm)

Robert Browning
by Michele Gordigiani
1858

Elizabeth Barrett Browning
by Michele Gordigiani
1858

back

embracing new media and technology in his work. The web artist Barminski exploits the full power of sound and animation to present his idiosyncratic view of popular culture using Macromedia's Shockwave.

We exist in an environment where our senses are constantly bombarded with sounds, words, and images. Designers, artists, and developers are responsible for the many forms of information and entertainment that we experience, but must constantly reset their working parameters to keep abreast of new developments. Multimedia designers may well be musicians, fine artists, film- and video-makers, writers, or editors. Graphic designers especially, however, find that their visual language, together with their experience in managing words and images, provides them with an excellent basis for multimedia work.

Below: **Multimedia means the designer is free to create a high-quality sensory experience using dynamic video and audio. Large, high-resolution moving images such as this are impractical to transmit over the Internet, but will not tax the relatively huge data capacity of a DVD disc.**
Design by Tomato Interactive, UK

MULTIMEDIA AND WEB DESIGN – THE DIFFERENCES
Much of the technology used to create multimedia projects is similar to that used to create webpages, but there is one major difference. Multimedia work is not constrained by the limitations of the Internet.

Unlike the Internet, in which the all-important download time is reliant on the unpredictable speed of modems, broadband connections, and web servers, multimedia – whether in the form of a DVD-ROM or a touch-screen museum installation – is only limited by the speed the computer reads the information from the disc. The advantages of this are clear. First, the viewer gets 'real time' playing, with no jerkiness in video playback or lack of responsiveness in interaction; second, far larger file sizes are permissible, enabling a greater range and quality of content. Video and audio are notoriously storage- and bandwidth-hungry, but a DVD can deliver CD-quality stereo – even full surround sound – and better-than-TV-quality video, impossible to stream over most people's Internet connections.

REAL TIME PLAYING
'Real time' playing has to be qualified: the speed at which video can be played from a DVD-ROM or from the computer's hard drive depends on the processing power and internal architecture of the machine, factors which also affect the responsiveness of interactive elements. Today's personal computers, however, have reached a point where multimedia designers are barely limited by performance constraints. With the vast majority of systems now easily capable of playing full-screen video at 25 frames per second, choices regarding video quality and compression are more likely to be influenced by the 4.7Gb capacity of single-layer

recordable DVD media. Even this is rapidly being rendered obsolete by dual layer technology, and discs with much greater capacity are only a few years away. Nonetheless, where multimedia is to be delivered to end users' machines (rather than displayed at fixed kiosk points), it is vital to cater for the broadest audience possible. The continuing growth in computer ownership partly reflects the increased availability of low-cost consumer models which often cut corners in areas such as graphics processing. In this respect the multimedia designer faces some of the same issues as web designers.

THE POINT OF DELIVERY
Multimedia is often delivered over a closed network using a powerful central computer to send the work to smaller satellite machines. This is much more efficient than using the Internet, because data is transferred across a high-bandwidth local area network (LAN) – whether cabled or wireless – rather than meandering around the Internet. This kind of set-up can be used for 'Intranet' systems (web-style pages distributed only within a company), company data, training workshops, in-store information points, and similar restricted environments.

Multimedia products usually offer a broader, richer, and more expanded range of outcomes than web products, which by their very nature are anchored to the more stifling constraints of the Internet. Interactive television, although barely out of its infancy and currently burdened by low screen resolution, provides a particularly exciting prospect for multimedia designers over the next few years.

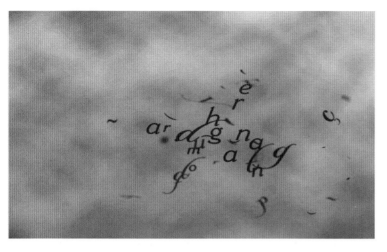

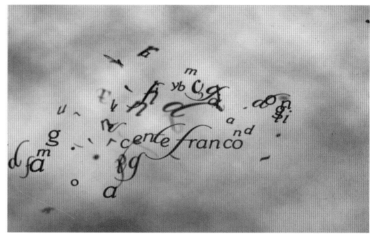

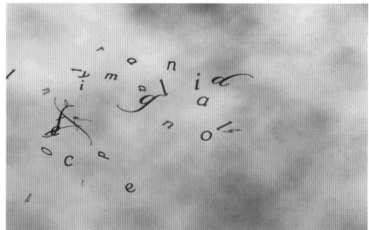

Above: InterStitch created this title sequence for the feature documentary *Daughter from Danang*. In the film, a grown woman flies from America to Vietnam to reunite with her lost family and culture.

The title sequence bridges that journey with animated letterforms which blow through clouds and sky. Each letter was animated individually in Adobe After Effects and then composited with an environment of digitally created clouds and wind.
Design by InterStitch, USA

This page: The *Sunday Times* is probably the bulkiest of the British Sunday newspapers, but one of its colour supplements is only the size of a CD-ROM. *The Month* contains interviews, features, listings, reviews, and promotions, all laid out in a style matching the paper's other sections. Hyperlinks to web content enable users to access extra material and order featured products. With a print run of over 1.5 million, this is multimedia for the mass market, and content is formatted to work on the widest possible range of home computers.

Design by Mook, UK

Sonic © Sega

THE DESIGN PROCESS The multimedia design process is by definition diverse, and the designer has to adopt many roles. Working through ideas and concepts on paper is useful, and defining the project parameters is essential. Many multimedia prototypes are very complex with the integration of sound, moving image, video, and graphics presenting the designer with a formidable challenge.

Almost without exception, multimedia models are non-linear, that is, they present an interface to the user that is composed of multiple choice options and paths to select. A well-designed navigation structure will significantly improve the enjoyment and accessibility of a piece of work. Good navigation design is an artform in itself and certainly should not be undervalued. The problems associated with user boredom, characteristic of web publishing, are not so prevalent in multimedia work. It is assumed that a potential audience will be more focused and, as the medium delivers a quicker response to user interaction, not need to wait so long for on-screen content. This distinctive quality of CD-ROM multimedia products should be balanced against the fact that they are less easy to update than webpages.

HIGH EXPECTATIONS

Client expectation can present problems for the designer. The nature of multimedia allows for a rich and varied content, but the time and cost in preparing this content can be significant. So how does a designer positively engage the client whilst at the same time highlighting the potential pitfalls and limitations of the medium? Clients who are not fully conversant with the scope of the medium often anticipate an 'all singing, all dancing' product. One solution is to present a scaled range of product levels, offering the necessary graphics, navigation structure, and production methods necessary to complete the work to a satisfactory standard for a lower budget. A menu of additional options, such as more video, larger-format video, and more animation

and sound can then be offered. The onus is then on clients to balance their expectations with project budgets. Providing a demonstration of a range of options will be very helpful in this process.

If a designer is part of a large organization with access to many technical resources, many of these issues are more-easily solved. The 'internal' client may well be aware of the possibilities and options available from the start. For the freelance designer there is a more challenging task, as all the resources will have to be independently sourced. This is why many multimedia designers build up contact lists of programmers, video editors, and sound designers to call upon. This aspect alone encourages an interdependent approach to multimedia design processes. Designers can increase their skills and expertise by working in a 'design community', sharing their knowledge and learning from others. This makes for a very exciting and challenging career shift for many designers switching from traditional print and publishing backgrounds.

AUTHORING APPLICATIONS AND THEIR ROLES In the professional market, Macromedia Director is well established as the dominant authoring package. It allows the designer to manipulate sound, graphics, moving image, and video in a single editing environment without the need for further plug-ins. Director uses Lingo, its own powerful scripting language, for complex 'behind-the-scenes' programming actions that provide a rich resource for user interaction.

DIRECTOR

Macromedia Director uses a metaphor of a theatre production, comprising a 'stage', 'cast members', and a 'score'. For designers this is an excellent format, as it demystifies what is potentially a complex workspace. The screen functions as a stage upon which the designer can directly place cast members from a database of elements (graphics, sound, video, etc). The cast are then orchestrated within the score – a multi-layered traditional animation timeline – to animate frame by frame. Cast members become 'sprites' when they are placed on the stage, leaving their original files untouched in the cast database. Sprites can be modified on the stage without increasing the file size of the finished movie. They can be animated, resized, made transparent, and scripted to perform and respond to user interaction using Lingo. To appeal to programmers with experience in the web market, Director has also gained a JavaScript-style scripting language.

Finished productions can be made into stand-alone cross-platform presentations delivered using a 'projector' program. The projector launches the Director movie, which can be set to fill the whole screen for a TV-like experience.

Used effectively, Director can provide a complete digital production solution for multimedia CD-ROM, DVD, and touch-screen installations. In web publishing, Director is used by online games developers who exploit its option to export projects in Shockwave movies, played back using browser plug-ins. Equally, multimedia developers use Flash to produce material for projects not destined for the Web.

Macromedia actively encourages a web community of third-party developers who test, share, and expand Director. They, in turn, have helped it to become extremely versatile for integration with other formats such as Adobe's PDF, Apple's QuickTime, and HTML. For example, a CD-ROM production could include a 'live link' to a website or have the option to open and view PDF files while the Director movie is running on the user's computer in the background.

AFTER EFFECTS AND ITS RIVALS

Adobe After Effects is the traditional market leader in broadcast-quality composite digital video production. It now exists in a competitive market which has seen the cost of video compositing and special effects fall dramatically. Using the latest Macs and PCs, real-time editing can be achieved in software without investing in high-priced hardware add-ons. Other compositing titles include Pinnacle Commotion Pro, Discreet Combustion, Boris Red, and Apple Shake. General purpose video editing programs including Adobe Premiere and Apple Final Cut Pro, along with video-based animation tools such as Apple Motion, can also be used to edit content for multimedia presentations.

Graphics, sound, music, and video can be imported and edited to create a layered composition which can be exported in any of the popular video playback formats or exported to a professional video post-production system, such as Avid's Media 100, for further manipulation. After Effects can also use a range of Photoshop plug-in filters to apply effects and transitions.

This type of software is frequently used to create title sequences for TV and multimedia presentations. Although mainly non-interactive, it can be exported for web use and include some interactive elements.

Left and above: **Director provides a complete multimedia authoring environment. A wide range of input formats is supported, including DVD Video, and productions can be output for both Mac and Windows platforms from the same files. A new scripting language with syntax similar to JavaScript makes Director's advanced capabilities accessible to a wider range of creative professionals.**

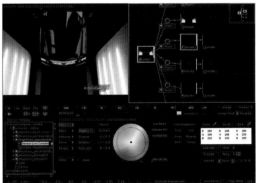

Left: **While Flash's efficient vector-based graphics are ideal for online work, audio and video can also be integrated into Flash movies and enhanced with interactive elements and links. The results can be stored at high quality for playback within off-line multimedia presentations.**

Above: **Discreet Combustion is one of a growing number of sophisticated compositing programs which, while not specifically designed for interactive work, can bring new depths of richness to all kinds of multimedia presentations.**

chapter 02. design for multimedia 173

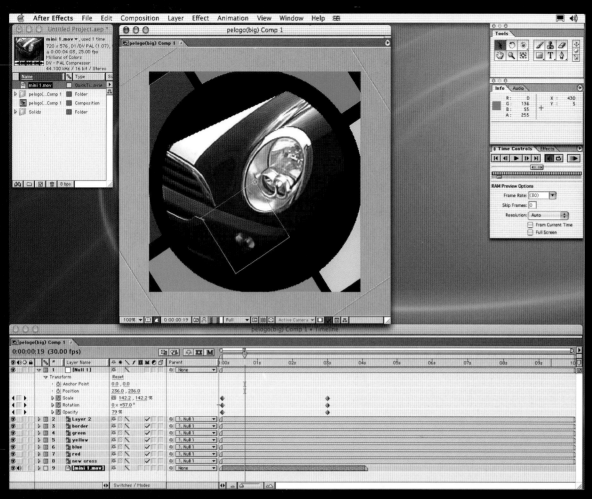

Left and above left: **Adobe After Effects** is a video compositing application that provides tools for manipulating layered video clips in conjunction with graphic and text elements. It is used extensively in video post-production for animated trailers, title sequences, and any project that requires the merging of video and animated graphics in a dynamic way. Keyframes control each element in the composition, allowing the user to specify position size, opacity, and a vast number of other attributes at any point in time. After Effects then calculates the values of these parameters for every other frame, a process known as 'tweening'.

part 03. design for screen

PLANNING AND PRODUCTION Multimedia planning and production can be loosely divided into two stages. Initially, as with both paper-based media and web design, there must be co-ordination of content, design, and production resources. The production phase then includes rigorous testing to ensure the product functions correctly on whichever platform or platforms it is to be delivered to.

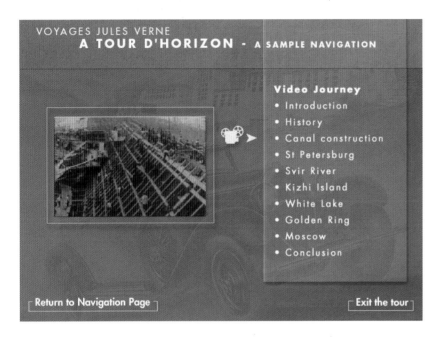

Above: a screen from a promotional CD-ROM for Voyages Jules Verne Travel. The re-purposing of existing promotional or advertising material, supplied by a company, can be effectively implemented into a multimedia production. Posters, photographs, and video can be re-edited with Adobe Photoshop and Premier to sit within a new production.
Design by Phil Taylor and Phil Jackson, UK

Multimedia projects are generally large undertakings, with many unforeseen issues unfolding during the production and authoring stages. It is essential to establish a fixed price for the initial design and concept stage, then build in a tiered fee structure to cover production costs dictated by any revised expectations or supplementary requirements of the client. Sub-contracting is commonplace and should be thoroughly researched and planned. For example, using advanced Lingo scripting in Director will often require out-sourced programming expertise, even for the experienced Director user.

The fact that relevant content may be available in an existing format does not mean it can be incorporated into a new multimedia project at negligible cost. Converting or 're-purposing' content can be a time-consuming and expensive process. Text usually presents few problems, as it can be easily stripped from existing documents and reformatted. Images originally scanned for print can be resized, converted to RGB and compressed. Video may need to be digitized from analog sources, and even if it exists in digital format will require transcoding and recompression according to the distribution medium. Where video content exists on an earlier digital product, such as an interactive CD, the original uncompressed files will need to be sourced for conversion. Despite advances in technology, video is one area where processing on desktop computers is likely to be a laborious affair.

TEST! TEST! TEST!

Testing is absolutely vital for multimedia productions. Web publishing has its challenges, with varying browsers and monitor resolutions, but multimedia for mass distribution has all these and more. A typical DVD-ROM will have to function on computers with different specifications of hardware on varying revisions of operating system software and be compatible with third-party applications.

The choice of video format (such as QuickTime or AVI) and codec (the specific algorithm used to compress and play back the video stream) affects file size, compatibility, and playback performance. Not all machines are equipped to play back video in all formats without the user adding new software. The developer should first consider player architecture: Windows Media, Apple QuickTime, and RealMedia each have their own merits and installed base of users. Beyond this, the choice of codec will be influenced by the video image quality required, any restrictions on file size imposed by the capacity of the media, and likely playback performance on users' systems.

Broad compatibility is one of the most sought-after goals in multimedia. Although PCs represent the largest market, the many cross-platform tools and technologies available make Mac compatibility relatively easy to achieve. Professional developers often have a testing room set aside with a range of older machines – of both platforms and varying specifications – to test a product for flaws and conflicts.

CASE HISTORY

WOODWARD PORTRAIT EXPLORER
NATIONAL PORTRAIT GALLERY, LONDON

The Woodward Portrait Explorer is a permanent touch-screen installation designed by Cognitive Applications, based in the UK and the US. The Portrait Explorer system extends the approach of the acclaimed Micro Gallery guide in the National Gallery, in London.

The installation functions primarily as an informative guide for visitors to the gallery, with insights into thousands of works of art in the collection, video interviews with artists, and many other interactive features.

Designing a multimedia system for public use, such as in a gallery, requires careful planning and execution. Typically, an interface design will employ visual metaphors as navigational icons. Presenting a 'human' interface is critical to the usability of the multimedia system. With web design the interface has to exist within the constraints of browser configurations and limitations, and can be altered by the end-user. Touch-screen installations run directly from a hard drive or CD and so permit greater control for the developer. This requires the application of considered and tested design concepts. For example, if the design calls for finger/touch interaction to activate a cursor instead of a mouse, larger buttons will be needed on the screen. The familiar metaphor of 'push-buttons' with drop shadows may seem out-moded in today's computer-driven design, but in an established, traditional gallery setting they may be critical in ensuring that the system is accessible and user-friendly to a wider public.

Rory Mathews, the Design Director at Cognitive Applications, UK, considered three important questions before designing the museum installation:

* What is the subject matter?
* What environment will the system be seen in?
* What are the aims of the system?

The most fundamental question concerning the Portrait Explorer system was, 'What, in essence, is an art gallery about?' The answer to this was, 'To provide an environment in which to present works of art, and to allow the opportunity for the visitor to expand their knowledge through exposure and education'. The system would need to accommodate a wide range of people and not exclude anyone within the 'typical visitor' profile, which does not really exist in a large, open-access public space. An interactive multimedia system would need to be in tune with this environment and aligned to these aims. The Portrait Explorer system was designed to offer a refined interface that achieved these aims through an exhaustive reappraisal of the objectives during the design process.

THE MAIN SUCCESFUL CHARACTERISTICS OF THE SYSTEM

* The system has its own visual identity, but complements the character of the museum and its collection.
* The system's graphic design, interface design, and technology are designed to be as easy to use as possible for the ordinary user.
* The design does not compromise the integrity of the works of art by gratuitous use of animation or image manipulation.
* The design will always be complementary and sub-ordinate to the works of art discussed in the system.
* Because the system is designed without modish design or technological gimmicks it will not become dated quickly.

A visitor to the National Portrait Gallery can enrich their experience greatly through interacting with the Portrait Explorer system. Through the considered use of animation, video, and image manipulation, Cognitive Applications have built a successful, interactive experience.

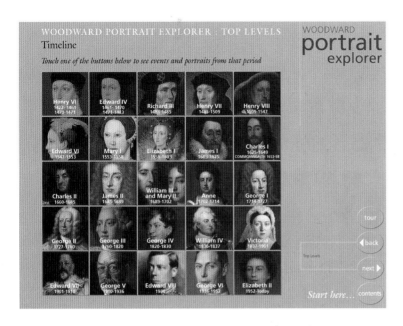

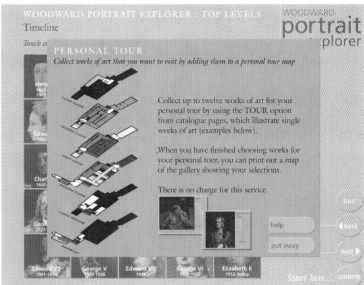

These screen shots demonstrate the careful planning necessary to produce an involved project such as the Woodward Portrait Explorer. The aim of any ambitious site-specific multimedia installation is to complement the museum's collection and enrich the visitor's experience. The Woodward Portrait Explorer succeeded in this by offering a varied mix of educational, informative, and entertaining stimuli with which the viewer can interact.

Computer and video game graphics have come a long way since 'Pong'. Visually, the 1972 gaming pioneer made do with two white rectangular 'bats' and a square white 'ball', on a plain black background. Created in the days before microprocessors, its graphics were hardwired by an engineer.

Today, however, game development is a global creative industry employing tens of thousands of writers, musicians, game designers, and artists. User-friendly professional tools have enabled non-engineers to create the vast amount of visual content required for a state-of-the-art title, in high-resolution and millions of colours – using many of the same techniques as conventional, non-interactive graphic designers and fine artists.

Game development is a highly team-orientated industry with people from all technical disciplines working together over a long period of time to bring a game from concept to final production. Often, a team will be split evenly between the three departments of art, programming, and game design, with a single producer in overall charge, though the divisions vary massively depending on the game. Each department within the team will function as a tightly-knit unit, with individuals assigned their own areas of focus or specialization.

A single artist famed in a different field – comic-book art, for example, or film design – is very occasionally brought in to a game project as a 'star' attraction, and will probably contribute their work independently of the team; but it is extremely rare to see one person given any sort of headline credit for a game, especially on the art side.

There are some basic technical specializations within most game development art departments – but it is important for any artist to be flexible, and to at least have an understanding of the other elements which together make up the finished graphics. Broadly, there are four areas of game art: conceptual, 2D, 3D, and animation.

Conceptual artwork will be sketched in the earliest stages of a game's development to establish the basic look of characters and environments, and later it will be fleshed out in detail to storyboard in-game sequences or cinematic 'cutscenes'.

PART 03. DESIGN FOR SCREEN

CHAPTER THREE

DESIGN FOR GAMES

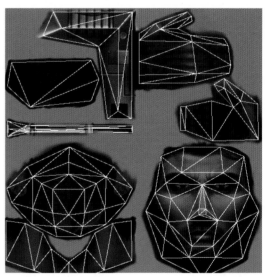

This character model from Epic's *Unreal* shows the unique difficulties that artists face when working with 3D. Although there are some applications that allow you to paint directly onto a 3D model, most 3D graphics are created as 'skins' that are then wrapped around the 3D model. Flattened skins look very odd, and it can take an untrained eye a while to work out how the graphic will look on the model. Luckily, there are applications available that show the model updated in real time as you work on the flat graphic.

Below: **Today's games for the PC, Mac, and TV-based consoles present almost photo-realistic immersive worlds containing thousands of scenes, objects and characters that must each be** modelled in three dimensions. As with a movie, the design of authentic buildings, clothing, vehicles, weapons and accessories is painstakingly researched.
Design by Activision, USA / Aspyr

Above: **User interface design is as important to many games as the action. In The Sims 2, graphic icons depict characters' thoughts, giving players insight into their behaviour (as well as amusement).**
Design by Maxis, USA / Electronic Arts

'Finished' 2D work is required for the creation of on-screen display elements (scores, meters, indicators, and icons), or menu-based interface screens. Very recently, Flash has become a viable cross-platform development environment for this kind of 'front end' work. Generally, though, 2D images are created and manipulated in a graphics editing package such as Adobe Photoshop. This is certainly the tool most often used for the creation of the fundamental building-blocks of contemporary game graphics: 2D textures, which will be overlaid onto flat polygons in the game's 3D-rendered world.

Although there are a small number of popular modern titles which don't create a fully-3D game space, they are very much in the minority. Hardware advances over the past seven or eight years have resulted in the normalization of this once-revolutionary approach.

Technical challenges still abound, however, and any 3D artist has to work strictly within the confines established by the game 'engine' written by the programming team. This will determine, for example, how many individual polygons can be used to build any particular character or object, without affecting the game's performance.

The most prevalent professional tools for 3D and animation work are Discreet's 3D Studio Max, NewTek's LightWave, and Maya from Alias. Using any of these packages, artists have total modelling control over every detail of the landscapes, architecture, objects, and characters that populate today's interactive 3D worlds – totally immersive 'virtual realities' undreamed of by those first 'Pong' players a few decades ago.

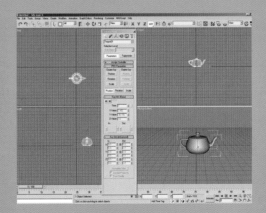

Left: **Discreet's 3D Studio Max is the world's best-selling 3D animation and modelling package. It is used for a wide variety of purposes, from movie animation to architectural design, but is notably popular among game developers.**

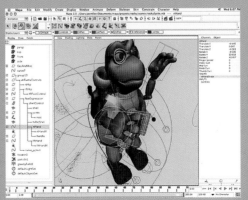

Left: **Maya, from Alias, is very widely used in game development and is also prominent in the fields of film and broadcast television. The package's power, speed, and flexibility are reflected in a hefty price tag, but a free 'learning edition' allows designers to experiment with the software before committing to a purchase.**

TYPE
COLOUR
IMAGE

Type is one of the graphic designer's core tools. With attention to detail, the designer can use type to communicate appropriately, to suggest mood and character, and to contribute to page or surface layout dynamics. However, type does need to be handled with care and understanding.

Designers should not only have an appreciation of the aesthetic values of type (see Part 1, Design Basics), but also know how type is stored, controlled, and output digitally. All these issues have a direct bearing on how type is printed and displayed on screen.

A typeface is an alphabet (along with numerals and punctuation) considered as a designed or aesthetic visual entity. A font is a collection of letterforms in that typeface, and is stored in one file on the computer. One font may contain the alphabet in upper and lower case, with related numerals and punctuation, plus any number of alternative or additional characters and symbols (see page 48). Several fonts will be required to use a typeface effectively for text setting, typically including at least italic, bold, and bold-italic variants. Many typefaces are available as 'families' of several dozen fonts.

Font-related issues are among the most common causes of problems when collaborating on documents with other users, sending desktop publishing files to press, and even keeping the designer's own system running smoothly. The following brief overview should help to clear up any confusion and avoid the potential pitfalls.

PART 04. TYPE/COLOUR/IMAGE

CHAPTER ONE

TYPE

áéèüöçôåñ˘

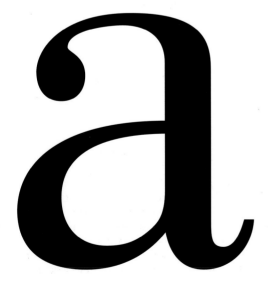

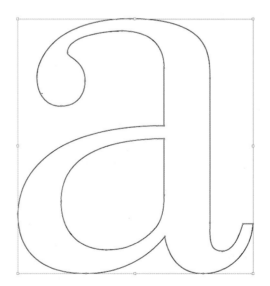

Above: The common accents used in most Latin alphabets can be obtained on the Mac by pressing Option plus another key before typing the character that you want to accent. For example, to place a circumflex over an e (ê), hold down Option and press i, then let go of Option and type e. The keys to generate accents are identified by a white outline in *Keyboard Viewer* (see opposite, top).

Left: Every character in a font is decribed by a set of vectors, its 'outline' description.

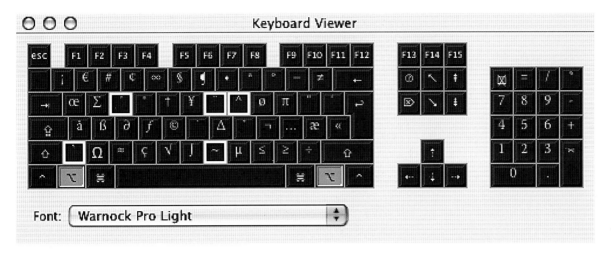

BITMAPS AND VECTORS

Letterform information can be stored digitally in bitmap or vector form. Bitmap data – effectively a black-and-white image – is fine for screen display at a fixed size, but gives a 'pixellated' appearance when scaled up. Vector or 'outline' descriptions of each character provide scalable forms which can be displayed and printed at any size, provided that the computer or printer has the means to 'rasterize' the outlines to a bitmap (all screen or printer output is ultimately bitmapped). The outlines are filled with black or whatever colour you choose for the text.

In the early days of scalable type on desktop computers – dating from the launch of PostScript in 1985 – the processing power was not available to rasterize outline fonts 'on the fly' for screen display. Instead, characters were represented on screen by bitmapped fonts in a fixed range of sizes, and outline fonts substituted on printing. This meant that what you saw on screen often bore little resemblance to what appeared on paper. Later, outline fonts could be rendered on screen using Adobe Type Manager (ATM).

Today, font display is handled by the computer's operating sytem, whether OS X or Windows. (Users with obsolete versions of these will still need ATM.) You can be sure that, with very few accidental exceptions, the shapes and positions of the characters you see on screen in your page layouts will be precisely reproduced when you print.

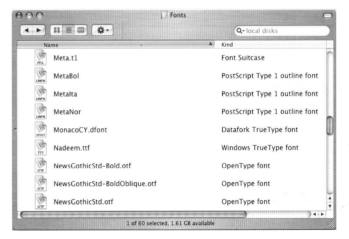

Above and left: Font files on the Mac are identified in *Finder* windows by their icon and 'Kind' attribute. PostScript fonts traditionally comprise an outline file for each instance along with a 'suitcase' of bitmaps for the set, although Mac OS X can recognize the outline files, and render them on screen and in print without the bitmaps present. Double-clicking a compatible font file shows a visual preview of the font. An option to install it appears if the font is not already installed.

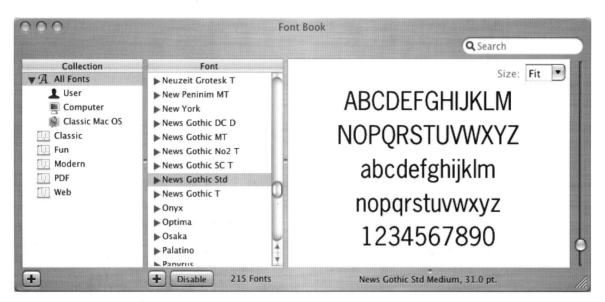

Left: Mac OS X includes the Font Book utility to help install, organize, and manage your fonts. It can be found in the *Applications* folder. Fonts within OS X can be installed and turned on and off; fonts can also be added to Classic from here, but they can only be managed from within Classic.

Designers producing materials for the screen, such as web graphics, have different concerns. At small sizes, the area into which a letterform is to be rasterised may contain only a few pixels. Using anti-aliasing (see page 187, top right), a fair impression can be given of the shape, but the character will be fuzzy, and text set this way is hard to read. Bitmapped fonts, designed for on-screen use at a fixed size, are a better choice when text is set as a graphic at small sizes (this is also why operating systems have an option to anti-alias the fonts used for labels and buttons only above a certain size). For headings and other large text, an outline font rendered with anti-aliasing is ideal.

Below left: To install fonts under Windows XP, open the *Control Panel* from the *Start* menu and choose *Fonts*, then go to *Install New Font* on the *File* menu. For PostScript Type 1 fonts, click the '.pfm' file.

Below right: Some pairs of characters do not sit comfortably together. Type designers set up 'kerning pairs' – sometimes hundreds per font – to adjust the trickier combinations, but you will always need to fix a few instances yourself using manual kerning.

POSTSCRIPT TYPE 1 FONTS

PostScript, Adobe's page description language, can be used to store any kind of vector graphic from a simple shape to the structure of a complete page layout. Fonts for professional use, particularly with Macs, traditionally contain outlines in this language, and more specifically in a format known as Type 1. PostScript Type 1 fonts consist of two parts: a bitmap file for screen display, for the reasons explained earlier, and an outline file. (They may also have extra files with the extension '.afm' and/or '.inf'; these are rarely used by software.) Several bitmap files – contained in a 'suitcase' on the Mac – are usually supplied in different sizes. Older operating systems can use these to show characters on screen, and they will also be used if the outline file is missing. The outline font file is traditionally downloaded to the printer (which must have a

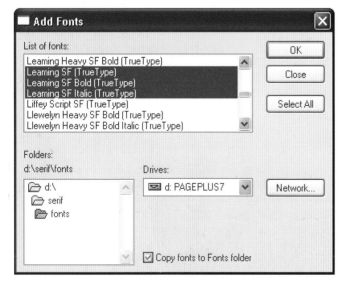

PostScript engine) to enable it to rasterize characters, but many applications now pre-rasterize their output in software, using the operating system's PostScript interpreter rather than the printer's. One advantage of this is that layouts can be output on non-PostScript printers; cheaper lasers, and almost all inkjets, fall into this category.

Although they contain the same information, Mac and PC PostScript font files are not interchangeable – you need the right ones for your computer platform.

TRUETYPE

TrueType is a rival format to PostScript which was adopted as a standard by both Microsoft and Apple, although it only really caught on with Windows users. A TrueType rasterizer is built into both Macintosh and Windows operating systems. TrueType fonts are held in a single file which can contain variants such as regular, italic, bold, and bold italic. From Mac OS 8.5 onwards, Macs can use the same TrueType file format as PCs, with the extension '.ttf' or '.ttc'. However, Macs also have their own TrueType format, '.dfont', which is not compatible with Windows.

OPENTYPE

OpenType, a relatively new font format from Adobe and Microsoft, can contain TrueType and PostScript data, and works on both Macs and PCs. OpenType fonts have the extension '.otf'. Despite the undoubted benefits, such as the inclusion of extended character sets and alternative glyphs (see page 48) in a single font file, so many pre-OpenType fonts exist that adoption of the new standard can only proceed fairly slowly. Significantly, though, Apple is supporting it and supplies OpenType fonts with the Mac OS.

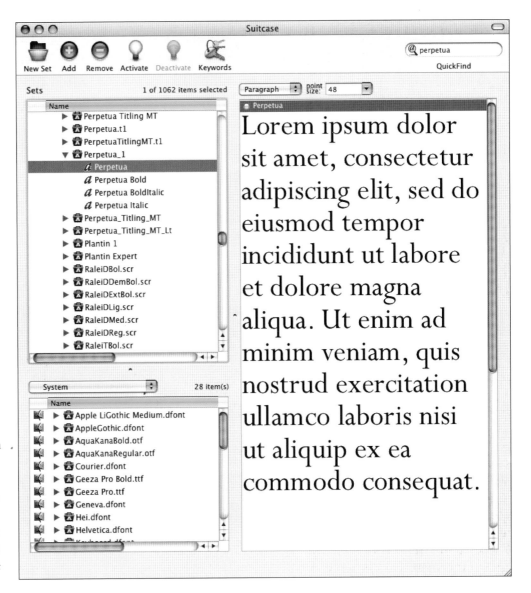

MULTIPLE MASTER FONTS

Multiple Master fonts, developed by Adobe, contain several sets of outlines that represent either end of up to four 'design axes': weight, width, style, and optical size. Using a software utility, designers can create custom fonts by choosing points between these extremes. The result is not a distortion of the original letterforms but a newly generated font. Sadly, only a few Multiple Master fonts have appeared, and they are not directly supported in either Windows or the Mac OS.

WHERE ARE MY FONTS?

TrueType and Type 1 fonts can be installed and used on the same system and even within the same page. To avoid confusion, it is safest not to install the same font in more than one format. When using PostScript Type 1 fonts, always make sure you have the outline font as well as the bitmap. In general, you should stick to Type 1 fonts in documents that are to be

Above: Font management software such as Extensis Suitcase can help rationalize the large number of fonts likely to be found on a designer's system. User-defined 'sets' arrange fonts by type, usage, client, or job. Sets or individual fonts can be activated and de-activated as required, rather than having a huge number constantly installed, which can slow down the system and cause conflicts between copies of the same font. Some of this functionality, however, is now built into Mac OS X and, to a lesser extent, Windows.

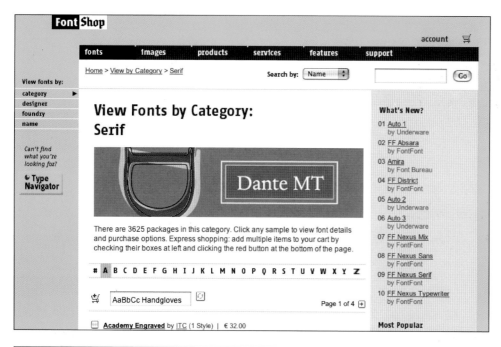

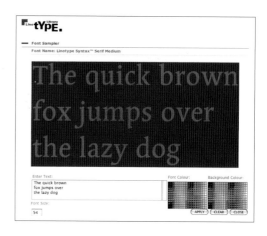

Above: Most sites include a facility to try a few words of your choice in any font. Linotype's has the option of setting foreground and background colours to check legibility.

Above: The World Wide Web is a great place to shop for fonts. Most leading suppliers have excellent e-commerce sites where you can browse thousands of typefaces. Any fonts you choose to buy can be downloaded immediately.

sent for commercial printing, but TrueType and OpenType fonts are increasingly accepted by prepress equipment.

In Windows, installed fonts are normally stored in the Fonts folder inside the Windows folder on the main hard disk, although they can be kept elsewhere. In Mac OS X, fonts are normally only available for use if they are stored in one of four Library folders, depending on whether they are essential system fonts; to be used by everyone with access to the Mac; only for one named user; or stored on a network server. A built-in utility called Font Book makes this clearer than it

sounds, and also allows installed fonts to be turned on and off. Fonts used in OS X's Classic mode, which provides access to OS 9 for older programs, are stored in the Fonts folder inside the OS 9 System Folder.

FONT PROBLEMS

Font problems are less common than they used to be, but graphic designers are particularly prone to them, simply because they tend to have more fonts and do more with them than other users.

'Jagged' type on screen is caused by missing PostScript outline files; try using Find (Mac OS) or Search (Windows) to see if they have simply ended up in the wrong folder. With older systems, another possible cause is that ATM is switched off.

When you click the Italic or Bold button in software, the result may be that the selected text is reset in the corresponding italic or bold font, which is correct. If no such font is present, though, or if (in the case of Type 1 fonts) the software does not know which file it is, then all that happens is that the ordinary letterforms are either slanted to simulate italic or offset for bold. Not only are these effects unsightly, but they may not print. To be safe, choose the italic or bold version of the font from the font menu, unless it is a TrueType font which has them in a single file.

jaggies

jaggies

Anti-aliased font   Bitmap font

Above: Anti-aliasing creates a smoother impression when vector outlines are rendered as a bitmap. It is particularly effective at small sizes, but on screen these are better handled by carefully created bitmap fonts, which appear sharper.

Above: 'Jaggies' is the name given to to the crude pixellated rendering of type on screen which occurs when bitmapped fonts are enlarged. Smooth results are obtained when working from the outline information in OpenType, PostScript, or TrueType fonts.

Some fonts may not be listed alphabetically where you expect, usually because their makers have added a variant prefix, as in 'I Bodoni Italic', or a foundry name, as in 'ITC Garamond'.

If you open a previously laid-out document and find text looks wrong or has moved, there are two possible causes. Either you do not have the correct font installed, and the software has substituted another; or you have more than one version of the font, perhaps from different makers, and the wrong one is active. Sort this out before editing the document.

When you send a job to a bureau or printer, always include the fonts, either by embedding them, if using PDF, or by sending all of the necessary font files with the document and image files. The latter route is technically an infringement of copyright unless the contractor already owns the exact same font, but it is common practice and the font companies have never come up with a workable alternative.

Sometimes the the bureau or printer may report that a font is missing, even though you have no recollection of using it. A blank line or single character in a font – even a space – will throw up an error if that font is missing. Many programs let you check the fonts used in a document and switch any mis-styled characters to one of the fonts intentionally included.

FONT COPYRIGHT

Remember that fonts are protected by copyright law. When you 'buy' a font, you only acquire a licence to use it, usually on one to five computers. You should not pass fonts to friends, colleagues, or contractors. It is very common practice to do so for one-off jobs where it would be uneconomical for everyone in the production chain to buy their own copy, but you should be aware that there is no legal protection for this. Embedding fonts in PDFs largely obviates the problem.

IMPROVING TYPE ON SCREEN

Good digital typeface designers tweak the 'hinting' in their fonts to help computers rasterize characters clearly and accurately at low resolutions. The quality of hinting varies greatly between fonts, but some are sold specifically as being optimized for use at the relatively low resolution of the monitor. Ideally the weight, width, spacing, and stroke variation should all be considered in this light, as well as the hinting.

When you rasterize type in a program such as Photoshop, you can choose between different anti-aliasing methods – for example, Smooth or Crisp – to tweak the appearance of the resulting letterforms. This option should not be overlooked when setting type as graphics for website navigation and headlines.

The future of type in on-screen media could lie in a system such as Bitstream's TrueDoc. This allows fonts to be embedded in multimedia content, and rasterizes them to the screen using 'subpixel' technology, which noticeably improves sharpness and accuracy. At present, however, there is little sign of any such system being adopted as the norm.

04.02

The appropriate and emotive use of colour is integral to the competence of the digital graphic designer. In our consumer-led, information-rich, entertainment-orientated society, the designer must understand thoroughly both the nature of colour and the way in which it works in order to use it effectively.

There are several reasons why the nature and the workings of colour are important (see also Part 1, Design Basics). First, when designing on screen with colour (and when screen colour is actually used in web and multimedia projects), that colour is transmitted directly from a white light source. However, when colour is reproduced through the use of printing inks, the colours are not transmitted but reflected. Crucially, the range of colours that can be printed with inks is smaller than and different from the range that can be created from white light on a computer monitor. So the final digital file, particularly one used for print, must contain reliable information about colour output.

PART 04. TYPE/COLOUR/IMAGE

CHAPTER TWO

COLOUR

WHERE DOES COLOUR COME FROM?

All colour comes from pure, white light. Most of us have seen light passed through a glass prism and split into the colours of the spectrum. The colours seen from the prism are transmitted directly onto the retina and are not reflected from any surface. The computer monitor is a source of artificial white light and the colours seen on a monitor are also transmitted directly onto the retina.

Since all the data that constructs computer imagery is digital, monitors need a method whereby all the colours of the spectrum can be quickly simulated. The method used displays only the three primary colours that make up white light, in a grid of pixels. By using up to 256 different intensity levels of each of the primary colours to display each pixel, it is possible to arrive at a total of 6.7 million colours (256 x 256 x 256). The three primary colours used are red, green, and blue, known as RGB for short. If we created products only for screen viewing, what we need to understand about primary colours could stop there. However, most designers also produce design for print, so they have to simulate colour through printing inks. Ink colours are perceived by the viewer through the reflection of light from the printed surface. The RGB primaries apply exclusively to transmitted light, and for reflected light we need a second set of three colours. These are cyan, magenta, and yellow, or CMY.

Right: The use of colour for decoration, symbolism, and communication is an integral part of every human culture.

Left: This powerful poster by Nicklaus Troxler shows how vibrant colours contribute to the verve of the subject matter and helps to delineate the composition.

Additive colour

This diagram represents Red, Green, and Blue light falling onto a white surface. Yellow is formed when Red and Green overlap because there is additional light in that area. When all three colours overlap, we see white since all the components of white light are now present.

Subtractive colour

Here, three primary subtractive coloured inks have been printed onto paper. Each of these colours has one of the additive primaries subtracted so, where two overlap, two primary colours are subtracted leaving only one of the primaries visible. Once all three subtractive colours overlap then all three components of white light are absorbed; no light escapes and black is perceived. In practice a small amount of light does get relected and a true black is not achievable using only Cyan, Magenta, and Yellow. To correct this printers use a fourth ink, Black, to create deep shadow areas necessary for good colour-image reproduction.

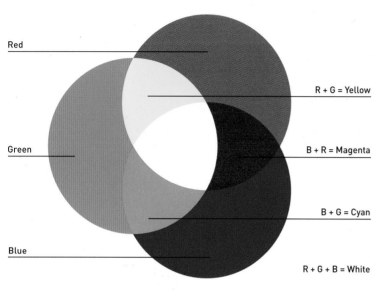

Red

R + G = Yellow

Green

B + R = Magenta

B + G = Cyan

Blue

R + G + B = White

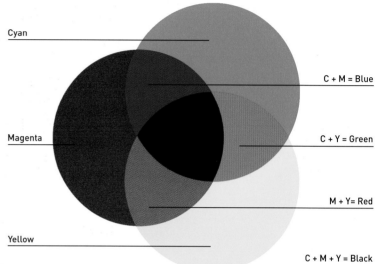

Cyan

C + M = Blue

Magenta

C + Y = Green

M + Y= Red

Yellow

C + M + Y = Black

TRANSMITTED OR ADDITIVE COLOUR

When one primary transmitted colour is combined with another, more light is perceived than with one colour alone. For this reason, red, green, and blue are referred to as the additive primary colours. All three colours add up to white. Thus, combining red light with green light, for instance, produces a colour that starts to approach white light (in fact, yellow). Similarly, a combination of red and blue produces magenta, and a combination of blue and green produces cyan. It will be seen that each primary additive (or transmitted) colour appears the way it does because each represents white light minus two primaries. Thus, for example, red is white light minus green and blue.

REFLECTED OR SUBTRACTIVE COLOUR

In our material world, everything we see has a particular colour because most matter absorbs white light (which we get, with varying degrees of purity, from sunlight and artificial light) to a greater or lesser extent. Black objects absorb all the white light that shines on them, whereas white objects reflect all the white light that hits them. What is generally understood to be an object's colour is, in reality, only the reflection of certain amounts of the three primary colours. It is a combination of these that is perceived and interpreted as a particular colour. For example, if an object appears red, it means that the material of which it is made is absorbing all the green and blue light, leaving only the red part of the spectrum to be reflected. Paints, inks and all other kinds of colouring pigment behave in the same way, by subtracting (absorbing) a certain amount of light and reflecting the rest.

Since pigments subtract colour from white light, it should be easy to see why red, green, and blue inks cannot be combined to mix colours for printing on white paper (which reflects the red, green, and blue that compose white light). Remembering that each primary additive colour is white light minus two other primaries, it should be clear that mixing any

Right: Photoshop's *Channels* palette shows how an image is composed in RGB or CMYK mode. On the right are the four channels of CMYK, which appear very much like the proofs taken from each lithographic printing plate. The channels displaying RGB are instantly recognizable by the areas of black in each channel which represent the absence of light. Note that the top images in these palettes are not channels themselves but provide a view of the combined channels.

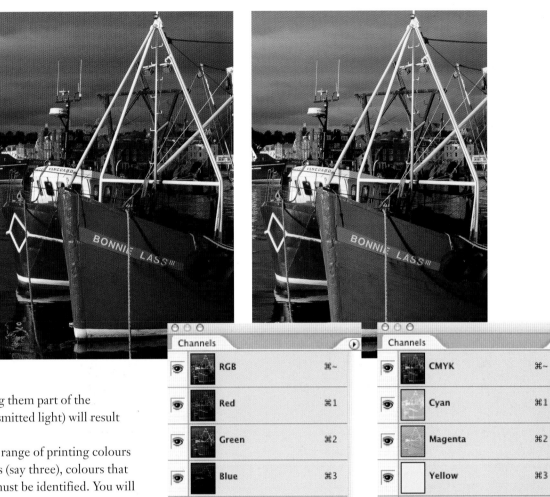

two primaries as pigments (making them part of the reflective surface rather than transmitted light) will result in colour being absorbed.

If the goal is to mix a wide range of printing colours from a small number of basic hues (say three), colours that absorb only one primary colour must be identified. You will recall that the secondary colours – cyan, magenta, and yellow – are each achieved by absorbing (subtracting) just one primary colour from white light. Similarly, mixing two secondary colours will absorb (subtract) two transmitted colours and leave the third. Thus, mixing cyan pigment with yellow pigment would produce green; mixing cyan with magenta would produce blue; and mixing magenta and yellow would produce red. All printing devices can therefore use cyan, magenta, and yellow as printing primary colours.

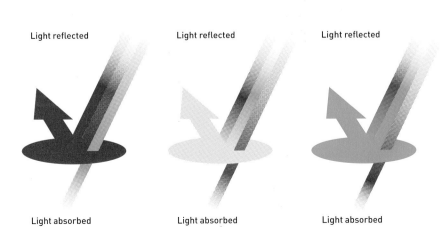

Light reflected   Light reflected   Light reflected

Light absorbed   Light absorbed   Light absorbed

RANGE OF ACHIEVABLE COLOUR Since the computer monitor generates white light, it is able to display virtually all the colours that the eye is capable of seeing. However, it is a fact of physics that (mirrors excepted) all objects absorb some light, even if only a very small amount. Thus the entire spectrum can never be reflected.

Above: Some of the brighter and subtler shades of colour will be lost when an image goes to CMYK printing. In these illustrations Photoshop's gamut warning is shown in green, revealing the shades that will be lost from the original RGB image when it ' printed in CMYK.

You may have noticed that the white of a computer screen is always so much brighter than the whitest of white printing papers. This is because paper does not reflect all the white light that falls on it. None of the many rich and vibrant pigments used in paints and inks can match the brilliance of the computer screen.

It is also impractical to use thousands of different coloured inks to reproduce coloured images. In printing, therefore, the three basic colours of cyan (C), magenta (M), and yellow (Y) are 'mixed' to simulate real-world colour as closely as possible. Black (K) ink is also added to boost shadow areas and make them crisper. Mixing is achieved by printing formations of tiny dots, each of a separate colour, that merge when viewed at reading distance. This method of reproduction is known as four-colour process (CMYK or just 'process'). The use of only cyan, magenta, yellow, and black thus produces a restricted range of vibrant colours known as process colours.

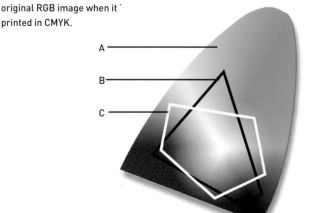

A
B
C

Left: The human eye is able to see a greater range of colour than either CMYK printing or RGB monitors are able to reproduce. Generally, more vibrant colours are available on screen than can be printed.

a = The visible spectrum
b = RGB monitor
c = CMYK process

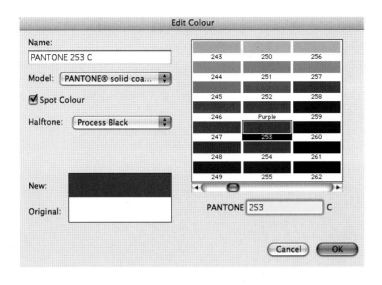

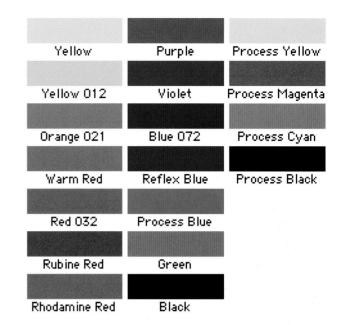

Above: It is absolutely vital that, when selecting colour from a palette in their graphic arts software, it is understood that (with the exception of pure Cyan) virtually all the PANTONE colours can be displayed on screen accurately, but they will not necessarily appear correctly when printed utilizing the four colour process method of CMYK.

PANTONE MATCHING SYSTEM

If a job only requires one or two colours, it would be unnecessary to run a four-colour press. A special colour of ink would be much more useful than a mix of cyan, magenta, yellow, and black. Many printers once held stocks of inks from a number of different ink manufacturers but, for practical reasons, the range of colours was somewhat limited. The PANTONE Matching System was devised to meet the needs of designers who want to specify a special colour. It is essentially a set of basic ingredients (standardized pigments) and a recipe book in the form of a colour sampler containing hundreds of colours that can be created by mixing the

specified amounts of the standardized pigments. By following these colour recipes, printers across the world can accurately mix and match any PANTONE colour from their basic stock and use it on their presses. The resulting colours are solid ink colours, known as spot colours or specials, and they are quite unlike the colours simulated by halftone dots in the four-colour printing process. Thanks to the stronger and wider range of pigments used, many PANTONE colour mixes can be more vivid and vibrant than those achievable using only cyan, magenta, yellow and black.

To give the digital graphic designer the widest range of colour choice, for print, almost all graphics arts software shows the full range of PANTONE colours as well as providing cyan, magenta, yellow and black (CMYK) controls for mixing process colours. The designer has the option of choosing either a PANTONE colour to be printed as a spot colour, or one to be simulated by cyan, magenta, yellow and black. Simulation can be successful but in many cases a good match cannot be achieved because the PANTONE colour is beyond the range achievable by the four-colour process (out of gamut).

Right: When a PANTONE colour is mixed according to the recipes shown on the swatch, it is *inks* that are being mixed to produce a single coloured ink. This is radically different from the simulation of a colour by the use of small dots of CMYK, which creates the illusion of colour change.

Left: Typical inkjet printer cartridges of black and CMYK. Some printers may have extra cartridges for pale cyan and pale magenta in order to increase the range of printed colour.

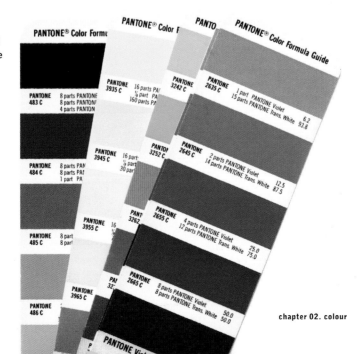

THE ATTRIBUTES OF COLOUR Whether colour is transmitted directly onto the retina or reflected from printed pigments, it has various attributes which can be measured and specified to define it. There are many different ways of describing colour, some useful for technical purposes, others more intuitive as a way of thinking about the appearance of colour and the relationship between different colours and shades.

Above: The Saturation level of the top picture is high and that of the bottom picture is very low.

The Brightness level of the top picture is low and that of the bottom picture is very high.

One of the most useful ways to describe colour is in terms of hue, saturation, and brightness (referred to as either HSB or HSL, 'lightness' replacing brightness). These terms underpin dialogues between users throughout the graphic arts industry.

HUE
Hue is essentially interchangeable with the word 'colour' as we normally use it. The colours of the spectrum are often displayed in a circle or 'colour wheel', and we can use basic names to identify each main colour: red, orange, yellow, green, blue, cyan, magenta, violet… When we refer to a colour as being 'orange', we are identifying its hue. Whether it is vibrant, dull, pale, or dark, we still recognize it as orange.

SATURATION
Saturation refers to the vibrancy and purity of a colour. The colours we see are made up from the three primary colours. A total absence of light – no red, green, or blue – of course is black. If there are equal, full strengths of red, green, and blue, white is perceived (white light, as you will recall from prism experiments at school, contains all the colours). As grey lies between black and white, it must be made up of equal amounts of less-than-total red, green, and blue. It is the fact that the amounts are equal that makes grey 'desaturated' – neutral.

If we now, for example, gradually increase the red element, while decreasing the blue and green, the grey will turn redder and eventually become a totally saturated red. The more balanced its red, green, and blue components, the less saturated a colour appears.

BRIGHTNESS
Brightness (sometimes referred to as lightness or tone) refers to how much light is present. Saturation or desaturation of a colour depends on the ratios of red to green to blue, not necessarily the overall quantity of light. If a large amount of light is used to create a colour, irrespective of the ratios of red, green, and blue, the colour will be bright (or light). If little light is used overall, then the colour is perceived as being dark.

COLOUR MANAGEMENT

In the digital realm, we can describe colour in terms of hue, saturation, and brightness by setting each on a scale, typically from 0 to 100 (a familiar scale to humans) or 0 to 255 (familiar to computers). But what exactly does this scale refer to? We could fire the electron guns in a CRT monitor in the proportions directly dictated by our HSB values, but the progression through the scale might be quite uneven, and the result would be different on each monitor.

Decades before the advent of desktop computers, it was realized that the industry needed a way to describe how colour appeared to the human eye and brain in such a way that a numeric colour specification would refer precisely to a certain perceived colour. The solution was the Munsell system, which formed the basis of new 'colour models' devised by the CIE, an international commission.

In the 1990s, the ICC (International Colour Consortium) – founded by Apple, Adobe, and other digital companies – devised an industry standard for swapping colour definitions accurately between digital devices. The particular way a device chooses to define colours, within the range of colours it can actually handle, is known as its 'colour space'. To be ICC-compatible, each device must come with a 'colour profile' that relates its colour space to a CIE colour space. Armed with a CMS (colour management system) and a profile for each device involved in production (including software programs), a computer can ensure colour images are transferred accurately from one device to the next, all the way from taking a digital photo, for example, to seeing it printed on a magazine page.

At least, that's the theory! In practice, few people know how to set up colour management effectively. Apple naturally added an ICC CMS to its own Mac operating system, under the name ColorSync, and most Mac products are ICC-compatible. Windows now also has a CMS built in, but Microsoft does not encourage anyone to use it. Instead, it recommends that every device should use the 'sRGB' colour space, a general purpose model. That would work fine, except that sRGB is not a very good colour space, and converting colour imagery (such as professional digital photos and scans) into it risks compromising quality.

Ideally, the colour profile of any hardware device shouldn't just be the preset or 'canned' one supplied by its manufacturer; you should test or 'calibrate' the device at regular intervals and recreate a profile according to its exact colour performance. This requires extra hardware and software. Calibrators for monitors are quite affordable, though, and professional designers should seriously consider investing in one. If the screen you are looking at is not representing colour accurately, there is little hope that the system as a whole will deliver the results you expect.

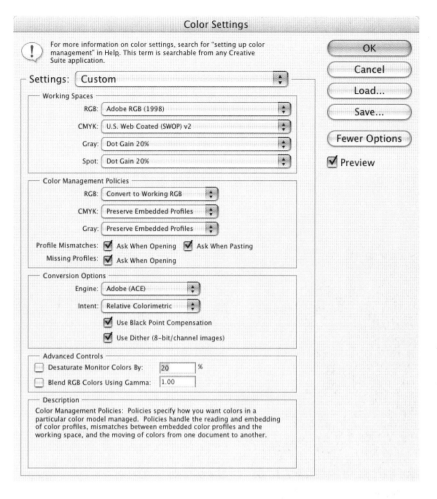

Above: Colour management only works if set up correctly, and the settings in your main graphics programs are the most important. Photoshop features this rather daunting *Color Settings* dialog box.

The first setting is your choice of RGB working space. This dictates the format in which all the colour information in an image is stored while you are working on it. A common mistake is to set this to your monitor's colour space, but that means the colour range of your monitor will limit the colour content of all your work – pointless when it is destined to be displayed and printed on other devices. Instead, the correct choice is a theoretical colour space that can represent the widest range of colour accurately, usually 'Adobe RGB (1998)'. The CMYK working space, however, should represent the actual printing press you plan to use, as you won't normally be editing images in CMYK mode.

Every colour graphics file you save should include a copy of the colour space it was created in, so that the next program or device can interpret it correctly. The *Policies* section tells Photoshop what to do when you open an image that lacks such an embedded profile.

Conversion Options govern the method used by Photoshop to perform all its colour conversion calculations. The settings shown here are generally appropriate.

Images created on the computer can range from a simple icon printed in one colour to a multi-layered photographic montage using all the colours of the spectrum. Different types of image include diagrams, charts, graphs, maps, technical illustrations, logos, icons, symbols, photographs, collages, montages, and photomontages, any of which might be incorporated into a design to inform or entertain, or both.

Images are designed in different styles, both for aesthetic reasons as well to meet production limitations. They may be in black and white, greyscale, or full colour, and may be produced as monotones or duotones. They may be square, rectangular, or geometrically shaped, or appear unbounded on the page or surface.

What images are, what they do, and how they are created are of considerable importance to the graphic designer. Image-making requires care, a rich visual language, a sense of purpose, and sensitivity to the way in which the outcome can affect the viewer.

Many graphic designers concerned with image-making are, or become, photographers and illustrators, with much of what they create being integral to their own designs. The graphic designer's motivation often springs from a client-generated brief, the parameters of which will often dictate the use of type and image.

WHERE TO OBTAIN IMAGES

Rich sources of copyright-free art are available on CD and the Internet, which, together with images generated by the designer, can provide a springboard for inventive, image-based design solutions. Collections of imagery can inspire the designer into developing, simplifying, or synthesizing them to support a project. This can often be detected in icon or logo design, where several visual references may have been modified and fused into a single graphic symbol.Much of the time, however, the graphic designer is the creative

PART 04. TYPE/COLOUR/IMAGE

CHAPTER THREE

IMAGE CREATION

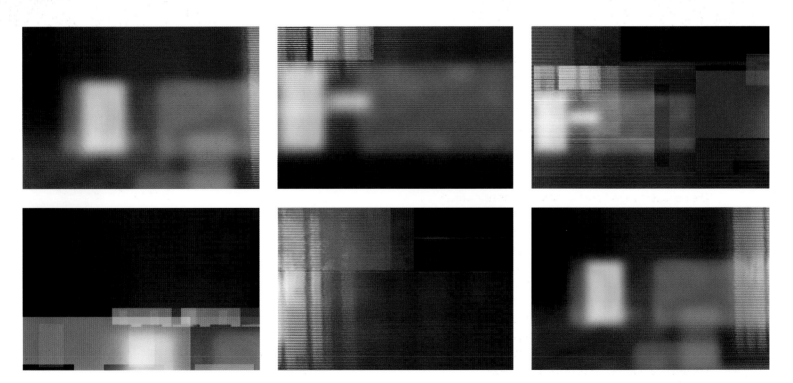

manager of visual components and uses images created by illustrators and photographers. A balance has to be maintained between giving the illustrator or photographer creative freedom and ensuring that the commissioned work complements the project. Building a good working relationship and establishing a rapport with other artists is essential to professional working practice and to getting the right results.

The advent of digital control over images has almost immeasurably expanded the creative scope of illustrators and photographers. With accessible, powerful software for creating and manipulating images at their fingertips, digital graphic designers can produce a wide range of graphic effects to incorporate into existing or newly created images. Respect for the integrity of other image-making professionals is, of course, extremely important. It is not ethical either to alter another professional's work or to manipulate it gratuitously. However, by agreement or in collaboration, it is possible to modify the original dimensions, mood, and meaning of an image.

Opposite and above: **Mood and atmosphere can be generated from creative image manipulation in a bitmap editing application. Qualities of layering, transparency, and depth are obtained by the inventive use of Photoshop functions.**
Designed for *MacUser* magazine by Tom Hingston Studio, UK

UNDERSTANDING DIGITAL IMAGE-MAKING The development of software for easy and creative image-making continues in leaps and bounds. Just when the designer exhausts all the tools of one program, an updated version hits the market, adding a plethora of new features.

BITMAP EDITING PROGRAMS

The industry-standard bitmap program, used by digital graphic designers, photographers, web designers, and the printing industry, is Adobe Photoshop. There are various other bitmap programs used by artists and illustrators, such as Paint Shop Pro and Corel PhotoPAINT, as well as specialist tools such as Corel Painter which, unlike other 'painting' programs, really does simulate paint – along with pencils, pastels, and many other real world art media.

Bitmap programs are used for creating single images, not multi-page documents. Their primary function is to adjust the colour values of the pixels that – in a grid of anything up to several million locations – make up every digital image, such as a photo from a digital camera. From a distance, of course, you don't notice the individual square pixels within an image, only the overall effect. Equally, you don't have to be aware that the software is modifying pixels; it appears to make subtle changes across all or part of a picture. Many different 'filters' can be used to adjust colour balance, increase the impression of sharpness, change the balance of light and shadow, and so on.

As programs become feature-rich, they attempt to be all things to all people, and in doing so may mask the fact that the behaviour of some aspects of image creation is not entirely compatible with others. It is easy to be overwhelmed by the multitude of features available, so it helps to have an appreciation of some of the underlying principles.

There are essentially two different types of image-making program: bitmap, also known as 'painting' or 'photo editing' software, and drawing, also referred to as 'vector'. The two ways of storing graphics are completely different, but they can be used within the same program and combined within the same artwork or layout.

Above: Libraries of images on CD or DVD are widely available, as well as web-based 'royalty-free' picture collections. Images are offered at varying resolutions to meet different requirements, and often the price will vary according to file size. Low-resolution images (72-96dpi) are suitable for screen-based work; high resolution (around 300dpi at A4 size) is required for commercial print quality; and extra-large images will be needed for full-bleed spreads or where part of the picture is to be blown up.

Right: Bitmap images (above right) may be available in full colour or as 'greyscales' printed in a single colour. Images with no gradations between black and white are called line art, sometimes also referred to as 'bitmap' images (right), although the correct term in this case would be '1-bit'. 'Bitmap' is also used to refer to one-colour digital images.

Alternatively, you can 'paint' with the mouse directly on to the part of the image you want to change, or more literally paint blobs and lines of colour onto a blank 'canvas'. Photoshop and some other bitmap editors now also provide vector drawing tools, and can store type as scalable vectors, 'rasterizing' it to a bitmap when you finish off your artwork.

BITMAP ADVANTAGES

Bitmap software is the best way to manipulate photographic and other 'continuous tone' images, such as paintings or scanned artwork. In the real world, hues and shades merge imperceptibly with each other in every direction. This 'continuous tone' effect would be impossible to reproduce using discrete shapes, as in vector drawing. Instead, the digital camera or scanner divides what it sees into a fixed grid of squares and measures the colour in each. When these colours are displayed on the monitor as pixels, they recreate the visual impression of the scene with its continuously varying tone. Software tools can alter pixel values in a gradual way, maintaining realism.

The amount of detail that can been seen in a scanned image (the same applies to any digital image) depends entirely on how many times per inch the scanner is made to record the colour values. This figure is the resolution. High resolution is obtained when pixel information is recorded at, say, 300 points across every inch (300ppi); a low-resolution scan might record 72 points per inch (72ppi).

Above: **Duotones are usually greyscale images overprinted black onto a copy of the image, which has been printed in spot colour to provide depth and interest. Generally the angle of screen for the black is set at zero and the angle of screen for the spot colour is set at 45°, which allows the colour to be more visible. Digitization of the image allows for considerable control of the tonal range across the black and spot-colour versions of the image.** Photo / Ed Seabourne

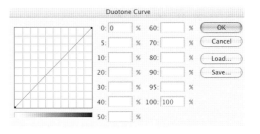

Below: **These images have been scanned at 300ppi, 150ppi, 72ppi, and 36ppi. The lower the scan resolution the less information captured and therefore the coarser the image. In order to display these images the same size, on screen or in print, we have had to enlarge the low-resolution images.**

Above: **The essence of a bitmap image is that shapes and images are made up entirely from the uniform arrangement of varying coloured pixels. There is no underlying structure to describe this shape.**

BITMAP DISADVANTAGES

Bitmap images have two disadvantages. First, in terms of digital storage, they are very space-hungry. The colour values of every pixel in the image – typically several million – must be identified and recorded. This large amount of information can be reduced to some degree by using 'data compression' techniques such as LZW or JPEG, but only up to a point. Second, because a bitmap image has no structure other than a sequence of pixels arranged in a grid, when you enlarge it the pixels just get bigger. The viewer will soon lose the illusion of a smooth image and become aware of the individual coloured squares. Unless the image can be recreated from scratch at a higher resolution (for example by re-scanning an analogue photo), you can never scale up a bitmap beyond a certain point without its visual quality suffering badly.

Left: Even apparently rough-edged images benefit from being created by vectors. This logo for Chronicle Books has been enlarged greatly from the same small-scale Adobe Illustrator file seen at the top left, but still keeps a clean, sharp edge. This would have been impossible from a small-scale bitmap file.

Below: Bitmap applications provide photo-realism and are useful for applying graphics such as logos or advertising into real-life situations. Here a corporate identity has been digitally applied to a photo of a vehicle so the look can be tested before implementing the design.

VECTOR-BASED PROGRAMS

Vector-based programs describe the shape of an object as a series of strategically placed points connected by lines controlled by mathematical formulae – rather like a 'join-the-dots' picture with the added benefit that the connections between points can be precisely described as straight or curved lines. The line is called a path or a vector. Paths can have thickness (stroke) and colour, and the shapes or objects they create can also be filled with a colour, gradient, texture, and so forth. Each object can be moved around a page independently which allows them to be arranged and rearranged, overlaying or underlying each other as appropriate. By altering the position of the points and the ways in which the paths connect them, the vectors and the resulting shapes they make can be re-formulated.

Vectors are an ideal way of describing the outline shape of letterforms, and in fact font files are essentially a collection of outline vectors.

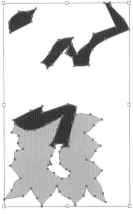

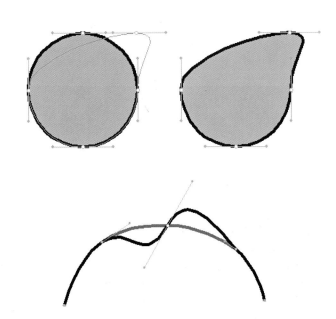

Above: Pamela Geismar of San Francisco's Chronicle Books was able to colour up the humorous illustrations of Thorina Rose, taking advantage of Illustrator 9's transparent colours, for the book *Office Kama Sutra*. It was essential to be able to lay transparent colours in *Multiply* mode to allow the grey tones to show through.

Above right: The fundamentals of vector shapes are points joined by straight or curved lines controlled by either moving these points or adjusting the curves between them by means of curve levers. All drawing applications use this method of creating simple or complex paths and shapes. It is well worth taking the trouble to master how to use the *Path* or *Pen* tools as they are absolutely essential to digital image creation.

Vector images allow for good-quality scaling both on screen and when output from a printer's RIP (see page 66). When a vector image is re-sized, the mathematical formulae ensure that all the points and paths are repositioned so as to maintain their original relationships. Since colouring is simply the filling-in of a defined shape, the scaled shape is automatically refilled. Objects described by outline information are memory-efficient, since a relatively compact set of numbers can describe quite complex shapes and colour fills. Vectors, however, cannot produce photo-realistic images, since realism needs a constantly shifting description of tone and colour that can be satisfactorily carried out only by the subtle changes in pixel colour achievable by bitmap techniques.

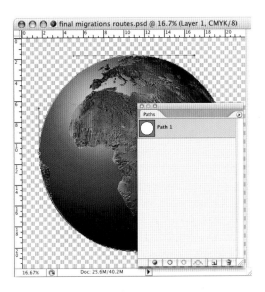

Above: Here, in a bitmap editing application (Photoshop), vectors are used purely as an aid for the user to create smooth shapes. Images may be selected and cropped to fit, or painted into the shapes. Once the vector has been used to carry out a function the resulting images are recorded in bitmap form.

Right: Freehand, as with other drawing applications, will create non-printing guides from user-drawn shapes. This is very useful when setting up perspectives and/or plans.

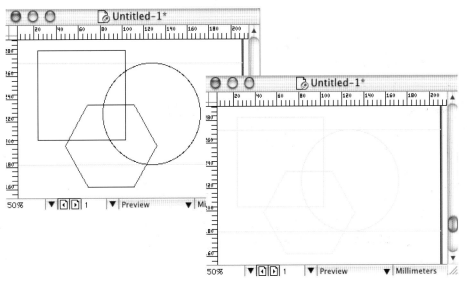

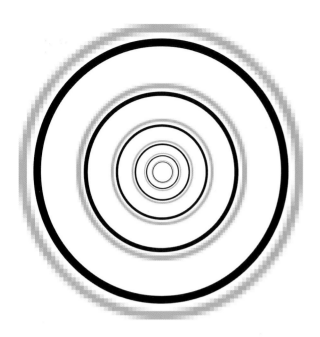

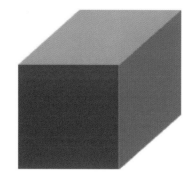

VECTORS AND BITMAPS TOGETHER

Most major graphic arts programs can handle both vectors and bitmaps, although they represent different imaging technologies. However, one or other technology generally dominates each program. For example, all page-layout and drawing programs are essentially vector-based, but they also have the ability to import bitmap pictures. The bitmap is usually contained within a placement holder, such as a 'picture box', that may or may not have a visible frame. Vectored objects such as typographic elements, graphic shapes, rules, drawn logos, and technical illustrations may lie over or under imported images.

Unless it is appreciated that an image composed of a grid of pixels is fundamentally different from a vector image, whose component parts are described as outlines and filled shapes, much confusion may occur. The designer may be left wondering why certain tools and functions do not work for both kinds of image.

Page-layout programs such as QuarkXPress and Adobe InDesign now have features that allow for quite a large amount of control over the imported bitmapped images

Above: A cube drawn in a vector application (left) has been 'rasterized' when opened in Photoshop (right). The process converts the vector drawing to a bitmapped (pixel-based) image.

Above left: A series of circles of increasing size produced from a single bitmap file, compared to those produced from a single vector file. It is not difficult to see which is which.

Below: Adobe Streamline is a useful application that can turn bitmap images into vector files. It places points and vectors to create outlines around significant bitmap areas of tone and/or colour. The resultant outlines can then be filled with colour using a drawing application like Illustrator.

beyond simply changing shape and size or applying tints, and can integrate vector and bitmap elements quite effectively, though less so than Photoshop. InDesign is the more advanced in this area. Adobe Illustrator and Macromedia FreeHand, both drawing programs, have the capability of modifying imported bitmapped images using various effect filters, and are also able to convert (rasterize) vector objects into bitmaps. Once rasterization has taken place, the vector information is lost and the result is merely a collection of pixels.

By contrast, Photoshop, a bitmap program, has very capable vector-based tools. One use of these is to enable the user to make accurate and smooth selections with the aid of paths. Additionally, text can be created using the outline (vector) information from the font files and still remain editable. In the end, however, vectors and editable text will need to be converted to bitmaps before they can be fully integrated into an image.

Working in the opposite direction, Adobe Streamline is a useful program that can process bitmap images and produce outlines (vectors) where colours and tone change. The trace or auto-trace facility in Macromedia FreeHand can be used in the same way, while Illustrator provides a more rudimentary facility.

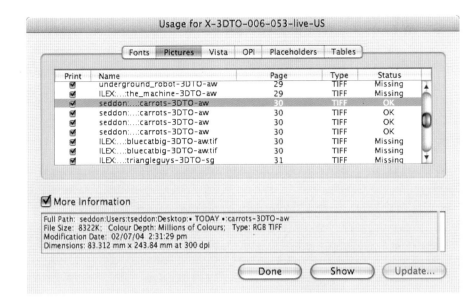

Usage for X-3DTO-006-053-live-US

| | Fonts | Pictures | Vista | OPI | Placeholders | Tables |

Print	Name	Page	Type	Status
☑	underground_robot-3DTO-aw	29	TIFF	Missing
☑	ILEX:....the_machine-3DTO-aw	29	TIFF	Missing
☑	seddon:...:carrots-3DTO-aw	30	TIFF	OK
☑	seddon:...:carrots-3DTO-aw	30	TIFF	OK
☑	seddon:...:carrots-3DTO-aw	30	TIFF	OK
☑	seddon:...:carrots-3DTO-aw	30	TIFF	OK
☑	ILEX:...:bluecatbig-3DTO-aw.tif	30	TIFF	Missing
☑	ILEX:...:bluecatbig-3DTO-aw.tif	30	TIFF	Missing
☑	ILEX:...:triangleguys-3DTO-sg	31	TIFF	Missing

☑ More Information

Full Path: seddon:Users:tseddon:Desktop:• TODAY •:carrots-3DTO-aw
File Size: 8322K; Colour Depth: Millions of Colours; Type: RGB TIFF
Modification Date: 02/07/04 2:31:29 pm
Dimensions: 83.312 mm x 243.84 mm at 300 dpi

(Done)   (Show)   (Update...)

Left: When images are imported to a layout or drawing document, it is usual for only low-resolution copies to be placed on the page as visual guides. When a printing device comes across a picture imported into a document it searches for the original, high-quality file. Seen here is Quark's *Usage* dialog box, which keeps track of where the originals of imported images are stored. One of the most common print 'problems' occurs when designers forget to send their original good-quality scans together with their document files.

Right: Seen here is a vector (left) and bitmap (right) version of the same image. In order to maintain a similar quality of reproduction when enlarged to 200% the bitmap image must be re-scanned at a much higher resolution than before, resulting in a much larger file size. By comparison, the same vector file may be used at any size without compromise to quality. Note, though, how bitmap images create smooth transitions throughout all the subtle tonal changes whereas vector images show well-defined, hard-edged shapes.

Native Adobe Illustrator
file enlarged 200% –
2.6MB

Native Adobe Photoshop
file enlarged 200% –
11.9MB

Native Adobe Illustrator
file – 2.6MB

Native Adobe Photoshop
file – 3MB

SCANNING AND RESOLUTION To work successfully with bitmap pictures, the impact of several different but interrelated technologies must be considered. In planning graphic reproduction the intended result needs to be established before the appropriate preparatory steps can be decided upon. In other words it is usually advisable to start from the output end and work backwards to the beginning.

SCANNING FOR PRINT

The Print section in Part II of this book explains how a printing plate must be made for each colour in order to transfer the colour-filtered components of the image onto paper. In four- or six-colour process, the coloured areas of an original image are analyzed for how much of each printing ink is required to simulate the colour at any given point. Then the location of each required ink colour is transferred to the appropriate plate as tiny, close-printing dots in a conversion procedure called halftoning. The dots in a full-colour halftone vary in size according to how much of their ink colour is required at a given spot, but even the biggest of dots is so small that it merges almost imperceptibly with the surrounding dots to create the illusion of a visually smooth change of colour, tone, and intensity.

Imagesetters (output devices used to generate reproduction-quality copy for printing) have a device resolution of up to 3000 dots per inch (dpi). For most printing work, halftone dots are required at a rate or output resolution of 150 halftone dots per inch. Dividing the imagesetter resolution by the output resolution, we find that a 3000-dpi imagesetter has 20 dots with which to construct the largest halftone dot required. Since these rates per inch are linear, the largest (100 per cent) halftone dot would be 400 dots in area (20 dots square) and a 10 per cent dot would be around 40 dots in area. That is more than enough to ensure fine reproduction.

The designer's file must obviously contain all the image detail to produce all the tiny halftone dots that represent how much ink falls where. In fully digital printing and direct-to-plate (DTP) imagesetting, the dots transferred to the plate come directly from the designer's file. More conventionally, there is an intermediate stage in which the imagesetter produces prepared photographic negative film, through which the plate's light-sensitive, emulsion-covered surface is then exposed to light. In this case, it is the film that comes directly from the designer's file.

In order to produce output at 150dpi (output resolution), the imagesetter must receive information at a minimum of 150 pixels per inch, or ppi (input resolution). If a picture file has been scanned at a lower resolution, there will be insufficient information to satisfy the imagesetter. In the absence of such information, it will make identically sized halftone dots until new information reaches it. For instance, if a file can only provide 50ppi (one-third of the necessary linear resolution), an imagesetter set to output at 150dpi must create three identical dots in a row both across and down. This results in a group of 9 identical dots which, when printed, will look like a little square to the naked eye. Worse, the whole image will be made up of these little squares. The way to avoid this is to scan at a high enough resolution to provide at least 150 unique pieces of information for the 150 demands made by the imagesetter.

That is the theory – but there is one small, added complication. Halftone dots are arranged at angles to each other, with a unique angle for each process colour. The objective is to ensure that any pattern in the dots does not distract the human eye, so that the image appears smoother and more realistic. Since images are scanned horizontally and vertically rather than at an angle, and since imagesetters lay down the dots from left to right, the requirement to work at an angle increases the demand for accurate information across the inch. For this reason, it is recommend that images should be scanned at between one-and-a-half times and twice the intended output resolution.

There is much confusion about the terminology regarding resolution. Dpi, ppi, lpi - what's the difference? It is quite common for lay persons and professionals alike to use dpi (dots per inch) to describe any type of resolution. Strictly speaking we use the term samples per inch (spi) when referring to scanned bitmaps – but now mostly ppi is used. Pixels per inch (ppi) refer to monitor displays and dots per ich (dpi) refer to particles of ink, toner, or light that are used by printing devices to create images. Halftone dots, created from the smaller printer dots (dpi) are arranged in lines to form a mesh, or screen, and so halftone screens are expressed in lines per inch (lpi).

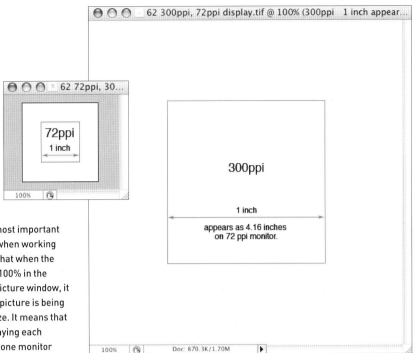

Above: One of the most important concepts to grasp when working with Photoshop is that when the application shows 100% in the bottom left of the picture window, it does not mean the picture is being viewed at actual size. It means that the screen is displaying each scanned pixel with one monitor pixel (pixel for pixel). It can be seen that if an image is scanned at 72ppi (the same resolution as a Mac monitor, which is fixed) then it will appear the correct size. If an image is scanned at, say, 300ppi, then the monitor will require 4.16 inches to show 300 pixels, resulting in a

bigger-looking picture. It is not possible to mix pixel resolutions in the one image so when images of variable resolutions are copied and pasted, they will appear to shrink or expand in order to fit the pixel grid of the host image.

Right: The ideal resolution for print work is 300ppi (top). If the resolution is too low or the image is enlarged too much – thereby reducing the effective resolution – then unwanted pixellation occurs (centre). If no halftone dots need to be created, as in line-art images – one may scan at the maximum resolution of the output device which could be as much as 3,000dpi. However a scan at 600ppi will normally be sufficient to obtain a visually sharp edge (bottom).

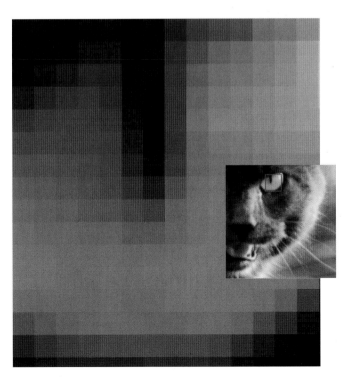

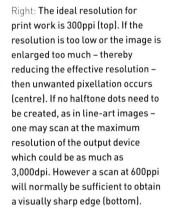

Left: When an area is enlarged on screen for a zoomed-in view, the application's software creates squares of identically coloured pixels to give the illusion of enlargement. Pixels are still displayed at the rate of 72ppi but the illusion is that they have 'grown'. A similar effect is seen when an image scanned at a low resolution is printed and there are not enough pixels per inch for every halftone dot required. So a few neighbouring halftone dots will use the same information and therefore appear identically, both vertically and horizontally. This results in little, visibly definable squares and the picture appearing pixellated.

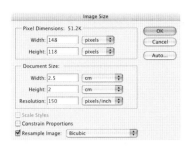

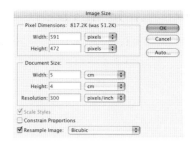

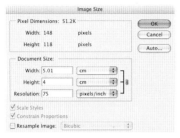

Above and right: Image size and resolution are interlinked. When an image is scanned it may be expressed in two ways. First, by how many pixels it measures horizontally and vertically. This need not dictate how big it will print, just how many bits of information record the picture. Secondly, we are able to give the picture a physical size so that when sent to a printer there is some reference as to how big the picture should be reproduced. Above left are two versions of a picture that has been scanned once - its pixel size is 148pixels x 118pixels. The top picture is described physically 2.5cm x 2cm at a resolution of 150ppi whereas the lower picture is described 5cm x 4cm at a resolution of 75ppi. This is very similar to looking at a mosaic on a wall close to or from a distance - the number of squares that make up the picture do not change, it is the viewing distance that makes the picture appear biggger or smaller and coarser or smoother respectively.

By contrast the picture on the top right has been given the same physical dimensions as the one on the lower left but has been scanned at a far higher resolution (300ppi) so that the pixel size is 591pixels x 472pixels.

Most designers tend to err on the side of caution and stick to scanning at double the halftone rate. So, for most general commercial offset litho printing, pictures are scanned at 300ppi. There will be no quality problems if a picture is scanned at higher resolution, but equally there will be no quality improvement. However, there will be an enormous increase in file size and processing time, which will slow all processes down.

If an image is to be printed in solid process colour, requiring no halftone dots, it is known as line art. Theoretically, for the best results you could scan that image at 3000ppi to match every imagesetter dot. However this is impractical for file size reasons. For crisp results, line work should be scanned at about 600-1200ppi. Any extra quality obtained from scanning at much above this level of resolution is imperceptible.

The resolution of an image must be correct for the size at which it will be printed. It is no good scanning a picture at 300ppi and then enlarging it dramatically in a page-layout program. Your original picture file will still

contain the same information, but it will now be stretched two or three times beyond its original dimensions. This has the effect of substantially lowering the resolution relative to its new size. A small amount of scaling up or down may not result in print quality problems, but it is always best to scan a picture at the correct resolution for the intended output size. Fortunately, most scanning software allows the user to set a resolution and a scaling ratio. The scanner then ensures that the picture is scanned so that the resolution is correct at the new image size.

When buying a scanner, it is important to ascertain the highest resolution actually achievable. Some manufacturers claim a very high output, but this is sometimes achieved by interpolation – the software recalculates its best actual result to add more pixels per inch. Although interpolation will smooth out an image, it will capture no more detail, so always judge by 'optical' not 'interpolated' resolution. Interpolation also takes place when an image or parts of it are rotated or transformed in some way. Sometimes, owing to looming deadlines or unavailability of the original image, a designer will need to increase a picture's resolution directly in the file. PhotoShop can interpolate and increase the number of pixels in an image; if this proves necessary, the bicubic method should always be used for the best results.

FOR SCREEN PRODUCTS

Resolution issues for image use in webpages or multimedia production are much more straightforward than for print, since the designer knows that the audience will be viewing images on a monitor not dissimilar to the one on which the design was created – so the size you see is the size you'll get. At 96ppi, roughly the resolution of the average modern PC monitor, images contain just 9,216 pixels per square inch, about a tenth the size of a 300ppi file. Apart from bringing file size (with compression) down within a practical range for Internet transmission, this also means the designer's software will work faster than when editing high-resolution print files.

FILE FORMATS FOR BITMAPPED IMAGES Digital images can be saved in a variety of file formats, each of which has its own unique way of storing information and of handling digital data. Choice of file format is important to the digital graphic designer, since the one selected will have a bearing on the efficiency and performance of the stored image.

PICT (Macintosh picture file) is the Macintosh operating system standard format for saving bitmap information. It cannot store CMYK information.

BMP (Windows bitmap) is the Windows operating system standard format for saving bitmap information. It cannot store CMYK colour information.

TIFF (Tagged Image File Format) is the most widely used file format for print. It can store bitmap (black and white), greyscale and colour information (RGB, CMYK, or indexed colour) and include masking information. Furthermore, TIFF files can be compressed without losing data. Most programs can read TIFF files. The Macintosh and the PC use different versions of the TIFF format, but both versions can be read by Photoshop and re-saved for the platform required. Clipping paths, layers, and alpha channels (masks) can be saved.

JPEG (Joint Photographic Experts Group) is favoured for photographic images, especially on the Internet. It can offer high compression of file sizes, reducing them to a fraction of their original size. The drawback is the loss of information in the compression process: the greater the compression, the greater the loss. The user, who can make a trade-off between

Below: **File formats may, in Photoshop, be selected from the** *Save* **or** *Save As* **menu. Some file formats, such as Pixar or Amiga, are for more specialized computing systems and for most users may be ignored. Often, some file formats are 'greyed out' on the popup menu. This is because some file formats work only with RGB images and some only with CMYK images. When all of the file formats are 'greyed out', except Photoshop format, this indicates that the picture contains layers that will have to be flattened before the image can be recorded in any other file format. Note: to create GIFs the** *Export* **menu (under** *File*) **needs to be selected.**

file size and quality, can control the amount of compression. Repeated compression and decompression will make the quality worse.

EPS (Encapsulated PostScript) is a PostScript image file, which a desktop publishing program can use to print the vector and/or bitmap image stored in it, with a bitmap preview image included for on-screen display. Photoshop can open and save EPS files, and can save them with JPEG compression incorporated. Clipping paths can be saved, but not alpha channels or layers. EPS files are also able to hold instructions to the RIP about the appearance and output of halftones, duotones and so on. The only usual reason to save a bitmap as an EPS is to assure compatibility with and correct processing by a DTP program such as QuarkXPress.

GIF (Graphics Interchange Format) is a format normally only used for web work. It supports only 256 indexed colours. A useful feature is that, on saving, it is possible to select a colour to appear as transparent for cutout effects.

Hamlet.jpg

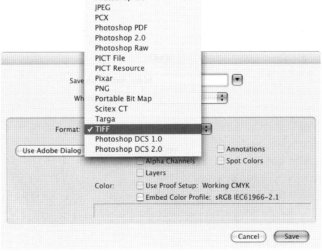

Far left: **Both Windows and the Mac OS automatically generate and display 'thumbnail' miniatures of image files in their desktop icons.**

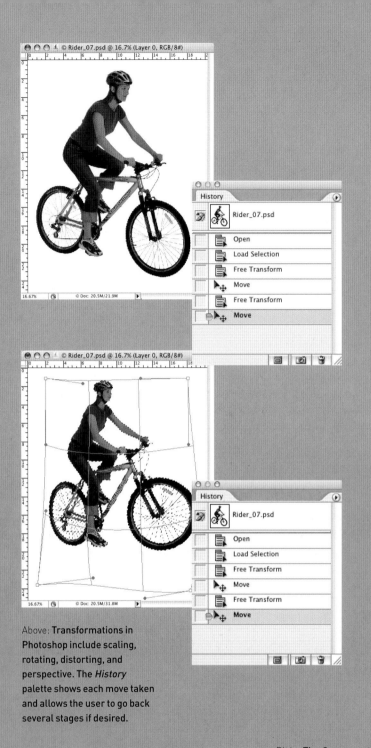

Above: **Transformations in Photoshop include scaling, rotating, distorting, and perspective.** The *History* palette shows each move taken and allows the user to go back several stages if desired.

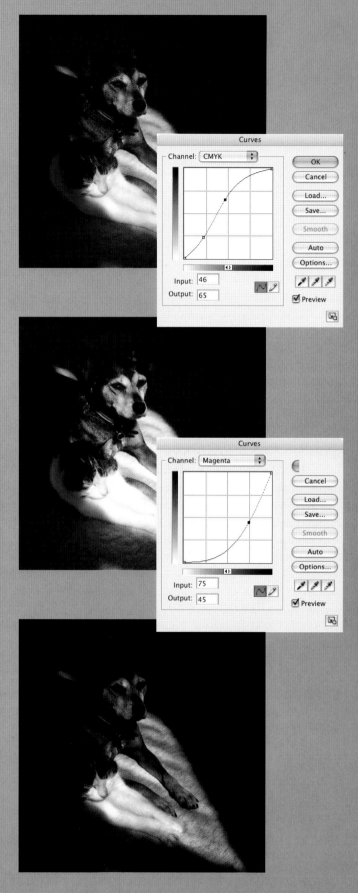

Right: The *Curves* control in Photoshop provides a very sensitive method of picture control by allowing the alteration of pixel brightness across all of the colour channels. Each channel may be controlled separately, facilitating the increase or decrease of that colour in any part of the the image between shadows, at one extreme, and highlights at the other.

WORKING WITH BITMAP IMAGES IN PAINTING PROGRAMS

Working on a bitmap image is much more flexible than working with the object-oriented, structured nature of vector shapes. Tools, generically termed 'painting tools', can be drawn across a field of tiny pixels to alter them in various ways.

Whether you have selected the eraser, pencil tool, or one of various brush styles, the tool is referred to as a brush. Its 'diameter' – the size of the area it affects – is measured in pixels, from 1 up to almost any size. Painting tools can also be assigned an opacity level to determine the extent to which the colour applied with the 'brush' overwrites existing pixels. The colour is chosen by setting the program's current foreground colour, although some brushes may use the background colour as well to create variation, or may have a preset colour scheme.

Brushes can either be set up as 'pens', consisting of an ellipse (a scalable vector shape) which can be angled for calligraphic effects, or based on a small bitmap image that is repeated along the stroke you paint.

A graphics tablet is a plastic-coated board, ranging in size from around A6 to A2 (though with a smaller 'active area'), accompanied by a stylus that is held like a pen. As you touch the stylus to the surface and move it around, its position is transmitted to the computer. This and various other parameters, such as pressure (how hard you press down) and tilt (the angle at which you hold the stylus), can be assigned to control aspects of the brush as you 'paint', allowing more subtle effects to be created.

CLONING

A special form of brush is the clone tool, sometimes called a rubber stamp. With this, you select a point within an image as the 'source'. When you start to paint, pixels from around this point are applied, so that you are effectively copying one part of the image over

another. Because the effect is seamless, this can be used to cover unwanted elements in a photo, or remove scratches and blemishes from scans, leaving the manipulation unnoticeable.

SELECTING

A number of selection tools, including rectangular and elliptical marquees, lasso and magic wand, can be used to isolate the area of the image you want to change. The edge of the area defined can be 'feathered' so that changes fade off gradually rather than leaving a hard outline. You can then apply an adjustment or effect to this entire area, or use it as a mask: brushes will have no effect outside the selected area.

TRANSFORMATIONS

Photoshop menus allow for either the whole image or a selected area to be rotated, mirrored, distorted, or inverted (colours reversed). More complex transformations are also possible.

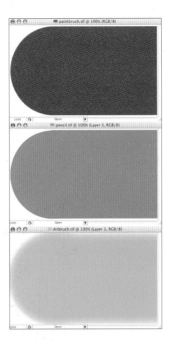

Above: **The three fundamental painting tools of Photoshop -** *Brush*, *Pencil*, and *Airbrush*. **Most significant is the default antialiasing of the** *Brush* **and** *Airbrush* **compared to the** *Pencil*. **Antialiasing is a technique used by software to place intermediate pixels of lighter tone between one colour and another to create an impression of smoothness. Antialiasing replicates the way the eye sees and helps create photo-realistic imagery.**

Right: **Probably the most useful painting tool in all of Photoshop's armoury, the** *Rubber Stamp* **tool (***Cloning* **tool) allows one part of an image to be painted across to another part. Combining subtlety of brush size and strength of opacity it is possible to eradicate unwanted material and replace it with other image-forming pixels. In the window to the right can be seen a circle, indicating the size of the active** *Rubber Stamp* **brush.**

Left: The *Replace Color* function in Photoshop allows a certain colour range within an image to be adjusted (by manipulating its hue, saturation, and lightness) without affecting other tones. The *Fuzziness* control dictates the extent of the area changed.

GLOBAL COLOUR ADJUSTMENT

Global colour adjustment allows the designer to modify either the entire image or a selected area for colour balance, brightness and contrast, saturation levels, colour replacement, and general fine-tuning. The effect can be adjusted in a dialog box, and calculations are carried out and implemented by the software according to the type of adjustment selected.

Right and below: *Layer Masks* are used to control the visibility of a layer. Seen here is a *Layer Mask* attached to Layer 1, which is permitting some of the image in the background layer to show through, creating a photomontage. Masks can be generated from the lightness values within an image, or painted from scratch.

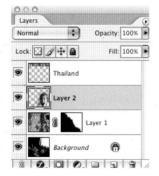

Below: The beauty of masks is that they can be saved and called up at any time to select a particular area of an image. Furthermore, a mask can be added to and subtracted from, using any of the usual painting tools, brush sizes, and/or opacities. The mask can optionally be shown as a red tint, allowing it to be edited with the image visible for reference.

Original image

'Quick mask'

Background pasted into mask

LAYERS

Layers exist to help create montage work as well as to allow changes and additions to a picture to be made without irreversibly altering it at each stage. Adding a layer is a little like putting a sheet of clear film over your image and painting onto it. The original image can be seen through the layer, and parts of the film can be cut out and discarded. Even better, areas of a layer can be 'masked' to allow the underlying image to show through, but are not actually deleted – by editing the mask, you can bring them back.

ALPHA CHANNELS AND MASKS

A colour file image has a 'channel' dedicated to each primary colour (RGB or CMYK). Extra channels – alpha channels – can be used to store masks as greyscale images. A mask can represent a selection: where there is white in the channel, those areas are selected, while areas that are black in the channel are unselected, and grey areas partially selected (so that any adjustment or effect applied will

Above: **Blending modes govern the way in which colours are applied to an underlying image, taking into account the values of the pixels over which they are being painted. The colour blue has been painted across half of the above pictures, but the blending mode selected has been changed for each. From left to right:** Colour, Overlay, Multiply, Saturation, **and** Luminosity. **The last two are interesting in that only one attribute of blue is being used to change the picture – that is to say, the pixels have been changed to match only the value of blue's saturation in one and only the value of blue's luminosity in the other.**

take partial effect, as if its opacity had been lowered). So you can use alpha channels to save selections made with the selection tools. An alpha channel saved within the final image file can be accessed by page-layout programs to create 'soft cutouts', where an irregularly shaped image is placed over other graphics or text and blends in seamlessly at the edges.

COLOUR ATTRIBUTES AND BLENDING MODES

In applying colour using brushes or global fills, it is possible to paint with attributes of colour rather than with the colour itself. For instance, if a vibrant red is selected from the palette and a brush set to the blending mode *Luminosity*, the underlying pixels will not change to red when painting starts but will simply be brightened or darkened to match the luminosity of the red. If a colour is applied with the *Colour* blending mode, the underlying pixels will change hue but the image's light and shade qualities will remain unchanged. There are many different blending modes to choose from

(the range has gradually grown in successive versions of Photoshop), each one affecting the underlying pixels in its unique way.

SPECIAL EFFECT FILTERS

Filters apply effects to images or selected areas, enabling many interesting and novel results to be achieved quickly. Photoshop and other image editors are supplied with a wide range of useful standard filters, many of them highly controllable using several parameters set numerically or by dragging sliders in a dialog box. A real-time preview is usually provided so that you can adjust the effect by eye before applying it to the image, which may take longer. Hundreds of other filters are available from third-party manufacturers such as Alien Skin, Auto FX, and Extensis.

   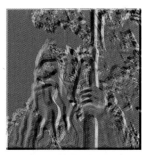

Left: **Just some of the many filters and effects available to modify images. Combinations of filters and the use of a filter several times over provide interesting and more extensive results. From top left, clockwise: original picture,** Frosted Glass, Find Edges, Emboss, Feather Edges, Wind Blast, Color Halftone, Pinch.

WORKING WITH DRAWING (VECTOR) PROGRAMS The vectors used in drawing programs are called Bézier curves. All drawing programs handle Bézier curves in a similar fashion: a pen tool allows the user to set a series of points on the page, and these will automatically be joined by lines.

The shape of these lines is dictated by the way in which the pen is manipulated by dragging and clicking the mouse. Each point or 'node', when selected, will display one or two non-printing 'handles'. A given point may be selected later and the handles manipulated to modify the curves. The points themselves can also be repositioned at will.

Drawing programs give the digital graphic designer many powerful tools with which to create complex shapes, to apply special effects, and to speed up otherwise laborious tasks. Not all programs offer identical tools, although most of them do share a core set of features. The menus and terminology employed may also differ, as may the graphical presentation of tools. For example, both Illustrator and FreeHand can convert type into points and vectors; the operation is called *Create Outlines* in Illustrator, but *Convert to Paths* in FreeHand.

Left: Just a few ways of using type in a drawing program. The type may be converted to paths in order to make adjustments to the letterforms. The shape of type converted to paths may be used as a picture mask and drawn shapes (in this case type) may be rasterized into a bitmap image so that bitmap filters can be used. Of course, once an image has been rasterized it will no longer have any vector structure.

SOME OF THE FEATURES OFFERED BY DRAWING PROGRAMS

✱ Typographic functions are comparable with those found in leading page-layout programs, so that all character and paragraph formatting and spacing can be applied, together with layout functions such as multiple columns and text flow.

✱ Text can be converted to paths so that letterforms can be used in the same way as any other hand-drawn object.

✱ Shapes may be stroked (given a coloured outline), filled, cut, rotated, skewed, distorted, duplicated, mirrored, scaled, and added to. They may also be grouped, fused, cropped or used to crop others, used as a mask, used to contain a picture, and used to make patterns.

✱ User-defined colour palettes can be made up from RGB, CMYK, and HSB models as well as from colour libraries such as PANTONE.

✱ Many guides, grids, and views are available to support image construction. Views such as 'artwork' mode show only points and paths, without colour or fills, to help to clarify highly complex pictures and speed up screen rendering.

✱ Layers can be used to build up images in coherent groupings. These may be locked against accidental deletion and may also be hidden while other layers are being worked on.

✱ Numerous filters are available to create special alterations and effects with shapes or groups of shapes.

✱ Shapes or groups of shapes can be rasterized, which enables them to be used with an imported bitmap image.

✱ A range of bitmap-only filters may be applied to any imported bitmap or rasterized image.

✱ Multiple blends may be used between two shapes to act as a morphing technique.

✱ Spacing and alignment tools allow for swift arrangement of disparate elements.

Finished drawings should be saved in the 'native' format of your drawing program to ensure all features can be read back in. For transfer to other programs, such as a DTP package, all type should be converted to outlines and the drawing saved as EPS (encapsulated PostScript). Illustrator's native format is an adaptation of this standard format, and files from earlier versions of Illustrator can thus be read by many other programs. The advanced features recently introduced into drawing packages, however, cannot be saved as regular PostScript. It may be possible to export as an EPS with certain effects converted to simpler vector forms (with the same final appearance, though no longer editable) and others rasterized to bitmap images incorporated within the file. Output errors are not uncommon, and in some cases the best option is to rasterize the whole drawing to a 300dpi bitmap image at the required size.

Above and right:
Illustrator Lawrence Zeegen uses FreeHand to assemble and manipulate a combination of bitmap and drawn images. When displayed in 'artwork' form it is easy to see the entire structure and layout of object-oriented components.
Design by Lawrence Zeegen, UK

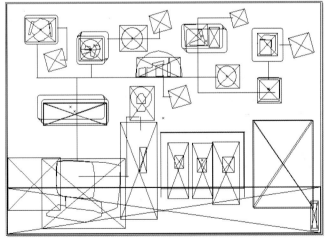

GLOSSARY

animation The process of creating a moving image by rapidly switching from one still image to the next. Traditionally achieved by drawing or painting each frame, now possible with a variety of software (qv) running on personal computers.

antialiasing The strategic insertion of pixels (qv) of various shades into a bitmapped graphic (qv) to smooth out 'jagged' transitions between contrasting tones, for example along a diagonal line.

ADSL Acronym for 'asynchronous digital subscriber line', a form of broadband (qv) Internet (qv) connection created by boosting the capacity of existing copper telephone wires. Typically the speed achieved for uploading (sending files out from the user's computer) will be half that for downloading (receiving files, including webpages being viewed by the user), hence 'asynchronous'. The more general term 'DSL' is more commonly used in North America.

Apple Macintosh The brand name of Apple Computer's range of PCs (qv). The Macintosh (or 'Mac') was the first personal computer to make use of the graphical user interface that had been pioneered by Xerox at the Palo Alto Research Center. The use of this interface provided the platform for the software (qv) applications that gave rise to desktop publishing, revolutionizing graphic design.

authoring tool Software (qv) for creating interactive presentations or websites. Such programs typically include text, drawing, painting, animation (qv), and audio features. These are combined with a scripting language that is used to determine how each element of the page or screen behaves – for example, it may be used to ensure that a movie is played when a certain button (qv) is pressed.

bandwidth The measure of the speed at which information is passed between two points (for example, between two modems (qv) or from memory to disk). The broader the bandwidth, the faster the data flow. Bandwidth is usually measured in cycles per second (hertz) or bits per second (bps).

Bézier tools Vector-based (qv) drawing tools, employed by most graphics programs. A pen tool allows the user to place a series of points on the page; the points are then automatically joined by a line. Two 'handles' on each point control the curve of the line.

bit A contraction of 'binary digit', the smallest unit of information that a computer can use. A bit may have one of two values: on or off, 1 or 0. Eight bits form a byte.

bitmap An image composed of dots, such as a digital photo. A bitmap is a table of values corresponding to the pixels (qv) that make up the image. 'Bitmap fonts', for example, contain such an image of each character, with each pixel represented by one bit, which can be either black or white. Colour images typically use at least 24 bits (three bytes) for each pixel, allowing millions of colours to be represented. The finite number of pixels in a bitmap limits the maximum size at which it can be reproduced at acceptable visual quality, unlike vector (qv) graphics.

bleed The margin outside the trimmed area of a sheet, which allows for tints, images, and other matter to print beyond the edge of the page. For printing without bleed, the designer must leave a blank margin around the page.

body text The matter that forms the main text of a printed book, excluding captions (qv), headings (qv), page numbers and so on.

brand guardian A person who is employed, usually by the client of a design or advertising agency, to ensure that the corporate brand identity of the client company is consistently presented.

broadband Used to describe any telecommunications link with a high bandwidth (qv), enabling a fast rate of data flow; specifically, a digital Internet connection made via ADSL (qv) or cable modem (qv).

browser An application that enables the user to view (or 'browse') web (qv) pages across the Internet (qv). The most widely used browsers are Netscape Navigator and Microsoft Internet Explorer. Version numbers are particularly important in the use of browsers, as they indicate the level of HTML (qv) that can be supported.

button An interface control, usually in a dialog box, that is clicked by the user to designate, confirm, or cancel an action. Default buttons are usually emphasized by a heavy border and can be activated using the Return or Enter keys.

cable Shorthand for a broadband (qv) Internet connection made using digital land lines installed by a cable telecoms company. In domestic installations this is typically sold as a package with digital cable TV, but provides a separate connection point for a personal computer.

cable modem A book-sized box that connects a computer to a cable (qv) service. Also known as a 'digital modem', although not strictly a modem (qv) at all.

CAD Acronym for 'computer-aided design'. May refer to any design carried out using a computer, but usually to three-dimensional design, such as product design or architecture. Software (qv) may control the entire process from concept to finished product, sometimes termed CAD-CAM (computer-aided manufacturing).

caption Strictly speaking, a caption is a headline printed above an illustration, identifying the contents of the image. However, the word is now used to describe any descriptive text that accompanies illustrative matter, usually set below or beside it at a small size. Not to be confused with 'credit', the small print beside a picture that identifies the illustrator, photographer, or copyright holder.

CD-ROM Acronym for 'compact disk, read-only memory'. A CD-based method for the storage and distribution of digital data. Based on audio CD technology, CD-ROMs can store up to 650 megabytes of data, and are available in record-once (CD-R) or rewritable (CD-RW) formats for computer use.

character A letter of the alphabet, numeral or typographic symbol. The table of contents of a font is its character set.

CMYK In four-colour process (qv) printing, an abbreviation for cyan, magenta, yellow, and black (black being denoted by 'K' for 'key plate').

ColorSync Apple's colour management (qv) system.

colour management The process of controlling the representation and conversion of colour information. The designer's computer should have a colour management system (CMS) such as ColorSync (qv) which is used by software to help ensure colours appear consistently on all devices, including the monitor.

compression The technique of rearranging data so that it either occupies less space on disk, or transfers more quickly between devices or along communication lines. Different kinds of compression are used for different kinds of data: applications, for example, must not lose any data when compressed, whereas images, sound, and movies can tolerate a large amount of data loss.

contrast The degree of difference between tones in an image (or computer monitor) from the lightest to the darkest. 'High contrast' describes an image with light highlights and dark shadows, whereas a 'low contrast' image is one with even tones and few dark areas or light highlights.

corporate identity A design or set of designs for use on corporate stationery, livery, etc.

CSS Abbreviation for 'cascading style sheets'. These extend the capabilities of HTML *(qv)*, allowing the web *(qv)* designer to exercise detailed control over layout and typography, applying preset formats *(qv)* to paragraphs, page elements, or entire pages. Several style sheets can be applied to a single page, thus 'cascading'. Correct use of CSS helps create pages that display as intended in all browsers.

default settings The settings of a hardware device or software *(qv)* program that are determined at the time of manufacture. These settings remain in effect until the user changes them; such changes will be stored in a 'preferences' file. Default settings are otherwise known as 'factory' settings.

digital press A printing press that outputs pages directly from digital files, typically using some form of inkjet technology.

Director Macromedia's multimedia authoring software *(qv)*.

display type Text set in large-size fonts *(qv)* for headings *(qv)*, or any matter that is intended to stand out. Fonts too ornate for general text, or specially designed for larger sizes, are referred to as display faces.

download The transfer of data from a remote computer – such as an Internet *(qv)* server – to a PC *(qv)*.

dpi Abbreviation for 'dots per inch'. A unit of measurement used to represent the resolution *(qv)* of devices such as printers and image setters. The closer the dots (ie, the higher the value), the better the quality. Typical values include . 300dpi for a laser printer, and 2450dpi+ for an imagesetter. Dots per inch is sometimes erroneously used as a value when discussing monitors or images; the correct unit in these cases is ppi (pixels *(qv)* per inch).

Dreamweaver Leading web design software *(qv)* from Macromedia.

DSL See *ADSL*.

DVD Abbreviation for 'digital versatile (or video) disk'. A storage disk similar to a CD-ROM *(qv)*, but distinguished by its greater capacity (up to 17.08 gigabytes).

embedded fonts Fonts *(qv)* that are fixed within files, meaning that the original font folder does not need to be provided in order for the file to be printed or set.

embossing Relief printing or stamping in which dies are used to impress a design into the surface or paper, leather, or cloth so that the letters or images are raised above the surface of the paper.

EPS Abbreviation for 'encapsulated PostScript'. A graphics file format used primarily for storing object-oriented or vector *(qv)* graphics. An EPS file consists of two parts: PostScript *(qv)* code, which tells the printer how to print the image; and an onscreen preview, usually in JPEG *(qv)*, TIFF *(qv)*, or PICT format.

film The material that provides the template for printing plates. A cellulose acetate-based material, coated with light-sensitive emulsion so that images and text can be recorded photographically.

finishing As the name implies, the final part of the print production process. It encompasses various

processes, including collating, trimming, folding, binding, embossing *(qv)*, laminating *(qv)*, varnishing *(qv)*, and so on.

Fireworks A web-specific graphics production tool by Macromedia.

Flash Macromedia software *(qv)* for producing vector *(qv)* graphics and animations for web *(qv)* presentations. Flash generates small files that are quick to download *(qv)* and, being vector-based, the graphics may be scaled to any dimension without an increase in file size.

font A complete set of type characters of the same size, style and design.

format In printing, the size or orientation of a book or page.

four-colour process Any printing process that reproduces full-colour images which have been separated into three basic 'process' colours – cyan, magenta, and yellow – with a fourth colour, black, added for greater contrast. *See also CMYK.*

frame (1) A decorative border or rule surrounding a page item.

frame (2) In page-layout software *(qv)*, a container for text or image.

frame (3) On the Web *(qv)*, a means of splitting a page into several areas which can be updated separately.

FreeHand Vector-based *(qv)* drawing software by Macromedia.

Freeway A website layout program produced by SoftPress.

GIF Acronym for 'graphic interchange format'. A bitmapped *(qv)* graphics file format that compresses *(qv)* data without losing any, as opposed to JPEG *(qv)*, which discards data selectively.

glyph A letter, number, or symbol in a particular typeface, referring to its visual appearance rather than its symbolic function. Any number of alternative glyphs may represent the same character *(qv)*.

gobo A metal or glass disk with designs printed onto or cut into it, for use with a projector or spotlight.

GoLive A website design program by Adobe.

graphic A general term that is used to describe any illustration or drawn design. May also be used for a type design based on drawn letters.

grid A template *(qv)* – usually showing such things as column widths, picture areas, and trim sizes – used to design publications with multiple pages, to ensure that the basic design remains consistent.

hairline rule The thinnest line it is possible to print, with a width of 0.25pt.

halftone The technique of reproducing a continuous tone image, such as a photo, on a printing press by breaking it up into a pattern of equally spaced dots of varying sizes.

heading A title that appears at the top of a chapter, or at the beginning of a subdivision within the text.

hierarchy of information The technique of arranging information in a graded order, which establishes priorities and helps users to find what they want.

hinting In typography, information contained within outline fonts *(qv)* that modifies character shapes to enhance them when they are displayed or printed at low resolutions *(qv)*.

HSB Abbreviation for 'hue, saturation, and brightness'.

HTML Abbreviation for 'hypertext mark-up language'. A text-based page-description language used to format documents on the Web *(qv)* and viewed on web browsers.

hue Pure spectral colour that distinguishes a colour from other colours. For example, red is a different hue from blue. Light red and dark red may contain varying amounts of white and black, but they are the same hue.

GLOSSARY

hyperlink A contraction of 'hypertext link', a link to other documents that is embedded within the original document. It may be underlined or highlighted in a different colour. Clicking on a hyperlink will take the user to another document or website.

ICC The International Color Consortium, which oversees the most widely used standards for colour management *(qv)* systems.

Illustrator Vector-based *(qv)* drawing software by Adobe.

image map An image, usually on a webpage, that contains embedded links to other documents or websites. These links are activated when the appropriate area of the image is clicked on. Most image maps are now 'client-side', stored within the page's HTML *(qv)* code rather than accessed from a server.

ImageReady Software *(qv)* for the production of web-ready images, produced by Adobe.

imposition The arrangement of pages in the sequence and position in which they will appear on the printed sheet, with appropriate margins for folding and trimming, before platemaking and printing.

InDesign Leading desktop publishing software *(qv)* from Adobe.

ink A fluid comprising solvents and oils in which is suspended a finely ground pigment of dyes, minerals, or synthetic dyes, which provide colour. There are many different types of ink for the various printing processes.

inkjet printer A printing device that creates an image by spraying tiny jets of ink on to the paper surface at high speed.

Internet The entire collection of connected worldwide networks which serves as the medium of transmission for websites *(qv)*, e-mail, instant messaging ('chat') and various other digital services.

Internet Explorer Web-browsing software *(qv)* from Microsoft.

intranet A network of computers similar to the Internet *(qv)*, to which the public does not have access. Mainly used by large corporations or governmental institutions.

ISDN Abbreviation for 'integrated services digital network'. An obsolescent telecommunications technology that transmits data digitally via telephone lines.

ISP Abbreviation for 'Internet *(qv)* service provider . Any organization that provides access to the Internet. Most ISPs also provide other services, such as email addresses.

JavaScript Netscape's Java-like scripting language, which provides a simplified method of adding dynamic effects to web *(qv)* pages.

JPEG Abbreviation for 'Joint Photographic Experts Group'. This International Standards Organization group defines compression standards for bitmapped *(qv)* colour images, and has given its name to a popular compressed *(qv)* file format. JPEG files are 'lossy' (lose data during compression), but work in such a way as to minimize the visible effect on graduated tone images. Pronounced 'jay-peg'.

kerning The adjustment of space between adjacent type characters to optimize their appearance. Not to be confused with tracking *(qv)*, which involves the adjustment of spacing over a number of adjacent characters.

lamination The application of transparent or coloured, shiny, plastic films to printed matter to protect or enhance it.

layers In some applications, a level to which the user can consign an element of the design being worked on. Individual layers can be active (meaning that they can be worked on) or non-active.

layout The placement of various elements – text, headings *(qv)*, images – on a printed page.

leading The spacing between lines of type.

Lingo A powerful scripting language contained within Macromedia's Director *(qv)* software *(qv)*.

Mac OS The operating system used on Apple's 'Macintosh' computers.

master page In some applications, a template *(qv)* that includes attributes that will be common to all pages, such as the number of text columns, page numbers, and so on.

Media Player A widely used audio and video player application. Supplied with Microsoft Windows *(qv)* and also available for Mac *(qv)*.

modem Contraction of 'modulator–demodulator'. A device that converts digital data to analogue, and back, for transfer from one computer to another via standard telephone lines.

mounting The process of sticking artwork on to a thick piece of board, usually for display or presentation.

MP3 Abbreviation for 'MPEG audio layer 3'. A popular compressed *(qv)* audio file format.

offset lithography A common bulk printing method involving the use of photographic plates.

OpenType A relatively new digital font format that can contain either PostScript *(qv)* or TrueType *(qv)* data and allows large numbers of characters to be stored in one file.

PageMaker The original page make-up software, launched by Adobe. Now defunct.

PANTONE The proprietary trademark for PANTONE's system of colour standards, control and quality requirements, in which each colour bears a description of its formulation (in percentages) for subsequent printing.

PC Abbreviation for 'personal computer'. The term is generally used to denote any computer that is IBM-compatible and runs the Windows *(qv)* operating system (as opposed to the Mac OS *(qv)*, for example).

PDF Abbreviation for 'portable document format'. A multi-purpose format from Adobe that allows complex, multi-featured documents to be created, retaining all text, layout, and picture formatting, then to be viewed and printed on any computer with PDF 'reader' software (such as the free Adobe Reader) or, if correctly formatted, used for final output on a printing press.

Photoshop Powerful, industry-standard image manipulation software from Adobe.

pictogram A simplified graphic symbol representing an object or concept.

pixel Contraction of 'picture element'. The smallest component of a digitally generated image, such as a single dot of light on a computer monitor. In its most simple form, one pixel corresponds to a single bit *(qv)*: 0 = off, or white; 1 = on, or black. In colour and greyscale images (or monitors), one pixel may correspond to several bits: an 8-bit pixel, for example, can be displayed in any of 256 colours (the total number of different configurations that can be achieved by eight 0s and 1s).

plug-in Software *(qv)*, usually developed by a third party, that extends the capabilities of a program. Plug-ins are common in image-editing and page-layout software for such things as special effects filters. They are also common in web *(qv)* browsers for playing such things as movies and audio files.

PNG Abbreviation for 'portable network graphics'. A rarely used file format for images on the Web that provides 10 to 30 per cent 'lossless' compression (qv).

point The basic unit of Anglo-American type measurement. There are 72 points to an inch.

PostScript Adobe's proprietary page description language for image output to laser printers and high-resolution (qv) imagesetters.

pre-press Any or all of the reproduction processes that occur between design and printing, especially colour separation.

proof A prototype of a job (usually a printed document) produced to check quality and accuracy. An accurate on-screen preview of a job is known as a soft proof.

QuarkXPress Industry standard page-layout program.

QuickTime Apple Computer's audio and video delivery technology, compatible with both Windows (qv) and the Mac OS (qv).

raster Deriving from the Latin *rastrum* (rake), a 'raster image' is any image created as rows of pixels, dots, or lines in a 'raking' sequence, i.e. from top to bottom of a page, monitor, etc. On a monitor, the screen image is made up from a pattern of several hundred parallel lines created by an electron beam that 'rakes' the screen from top to bottom. The speed at which the image or frame is created is the 'refresh' rate, quoted in hertz (Hz), equal to the number of times per second. Converting a vector (qv) image to a bitmap (qv) for output on screen or printer is 'rasterization'.

Real Media A set of audio and video file formats and players from Real Networks, often used on the Web.

resolution The quantity of data points, such as pixels, with which an image, sound, or other phenomenon is stored digitally.

Higher resolution means better definition, clarity, and fidelity, at the cost of larger files.

RGB Abbreviation for 'red, green, blue'. The primary colours of the 'additive' colour model, used in colour monitors and for Web (qv) and multimedia graphics.

RIP Acronym for 'raster image processor'. Used by a printer to convert and rasterize (qv) page-layout data, typically in a PostScript (qv) or PDF (qv) file, for printed output, as a proof or on press.

rollover The rapid substitution of one or more images when a mouse pointer is rolled over the original image. Often used for navigation buttons on web (qv) pages.

rule A printed line.

Safari Web browser (qv) software from Apple, standard on Macs (qv).

sans serif The generic name for type designs that lack the small extensions (serifs, qv) at the ends of the main strokes of the letters. Sometimes called 'lineal type'.

saturation The variation in colour of the same tonal brightness from none (grey) through pastel shades (low saturation) to pure colour with no grey (high or 'full' saturation).

scamp A preliminary drawing showing a proposed design.

scanner An electronic device that uses a sequentially moving light beam and sensor to digitize artwork from paper or photographic film. Most scanners are flatbed, with a glass surface on which the original document is placed.

serif The short counterstroke or finishing stroke at the end of the main stroke of a type character.

ShockWave A Macromedia technology used for delivering Director (qv) presentations to browsers (qv) via the Web (qv).

silkscreen printing ('screen printing') A method of printing in which ink (qv) is forced through a

stencil fixed to a screen made of silk. Modern printers more commonly use a screen made of synthetic material .

software The generic term for any kind of computer program, as opposed to the physical hardware.

spot colours A printing colour that has been specifically mixed for the job, as opposed to using the four-colour process (qv) colours.

streaming A method of playing audio or video files as they are received (for example via the Web), minimizing initial waiting times.

tags Formatting commands in HTML (qv) and related mark-up languages. A tag is switched on by placing a command inside angle brackets <command> and turned off by the same command preceded with a forward slash </command>.

template A document created with pre-positioned areas, used as a basis for repeatedly creating other documents in the same style.

TIFF Acronym for 'tagged image file format'. A graphics file format used to store bitmapped (qv) images with no loss of data and optionally with extra features such as layers (qv). Widely used in graphic design and pre-press (qv).

touch screen A computer screen that responds to touch, avoiding the need for a mouse or keyboard. Often used for public access displays.

tracking The adjustment of spacing between characters in a selected piece of text. See also *kerning*.

traffic In an advertising context, elements of client business that an agency is handling.

trapping Settings in DTP programs that determine the interaction of overlapping colours. Also refers to printing problems when one solid colour completely overprints another. Trapping preferences are complex and best left to the service bureau or printer.

TrueType Apple Computer's digital font (qv) technology, developed as an alternative to PostScript (qv) and now used by both PCs (qv) and Macs (qv). A single TrueType file is used for both printing and screen rendering, while PostScript fonts require two separate files.

typography The art of type (qv) design and its arrangement on a designed page.

Unicode A system used to identify which glyphs (qv) in a font represent which characters (qv).

URL Abbreviation for 'uniform resource locator'. The unique address of any page on the Web (qv), usually composed of three parts: protocol (such as 'http'), domain name, and directory name.

varnish A liquid that dries to form a hard, usually shiny surface. Varnish can be applied on press to printed matter, especially covers.

vector A straight line segment of a given length and orientation. 'Vector graphics' – which can involve more complex forms than straight lines, such as Bézier (qv) curves – are stored as numeric descriptions that can be scaled to reproduce the same visual result at any physical size, rather than broken up into discrete pixels as in the case of bitmapped (qv) images.

Windows The PC (qv) operating system devised by Microsoft, which uses a graphical user interface (GUI) similar to the Mac OS (qv).

Web Also known as 'World Wide Web' (WWW). An amorphous entity comprising pages created in HTML (qv) and delivered via Internet (qv) servers to users' web browsers (qv).

XHTML A combination of HTML (qv) and XML (qv) used to create Internet content for multiple devices.

XML An acronym for 'extensible markup language', which is broader than HTML (qv).

BIBLIOGRAPHY

ART & DESIGN
Books
The Design Annual, Graphis International, New York
Albrecht, Donald, Holt, Steven, Lupton, Ellen, *Design Culture Now: The National Design Triennial*, Princeton Architectural Press, New Jersey, 2000
Berger, John, *Ways of Seeing*, Viking Penguin, London, 1991
Heller, Stephen, *Icons of Graphic Design*, Thames & Hudson, London, 2001
Hollis, Richard, *Graphic Design: A Concise History*, Thames & Hudson, London, 2001
Hughes, Robert, *The Shock of the New*, Thames & Hudson, London, 1991
Livingston, Alan, Livingston, Isabella, *The Thames & Hudson Dictionary of Graphic Design and Designers*, Thames & Hudson, London, 1992

Periodicals
Blueprint, Computer Arts, Creative Review, Design Weekly, Emigre, Eye, Flash Art, Frieze, MacUser, Wallpaper, Wired

PRINT
Books
Fawcett-Tang, Roger, *Experimental Formats*, RotoVision, Hove, 2001
Fishel, Catherine, *Paper Graphics*, Rockport, Gloucester MA, 1999
Foges, Chris, *Magazine Design*, RotoVision, Hove, 1999
Hochuli, Jost, *Designing Books: Practice and Theory*, Hyphen, London, 1997
Hurlburt, Allen, *The Grid*, John Wiley & Sons, New York, 1982
Koren, Leonard, *Graphic Design Cookbook*, Chronicle, San Francisco, 2001
Moser, Horst, *The Art Directors' Handbook of Professional Magazine Design*, Thames & Hudson, London, 2003

Pipes, Allan, *Production for Graphic Designers*, Laurence King, London, 2001
San, Lim Ching, *By Design*, HarperCollins, London, 2001
Zappaterra, Yolande, *Digital Lab: Editorial, Print and Electronic Design*, RotoVision, Hove, 2001

ADVERTISING
Books
Aitchison, Jim, *Cutting Edge Advertising*, Prentice Hall, London, 1999
Brierley, Sean, *The Advertising Handbook*, Routledge, London, 1995
Butterfield, Leslie (ed), *Excellence in Advertising*, Butterworth-Heinemann, Boston, 1997
Chaffrey, David, *Internet Marketing*, Prentice Hall, Harrow, 2000
Goddard, Angele, *The Language of Advertising*, Routledge, London, 1998
Pricken, Mario, *Creative Advertising*, Thames & Hudson, London, 2004
Williamson, Judith, *Decoding Advertisements*, M Boyars, New York, 1979

Websites
www.mediaguardian.co.uk;
www.pa.co.uk; www.dandad.co.uk;
www.adassoc.org.uk; www.aaaa.org;
www.americanadagencies.com;
www.aaf.org; www.adforum.com

PACKAGING
Books
Cliff, Stafford, *Fifty Trade Secrets of Great Design Packaging*, Rockport Publishers, Gloucester MA, 1999
Design Week Books, *The Packaging Design Book* (annual), Centaur Publishing, London, 2001
Fishel, Catharine, *The Perfect Package*, Rockport Publishers, Gloucester MA, 2000
Meyers, Herbert and Lubliner, Murray, *The Marketer's Guide to Successful Package Design*, NTC Publishing Group, Chicago, 1998

Phillips, Renee, *Packaging Graphics and Design*, Rockport Publishers, Gloucester MA, 2001

SIGNAGE
Books
Barker, P, *Sign Design Guide*, JMU Access Partnership & Sign Design Society, London, 2000
Follis, John and Hammer, Dave, *Architectural Signing and Graphics*, Whitney Library of Design, New York, 1979
Grayson, Trulove J, Sprague, C, Colony, S, *This Way: Signage Design for Public Spaces*, Rockport Publishers, Gloucester MA, 2000
Wildbur, P and Burke, M, *Information Graphics*, Thames & Hudson, London, 1999

EXHIBITION
Books
Carter, Rob, Majewski, Jan, et al, *Exhibition and Display Design*, RotoVision, Hove, 2000
Mijksenaar, Paul and Westendorp, Piet, *Open Here*, Stewart, Tabori and Chang, New York, 1999
Miles, R S (ed), *The Design of Educational Exhibits*, George Allen & Unwin, London, 1982
Pegler, Michael, *Contemporary Exhibit Design*, Visual Reference Publications, New York, 2001

WEB/MULTIMEDIA
Books
Bhangal, Sham, Rey, Patrick, *Foundation Flash 5*, Friends of Ed, Birmingham, 2000
Bolante, Antony, *After Effects 5 for Macintosh and Windows*, Peachpit Press, Berkeley, CA, 2001
Davis, Jack, Merritt, Susan, *The Web Design Wow! Book*, Peachpit Press, Berkeley CA, 1998
Greiman, April, *Hybrid Imagery*, Watson-Guptill, New York, 1990
Haskell, Barry G et al, *Digital Video*, Chapman & Hall, New York, 1996

Riley, Martyn J, Richardson, Iain, *Digital Video Communications*, Artech House, Norwood MA, 1997
Merritt, Douglas, *Television Graphics*, John Wiley, New York, 1987
Pitaru, Amit et al, *New Masters of Flash*, Friends of Ed, Birmingham, 2001
Poyner, Rick (ed), *Typography Now 2*, William Morrow, New York, 1998
Robbins, Christopher, *Director 8.5 Studio*, Friends of Ed, Birmingham, 2001
Rose, Carla, *Teach Yourself Adobe Photoshop 6 in 24 Hours*, SAMS, Indianapolis, 2000
Towers, J Tarin, *Dreamweaver 4 for Windows and Macintosh*, Peachpit Press, Berkeley CA, 2001
Velthoven, Willem (ed), *Multimedia Graphics*, Chronicle Books, San Francisco, 1996

Websites
www.adobe.com; www.computer
arts.co.uk; www.absolutecross.com
/tutorials/photoshop.htm; www.
deepspaceweb.com; www.design
dojo.com; www.designmuseum.org;
www.illustrator-resources.com;
www.photoshopcentral.com;
www.photoshop-cafe.com;
www.planetphotoshop.com;
www.magicpixel.com.au

FLASH reference sites
www.hillmancurtis.com;
www.waupaper.com;
www.linkdup.com;
www.amoebacorp.com;
www.design.net.uk; www.traffic-
movie.com; www. egomedia.com
www.deepend.co.uk;
www.turtleshell.com
www.coolhomepages.com

Commercial sites
www.hoover.co.uk;
www.newbeetle.co.uk;
www.vw.com; www.tothepoint.fi
www.yugop.com

INDEX

INDEX

PICTURE ACKNOWLEDGMENTS

Abbreviations: t **top;** l **left;** r **right;** b **bottom;** c **centre;** m **middle**

p2-3 Aston Leach /MacUser Magazine; **p12** Studio Myerscough; **p13** t Phil Bicker / DPICT magazine, b Cahan & Associates; **p14** t AMV BBDO Ltd, photography by Paul Zak, art director: Dave Dye, copywriter: Sean Doyle, account director: Oliver Forder, client: Hugh McCahey, b M&C Saatchi, creatives: Tiger Savage and Mark Goodwin, photography by Christopher Griffin; **p15** t Bartle Bogle Hegarty, London br design by Wieden and Kennedy / graphics by VgL, br Peter Stimpson / courtesy of MCV; **p16** t Area, br Summa, br Cahan & Associates; **p17** t Simon & Lars, b Veuve Clicquot; **p18** t Sussman/Prejza & Company Inc., b Ruedi Baur & Associates; **p19** tr commissioned by Edogawa Ward, design unknown, m Sussman/Prejza & Company Inc., b Niklaus Troxler; **p20** l Ralph Applebaum Associates Inc., r Design by IDEO; **p21** top: Pentagram: partner/designer: Peter Harrison (graphics), partner/architect: James Biber, architect: Michael Zweck-Bronner, design by Christina Freyss, photography by Bill Jacobson and Peter Mauss, Esto, b Poulin & Morris: photography by Tim Wilkes; **p22** tl Digit, courtesy of Habitat, r Identikal, b AllYourPrey; **p23** t Cuban Council, b Imagination for Guinness PLC; **p24** l Maddalene Beltrami and the Ospedale Maggiore di Milano, r InterStitch; **p25** l RTKL, tr EA, br Eidos; **p28** Lance Wyman; **p29** br Emery Vincent Design, tr: Carol Naughton & Associates Inc., br Niklaus Troxler; **p30** Produced by the

Whitechapel Art Gallery to coincide with the exhibition Live In Your Head (Feb-Apr 2000), design by Jo Stockham and Herman Lelie, concept and edit by Alistair Raphael; **p31** br Chermayeff & Geismar, tr Alan Fletcher, c Niklaus Troxler; **p32** Barney Pickard; **p33** t RTKL & Jonathan Spiers & Associates, b Tom Graboski Associates; **p34** l Williams Murray Hamm, r Pentagram: design by John Rushworth, design assistants: Vince Frost and Nick Finney; **p35** t Tenazas Design, br Niklaus Troxler, br Chronicle Books, USA; **p38** l Adobe Systems; **p39** Emery Vincent Design; **p40** l Chermayeff & Geismar, br Adobe Systems, tr Swifty @ Swifty Typografix, cr Gensler, b Barney Pickard; **p41** Regina Frank/SDA Creative; **p42** Wink Design; **p43** l Alan Fletcher, r Williams Murray Hamm; **p44** br Bryn Jones, t Chronicle Books **p45** t Cahan & Associates, b RTKL; **p46** Lippa Pearce; **p47** b Brian Coe; **p48** b Mauk Design; **p51** br Lance Wyman, tr Pippo Lionni; **p52** t Agenda, b Cahan & Associates; **p53** t Cahan & Associates, b Chronicle Books; **p54** l Grey Worldwide, r Cahan & Associates; **p55** t MetaDesign, br Alan Fletcher, br Cahan & Associates; **p56** l Alan Fletcher, r graphic and interior design by Ashdown Wood Design for 'Hang Out Laundry and Drycleaning', Sydney, Australia; **p57** br The Partners, br Summa, r design by Holmes Wood at Tate Gallery, London; **p60** l design by John Brown Citrus Publishing, r Teeranop Wangsillapakun, Segura Inc., Chicago; **p61** Why Not Associates, photography by Rocco Redondo and

Photodisc, courtesy of Royal Academy of Arts; **p75** Jeremy Leslie at John Brown Citrus Publishing for M-real, photography by Mischa Haller; **p77** Frederico d'Orazio, PlaatsMaken; **p79** t Dom Raban, Eg.G, br Lippa Pearce Design, br Jon Raimes, Foundation Publishing; **p81** t Pollard & Van der Water Golden, l SEA Design, r Epoxy, courtesy of Rolland Motif Paper; **p83** Jon Raimes, Foundation Publishing; **p84** Duckworth Finn Grubb Waters; **p85** t McCann Erickson, b Rainey Kelly Campbell Roalfe; **p86** Tribal DDB, Spain; **p87** t Brook Street, b DDB; **p88** Triangle Communications; **p89** t Impact FCA!, b Duckworth Finn Grubb Waters; **p90** r TBWA/Chiat/Day; **p91** Craik Jones; **p92** Tequila; **p93** c KLP Euro RSCG, b Benetton; **p95** BMP; **p97** Duckworth Finn Grubb Waters; **p98** Kenzo; **p99** t Pentagram, b Paul Smith Ltd; **p104** l SCA Packaging, r Fuji Seal Europe; **p105** tr Pemberton & Whitefoord for Tesco; **p110-11**: Richard Gooch, John Lewis Partnership; **p112** Pentagram; **P113** The Partners; **p114** t North Design, b Atelier Works; **p115** t MetaDesign, br Pentagram, br CDT Design; **p117** br Pentagram, tr Royal National Institute for the Blind, b architects: Allford Hall Monaghan Morris, design by Atelier Works; **p 118** t Atelier, b photography by Todd Gipstein, Corbis; **p 119** CDT Design; **p 121** Atelier; **p122-23**: CDT Design; **p124** design by Euroculture, courtesy Jean Michel Folon, Sabam 2001, photography by Thiery Renauld; **p125** br Guggenheim Museum, tr Event Communications, b Event Communications; **p 126**

Perks Willis Design; **p127** t Philip Miles Graphic Design, b Perks Willis Design; **p128** t Land Design Studios and The Chase, bl & br design by DEGW, courtesy of the Trustees of the Imperial War Museum, photography by Philip Vile; **p129-31** Exhibition Plus and Perks Willis Design; **p132-33** Exhibition Plus and Perks Willis Design, courtesy of the Natural History Museum, London; **p133** t illustration by Debbie Cook and Colin Mier; **p136** 2advanced Studios; **p137** t Emap, r Yugo Nakamura, l Poke; **p138** Nykris Digital Design, courtesy of the Tate Gallery; **p147** design by Lateral and NeoWorks, courtesy of five; **p154** tl design unknown, courtesy of New Line Productions, Inc., bl Biggles; **p155** tr Edge Modern; **p162** Nykris Digital Design, courtesy of the Tate Gallery; **p163** t Domani Studios, courtesy of the Whitney Museum of American Art; **p164-165** design by Headprecious Design; **p166** Cognitive Applications; **p167** Tomato Interactive; **p169** InterStitch; **p170** Mook, courtesy of the Sunday Times; **p175** Phil Taylor and Phil Jackson; **p177** Cognitive Applications; **p179** tl Activision, tr EA; **p188** photography by Bob Krist, Corbis; **p189** Nicklaus Troxler; **p197** Tom Hingston Studio, courtesy of MacUser Magazine; **p200** photograph by Ed Seabourne **p200** RTKL; **p201** t Pamela Geismar, courtesy of Chronicle Books; **p209** Lawrence Zeegen

Additional Photography by Rob Turner and Bob Gordon

Diagrams by bounford.com